Dangerous Thresholds

Managing Escalation in the 21st Century

**Forrest E. Morgan ■ Karl P. Mueller
Evan S. Medeiros ■ Kevin L. Pollpeter ■ Roger Cliff**

Prepared for the United States Air Force

Approved for public release; distribution unlimited

PROJECT AIR FORCE

The research described in this report was sponsored by the United States Air Force under Contracts F49642-01-C-0003 and FA7014-06-C-0001. Further information may be obtained from the Strategic Planning Division, Directorate of Plans, Hq USAF.

Library of Congress Cataloging-in-Publication Data

Is Available

The RAND Corporation is a nonprofit research organization providing objective analysis and effective solutions that address the challenges facing the public and private sectors around the world. RAND's publications do not necessarily reflect the opinions of its research clients and sponsors.

RAND® is a registered trademark.

Cover design by Ron Miller

© Copyright 2008 RAND Corporation

All rights reserved. No part of this book may be reproduced in any form by any electronic or mechanical means (including photocopying, recording, or information storage and retrieval) without permission in writing from RAND.

Published 2008 by the RAND Corporation
1776 Main Street, P.O. Box 2138, Santa Monica, CA 90407-2138
1200 South Hayes Street, Arlington, VA 22202-5050
4570 Fifth Avenue, Suite 600, Pittsburgh, PA 15213-2665
RAND URL: http://www.rand.org/
To order RAND documents or to obtain additional information, contact
Distribution Services: Telephone: (310) 451-7002;
Fax: (310) 451-6915; Email: order@rand.org

Preface

The subject of escalation has received little attention in U.S. strategic thought since the end of the Cold War. With prospects of conflict between nuclear-armed superpowers receding in memory, few policymakers, security analysts, or military leaders have worried about the danger of wars spinning out of control or considered how to manage these risks.

Yet there are important reasons to examine the dynamics of escalation in the current security environment. Although the United States retains its nuclear superiority and has demonstrated the ability to project overwhelming force in most conventional conflicts, strategic conditions have changed considerably in the past 15 years, and new adversaries have emerged. These developments could find the United States in escalatory situations that its leaders, schooled in ideas developed during the Cold War, are ill equipped to anticipate or manage. Understanding escalation is particularly important to the U.S. Air Force because of its unique ability to strike deep within enemy territory and the emphasis in Air Force doctrine on rapid strategic attack to achieve shock, paralysis, and escalation dominance.

The Air Force recognizes the importance of understanding and managing the risks of escalation. In 2004, Director of Air Force Strategic Planning Major General Ronald J. Bath sponsored a war game in which uncontrolled escalation occurred, surprising players and controllers alike. Because this experience was just one in a series of escalatory events occurring in major war games over the past several years, General Bath recommended to Air Force Chief of Staff General John P. Jumper that the RAND Corporation be tasked to examine the risks of escalation in the current security environment and offer recommendations on how the Air Force can best anticipate and manage those risks. General Jumper approved the recommendation, and RAND Project AIR FORCE was tasked to conduct a study later titled "Managing Escalation in the Post–Cold War Security Environment."

This monograph presents the findings of that study. It offers insights for air- and spacepower strategy and should also inform military operations and national security policy more generally. It builds on previous Project AIR FORCE work examining the risks of escalation and the potential impacts of U.S. policy in the current security environment: *War and Escalation in South Asia*, by John E. Peters, James Dickens, Derek Eaton, C. Christine Fair, Nina Hachigian, Theodore W. Karasik, Rollie Lal, Rachel M. Swanger, Gregory F. Treverton, and Charles Wolf, Jr., MG-367-1-AF, 2006, and *Striking First: Preemptive and Preventive Attack in U.S. National Security Policy*, by Karl P. Mueller, Jasen J. Castillo, Forrest E. Morgan, Negeen Pegahi, and Brian Rosen, MG-403-AF, 2006.

The research reported here was sponsored by the Director of Strategic Planning, Headquarters, U.S. Air Force, and conducted within the Strategy and Doctrine Program of RAND Project AIR FORCE.

RAND Project AIR FORCE

RAND Project AIR FORCE, a division of the RAND Corporation, is the U.S. Air Force's federally funded research and development center for studies and analyses. RAND Project AIR FORCE provides the Air Force with independent analyses of policy alternatives affecting the development, employment, combat readiness, and support of current and future aerospace forces. Research is conducted in four programs: Aerospace Force Development; Manpower, Personnel, and Training; Resource Management; and Strategy and Doctrine.

Additional information about RAND Project AIR FORCE is available on our Web site: http://www.rand.org/paf/

Contents

Preface iii
Figures ix
Summary xi
Acknowledgments xxiii
Glossary xxv

CHAPTER ONE
Introduction 1
Background 1
Contemporary Challenges 3
Purpose of This Monograph 4
Organization and Approach 5

CHAPTER TWO
The Nature of Escalation 7
Understanding Escalation 8
   Thresholds and the Subjectivity of Escalation 11
   Limited War 14
   Escalation Dominance 14
Dimensions of Escalation: Vertical, Horizontal, and Political 18
Escalation Mechanisms 19
   Deliberate Escalation 20
   Inadvertent Escalation 23
   Accidental Escalation 26
Complexity in Escalation 28

Motives for Escalation..29
  Instrumental Escalation.. 30
  Suggestive Escalation..31
  Other Motives for Escalation.....................................33
Dynamics of Escalation... 34
  Constraints on Escalation..36
Escalation and Instability in the 21st Century.................. 38
  New Escalation Options.. 38
  Perceived Political Fragility....................................... 40
  Windows of Opportunity and Vulnerability................ 40
  Indifference to Escalation Risks................................. 42
Anticipating and Managing Escalation........................... 43

CHAPTER THREE
China's Thinking on Escalation: Evidence from Chinese Military Writings...47
Introduction..47
Background and Conceptual Issues................................ 50
Understanding Chinese Views on Escalation and War Control............51
  The Conceptual Foundation of War Control..................52
  Operationalizing War Control: Military Measures to Contain Warfare........54
Assessing Chinese Escalation Behavior Through the Lens of the Second Artillery Doctrine..................58
Second Artillery Nuclear Operations and Escalation........61
  Key Nuclear Doctrine Concepts..................................63
  Additional Questions About Second Artillery Nuclear Operations......65
Second Artillery Conventional Missile Strike Campaigns...... 68
  Implications for Chinese Escalation Behavior................70
Chinese Views on Space Warfare and Escalation..............71
Conclusion..76

CHAPTER FOUR
Regional Nuclear Powers..83
Escalation Risks Inherent in Emergent Nuclear Capability..................85
Sources of Regional Instability....................................... 88

Instability and Risks of Escalation in Northeast Asia 89
Instability and Escalation in South and Southwest Asia 95
Risks of Escalation in the Ongoing Conflict Between India and
    Pakistan 97
Risks of Escalation Due to Domestic Instability in Pakistan 106
The Risks of Escalation in a Conflict with Iran 109
Conclusion 113

CHAPTER FIVE
Escalation in Irregular Warfare 117
Irregular Warfare's Many Paths of Escalation 118
Escalation in Stability Operations: Two Illustrative Cases 124
    Multiple Actors in a Complex Strategic Environment 126
    Multiple Conflicts Exist Simultaneously 127
    ROE and the Challenge of Complexity 129
    Dramatic Asymmetries of Power, Interest, and Commitment 131
    Irregular Warfare Undermines Traditional Escalation-
        Management Approaches 132
Escalation in the Global Jihad 133
    The Roots of Global Jihad 134
    The Escalation Dynamics of Global Jihad 135
    Escalation in Response to Global Jihad 141
Escalation Management in the Struggle Against Global Jihad 150
    Strategies in the Global Jihad 153
    Managing the Escalatory Effects of Global Jihad 154
Conclusion 157

CHAPTER SIX
Managing Escalation in a Complex World 159
The First Step in Managing Escalation Is Understanding Its Nature 160
    Deterring Deliberate Escalation 160
    Managing Inadvertent Escalation: A Matter of Clarifying
        Thresholds 163
    Managing Forces to Avoid Accidental Escalation 165
    Dominance as a Means of Escalation Management 165
    The Role of Technology in Escalation and Escalation Management ... 168

Managing Escalation Risks in Today's World 169
  Escalation Management in a Limited Conflict with China 169
  Managing Escalation in Confrontations with Other Regional
    Nuclear Powers 170
  Escalation Management in Irregular Warfare 172
Recommendations for the U.S. Air Force 174

APPENDIXES
A. China, Force, and Escalation: Continuities Between Historical
   Behavior and Contemporary Writings 177
B. Case Studies of Escalation in Stability Operations 197
C. Modified Method for Delphi Analyses 221

Bibliography 225

Figures

2.1.	Dimensions of Escalation	20
2.2.	Key Escalation Categories	29
5.1.	Incidents of Terrorism in Iraq Compared to Terrorism by Muslim Groups Elsewhere in the World Since September 11, 2001	147
5.2.	Incidents of Terrorism by Muslim Groups Since September 11, 2001	148
5.3.	Fatalities Resulting from Terrorist Attacks by Muslim Groups Since September 11, 2001	149
B.1.	Geographical Distribution of Religious Groups in Lebanon as of 1983	200
B.2.	Geographical Distribution of Somalia's Clans and Subclans in 1992	209
C.1.	Example of a Delphi Analysis Decision Tree	223

Summary

Background

Escalation can be defined as an increase in the intensity or scope of conflict that crosses threshold(s) considered significant by one or more of the participants. Escalation is a natural tendency in any form of human competition. When competition involves military confrontation or limited war, the pressure to escalate can become intense because of the weight of issues that bring actors into violent conflict and the potential costs of losing contests of deadly force. Escalation can be unilateral, but it is often reciprocal, as each combatant struggles ever harder to achieve victory or avoid defeat. Left unchecked, escalatory chain reactions can occur, raising the costs of war to catastrophic levels for combatants and noncombatants alike.

Cold War–era thinking about escalation focused on the dynamics of bipolar, superpower confrontation, and theories on how to manage it emerged as a branch of nuclear-deterrence literature. In that era, U.S. leaders could focus their attention on one principal adversary, the Soviet Union. Although the prospect of war with a nuclear superpower was frightening, anticipating and managing confrontations with Moscow was, in many ways, an easier task than those that U.S. leaders face today.

The current security environment is complicated by a wide range of threats that fall broadly into three interrelated but relatively distinct categories. Each of these threats entails a significant risk of escalation. First, the United States must remain prepared to manage potential confrontations with other large nuclear powers, such as Russia and, particularly, China. Second, the emergence of new nuclear-armed powers in regions in which the United States has important interests increases the risk of escalation in regional crises and challenges efforts to manage that risk should the United States choose to intervene. Finally, there is a risk of escalation from a range of irregular warfare threats resulting from the decline or failure of state authority in several strategically important regions; from the rise of a violent, transnational Islamist movement; and from advances in information networks that have enabled an international nexus of insurgent, terrorist, and criminal groups hostile to the United States.

Key Findings

The Nature of Escalation and Escalation Management

The first step to managing escalation is to understand its fundamental nature. Because escalation is an interactive phenomenon, one in which any party to a conflict can play a role, it can rarely, if ever, be *controlled*, in the normal sense of the word. However, by understanding the motives that drive escalation and the mechanisms through which it manifests, military and political leaders can anticipate the risks of escalation in a potential confrontation, recognize them as they emerge, and manage them by manipulating the tacit negotiations with opponents that characterize military confrontations and limited war. (See pp. 8–18.)

The escalation mechanism and motive that is most easily recognized and understood is *deliberate escalation* carried out for instrumental reasons. In this mode, a combatant deliberately increases the intensity or scope of an operation to gain advantage or avoid defeat. Combatants also deliberately escalate conflicts, or indicate that they are willing to do so, for suggestive purposes in an effort to send signals to an enemy. Deliberate acts of suggestive escalation may be done to punish enemies for earlier escalatory deeds or to warn them that they are at risk of even greater escalation if they do not comply with coercive demands. (See pp. 20–23, 30–33.)

The key to managing an enemy's propensity for deliberate escalation, whether instrumental or suggestive, lies in deterrence: discouraging an enemy from deliberately escalating a conflict by convincing that enemy that the costs of such actions will outweigh the benefits that may be accrued through escalation. Deterrence is most often associated with threats of punishment, and, indeed, that is the most direct way of manipulating an enemy's cost-benefit calculations. However, punishment-based deterrence may lack credibility in a limited conflict in which the adversary doubts that the other party has the capability or will to carry out a threat. (See pp. 22–23.)

More serious weaknesses emerge in punishment-based deterrence when there is significant asymmetry of stakes between parties to the conflict. An enemy that perceives that its stakes are high will be willing to bear greater costs and, therefore, will be less sensitive to threats of punishment. And if that enemy believes that the threatener's stakes are low, there may be doubt that the threatener is willing to bear the reciprocal costs of escalation or pay the political price of carrying out the threats.

Therefore, a more reliable strategy for deterring deliberate escalation is one that buttresses threats of punishment with visible capabilities for denial. Denial-based deterrence strategies entail discouraging an adversary from taking a prohibited action by convincing enemy leaders that such efforts can be countered sufficiently to deny their benefit.

The second fundamental mechanism that frequently causes wars to increase in scope and intensity is *inadvertent escalation*—that is, the mechanism that engages when a combatant deliberately takes actions that it does not perceive to be escalatory but are interpreted that way by the enemy. The cause of this phenomenon lies largely in the vague nature of escalation thresholds, which are inherently subjective and sometimes fluid. It is often difficult to divine what acts the enemy will consider escalatory, beyond the most obvious, such as attacks on the homeland, deliberate attacks on civilians or cherished sites, or the use of prohibited weapons. (See pp. 23–28.)

The key to managing risks of inadvertent escalation lies in clarifying thresholds—on all sides of a conflict. At or before the onset of a crisis, the United States should collect and analyze all available intelligence to determine where the enemy's salient escalation thresholds might lie. Such analyses should continue throughout a conflict. When likely thresholds are identified, U.S. leaders can respect them to avoid escalation or deliberately violate them if they conclude that escalation is affordable and will work to U.S. advantage. Either way, the choice to escalate or not becomes a conscious decision: It is managed. Similarly, U.S. leaders can reduce the risk that an adversary will inadvertently escalate a conflict by explicitly stating what actions the United States would consider to be seriously escalatory. As demonstrated in the first Gulf War, in which Saddam Hussein was warned against using chemical weapons, such statements carry an implicit threat of retribution and, therefore, simultaneously serve both to clarify thresholds and deter escalation.

The third fundamental mechanism of escalation is that which occurs by accident. *Accidental escalation* occurs when operators make mistakes, such as bombing the wrong targets or straying across geographical boundaries. It can also occur when leaders fail to set appropriate rules of engagement (ROE) or fail to maintain adequate discipline over the forces under their command. (See pp. 26–28.)

Although the risks of accidental escalation can never be completely eliminated, the key to mitigating them lies in effective force management. Leaders must assess the potential costs of escalatory acts, establish appropriate ROE, and enforce those rules among subordinate forces. The risk of accidents is further reduced with diligent training and exercise before engagement and effective command and control throughout the operation.

Escalation Dominance as a Means of Escalation Management

Because no nation today can rival U.S. power across the full range of nuclear and conventional military capabilities, some military and political leaders have concluded that the surest way for U.S. forces to manage the risks of escalation is to impose escalation dominance on their adversaries. The United States does, indeed, command a wide range of asymmetric strengths.[1] However, cases examined for this study suggest that escalation dominance is difficult to achieve against a committed adversary, even when the combatant seeking it enjoys vastly disproportionate strengths. More often, attempts to impose escalation dominance result in reciprocal escalation, as opponents seek ways to mitigate their enemies' advantage, prolong the conflict, and strive for asymmetric strengths of their own. (See pp. 15–17, 34–36.)

When escalation dominance does occur, it is more often the result of a combatant discovering, and effectively exploiting, some *asymmetric vulnerability* in an opponent, thereby imposing some cost that the opponent cannot avoid and is not willing to bear. For the United States, low stakes in some past conflicts have exposed such an asymmetric vulnerability in the form of casualty aversion, enabling adversaries to achieve escalation dominance on U.S. forces despite U.S. asymmetric strength in conventional warfighting capabilities. (See pp. 17, 40–42.)

Ironically, escalation dominance is most achievable when escalation management is of least concern. The United States might well achieve escalation dominance when confronting a state that possesses limited conventional capabilities and is not armed with nuclear weapons. However, if the United States confronts a significant regional power, particularly one armed with nuclear weapons, escalation-management concerns rise to the fore while prospects of escalation dominance become more remote. When enemies possess even a few nuclear weapons, attempting to impose dominance is a dangerous approach to escalation management. (See pp. 83–115.)

Technology and Escalation

The very essence of air- and spacepower lies in the orchestration of sophisticated technological capabilities, something that the U.S. Air Force does better than any other military institution in the world. It

---

[1] Although it has become fashionable to use the word asymmetric when referring to unconventional or covert attacks by weak states or nonstate actors, we use the word more literally. An asymmetric strength or weakness is simply a quality of one adversary that the other lacks in kind to a substantial degree. An asymmetric attack is one that exploits such a mismatch in capabilities or some undefended weakness, regardless of the nature of the weapon or tactic employed.

is almost axiomatic that *weapons do not escalate*; rather, *people escalate with weapons*. Yet, it is important to keep in mind that any technology that enables a military force to fight with more speed, range, and lethality will enable that force to cross escalation thresholds faster. In limited war, better technology can make a bad strategy more costly. (See pp. 160–169.)

Beyond that, deploying certain kinds of weapons to locations where they will be vulnerable may contribute to structural instability, making escalation more likely. Weapons or systems enabling capabilities that appear very threatening to adversaries but are difficult for U.S. forces to defend present tempting targets for escalation if deployed within reach of an enemy's strike assets. The U.S. military's growing dependence on space may be an example of such a structural instability, because the United States' orbital infrastructure enables U.S. forces in significant ways, yet that infrastructure is largely undefended, and portions of it may be within reach of more sophisticated potential adversaries (pp. 41–42).

On the other hand, lacking certain capabilities may also contribute to structural instability, prompting adversaries to escalate in ways against which the United States lacks proportionate responses. Leaving such options as the use of chemical or biological weapons available to an adversary risks exposing U.S. leaders to an *escalation dilemma*, forcing them to choose between allowing a painful enemy escalation go unanswered or responding with a disproportionate escalation that may entail undesirable military or political cost.

Managing Escalation Risks in Today's World

Military confrontations or limited conflicts with actors in any of the threat categories that characterize the current security environment would entail serious risks of escalation. Managing them will require strategies tailored for the kind of adversary engaged and the interests at stake. (See p. 169.)

China

A Sino-U.S. confrontation would present significant risks of inadvertent escalation if military forces were permitted to operate in keeping with their doctrinal tenets without regard for escalation thresholds. Chinese leaders and security analysts seem aware of the need to control escalation, as do their American counterparts, but operational military doctrines in both China and the United States emphasize surprise, speed, and deep strikes to seize the initiative and achieve dominance. Neither body of doctrine appears to consider how an adversary might react to such operations in a limited war: Indeed, each seems to assume that it will suppress enemy escalation by dominating the conflict. (See pp. 42–43, 47–81.)

Managing escalation in a limited conflict with China will require U.S. leaders to take a firm hand, not only in controlling their own military forces but also in clarifying thresholds and deterring the Chinese from violating them. At the onset of a crisis, U.S. leaders will need to assess each side's interests at stake and estimate the cost that the United States can bear in potential escalation. They will need to conduct an in-depth analysis of Chinese escalation thresholds and weigh the risks of violating them against operational necessity. At the same time, the United States should clearly state what forms of Chinese escalation are unacceptable and develop strategies for deterring Beijing from committing those acts. Because it may be difficult to make some threats of retribution credible in a limited conflict, such deterrent strategies should be fortified as much as possible via defensive capabilities to deny China success and benefits from attempted escalation. (See pp. 169–170.)

Regional Nuclear Powers

Newly emerging regional nuclear powers present escalation risks, in part, by virtue of their lack of doctrine and experience in nuclear force management. Moreover, such states initially lack survivable second-strike capabilities, and that generates "use-or-lose" pressures when they feel threatened. Historically, new nuclear powers have sometimes engaged in provocative behavior soon after achieving nuclear capability, suggesting that leaders of such states tend to overestimate the ability of nuclear weapons to deter conventional conflict. All this suggests that emergent nuclear states are more likely to make catastrophic errors than are longer-established nuclear powers: Their leaders and forces may precipitate a crisis and act unpredictably. Complicating matters, all the new and soon-to-be nuclear powers have bitter animosities with their neighbors and some are embroiled in ongoing conflicts. North Korea and Iran are hostile to the United States, and Washington has singled them out as rogues and members of an "axis of evil." Therefore, they may be anxious that the United States will attempt to impose regime change on them, raising risks of escalation should U.S. forces intervene in crises in their regions. Finally, some of these states have domestic problems that threaten their stability, and factions within them have known links to terrorist groups. (See pp. 84–96.)

Strategies for managing escalation risk in confrontations with new nuclear states will resemble those for conflicts with other nuclear powers, but they must hedge against a greater potential for miscalculation. U.S. statements about thresholds will need to be more explicit, and deterrent threats more pointed. Beyond that, the United States should focus on developing effective ballistic and cruise missile defenses, as well as other means of defending U.S. forces and regional friends from asymmetric attack. Threats and defenses alone may not deter enemy leaders who believe that their survival is at stake. For deterrence to hold, enemies must be reasonably confident that if they respect critical escalation thresholds, U.S. forces will as well. Therefore, in any limited conflict with regional nuclear powers, the United States may want to balance its threats with assurances. (See p. 113–115, 171.)

Irregular Warfare
The risks of escalation in irregular warfare are much broader and more diverse than was appreciated during the Cold War. Counterinsurgency and counterterrorist operations are prone to both vertical and horizontal escalation, incurring significant costs over time. Even seemingly benign peace operations can escalate into dangerous crises, as the 1983 U.S. experience in Beirut and the post–Cold War debacle in Mogadishu demonstrate. In all historical cases examined, state actors enjoyed dramatic asymmetric strengths in conventional force. Most of them attempted to employ those strengths to gain escalation dominance over their irregular adversaries. In doing so, they frequently scored impressive tactical victories and achieved a range of operational objectives; however, rarely did they succeed in applying their asymmetric

strengths in ways relevant to the strategic objectives in the conflict. In cases in which conventional force was effective, it was used primarily to provide security for populations threatened by terrorists or insurgents. Alternatively, when offensive operations were emphasized, conventional escalation ultimately served the irregular adversary's cause. (See pp. 118–124.)

Escalation management is inherently difficult with nonstate actors and is even more so with global jihadists. There are several reasons for this, not the least of which is that escalation management depends largely on deterrence. Jihadists are difficult to deter because it is difficult to make threats of punishment credible against elusive individuals and groups that reject the established order. Consequently, traditional two-player escalation management is disabled in the struggle with radical Islam, and limiting costs in this long-term conflict will require constraining and, ideally, eliminating the jihadists' ability to escalate the fight but doing so in ways that minimize the escalatory effects that U.S. and jihadist actions have on other actors in the environment (see pp. 150–155).

The United States should fashion and execute a strategy that maximizes its immediate security but does not, in doing so, jeopardize its victory in the more important, long-term political contest. Such a strategy should emphasize judicial and diplomatic actions and foreign assistance. The United States and its allies should avoid militarizing the conflict to the maximum extent possible. When military force is needed, the primary emphasis should be on providing security to populations threatened by terrorists or insurgents. Any employment of offensive force should be done with restraint and discretion to avoid antagonizing local populations. Failing to do this risks validating extremist propaganda and sowing the seeds of future escalation (see pp. 155–157).

Recommendations for the U.S. Air Force

Escalation management is largely a matter of sound policy and good strategy, functions that lie mainly in the realm of political and joint military leadership, but there are a number of things that the U.S. Air Force can do to organize, train, and equip its airmen to support these important tasks more effectively. This monograph offers the following recommendations (see pp. 175–176):

- *Identify and resolve potential escalation dilemmas.* The Air Force should conduct a thorough assessment of its current and future force structure to determine whether it provides the necessary flexibility to offer joint commanders proportionate responses to potential paths of enemy escalation. When gaps are identified, the Air Force should program new capabilities to fill them. When fiscal or political costs might preclude developing certain weapons that potential adversaries possess (such as chemical or biological weapons), the Air Force should concentrate on developing defenses against them and should work with combatant commands to develop strategies to deter their use.
- *Train air component commanders and their staffs on the principles of escalation management.* While developing military strategy is the purview of combatant commanders under the direction of political leaders, air component commanders and their staffs play essential roles in developing courses of action (COAs), evaluating prospective COAs, and conducting operational planning. Therefore, they have a fiduciary responsibility to advise joint commanders and policymakers on what escalation risks prospective COAs present and offer recommendations for managing those risks. To prepare airmen for that responsibility, they need to be taught that escalation management entails more than just establishing and enforcing rules of engagement. Determining enemy escalation thresholds should be an intelligence priority before and during the campaign planning process, and it should remain so as the fight progresses. Finally, commanders and planners should eschew plans that escalate in ways that offer tactical advantages at risk of great strategic cost.
- *Codify the principles of escalation management in airpower doctrine.* The Air Force should revise relevant passages in its doctrine to better acknowledge the risks of escalation and the need to manage

those risks. Doctrine should stress knowing the political limits of conflict and understanding why those limits are important. It should explain the relationship of thresholds to escalation and emphasize understanding the enemy's critical thresholds and how they can change over the course of the conflict. Finally, while the ability to impose shock, paralysis, and rapid dominance may be useful tools for the Air Force to bring to the fight, doctrine must acknowledge that they may not be appropriate tools to employ in some limited conflicts.
- *Teach escalation management in Air Force schools.* The Air Force should provide all airmen a firm grounding in the concept of limited war, the risks of escalation, and the principles of escalation management. These topics should be stressed in professional military education programs and at the School of Advanced Air and Space Studies. They should also be emphasized in war games and exercises.

Acknowledgments

The authors would like to thank the following individuals for their contributions to this study.

Major General Ronald J. Bath, Director of Strategic Planning, Headquarters, U.S. Air Force, provided the impetus for this work in a recommendation to Air Force Chief of Staff General John P. Jumper. General Bath sponsored the project and gave it his unfailing support. Similarly, Christopher Bowie, Assistant Director of Strategic Planning, provided helpful guidance and encouragement as the study developed, and his successor, Brigadier General Taco Gilbert, responded to the study's findings with a level of enthusiasm for which we are grateful. Colonel Rand Miller and Colonel Gail Wojtowicz were the project action officers. Colonel Wojtowicz's and Allen Moore's tireless efforts to get this work to key audiences are especially appreciated.

General (ret.) Charles Holland, Charles Swett, and Major Peter Garretson offered helpful comments and provided insights that were valuable in shaping the findings of this study.

At RAND, we thank the following colleagues for their invaluable participation in one or both of two Delphi analyses conducted during the course of this study: Robert W. Button, Daniel Gibran, John Gordon IV, Rollie Lal, Roger C. Molander, Bruce Nardulli, David Ochmanek, Toy Reid, Murray Scot Tanner, and Peter A. Wilson. We especially appreciate Peter Wilson's assistance in developing the scenario used in the second analysis and Sarah Harting's thorough and accurate documentation of events at both sessions. Thanks also go to Colonel Wojtwowicz, Mr. Moore, and Lieutenant Colonel Brian Copello for participating in the RAND Delphi analyses.

We would like to express our sincerest appreciation to our reviewers, Jasen J. Castillo, Eric Heginbotham, and Professor Emeritus Thomas C. Schelling. Their thorough reviews, thoughtful analyses, and insightful recommendations improved this work immensely.

Finally, we wish to thank Maria Falvo for her tireless administrative support throughout the project, and we extend our special appreciation to Lauren Skrabala for her diligent assistance in editing this manuscript.

Glossary

C4I	command, control, communication, computers, and intelligence
CFC	Republic of Korea–U.S. Combined Forces Command
指挥员的决定	commander's determination
遏制战争	containment of war
常规导弹打击战役	conventional missile strike campaigns
COA	course of action
DMZ	demilitarized zone
DPRK	Democratic People's Republic of Korea
威慑	deterrence
遏制战争	containment of war
反核威慑	*fan heweishe* [counternuclear deterrence or intimidation]
先机制敌	forestalling the enemy
战争形式	form of warfare
作战形式	forms of operations
FLN	Front de Libération Nationale

争取主动	gaining the political and military initiative
纲要	*gangyao* [a classified planning document]
GWOT	global war on terrorism
原则立场	guiding principle
后发制人	*houfa zhiren* [gaining mastery by striking after the enemy has struck]
IDF	Israel Defense Forces
IED	improvised explosive device
IRA	Irish Republican Army
LAF	Lebanese Armed Forces
LF	Lebanese Forces
LOC	line of control
MID	militarized interstate dispute
MNF	multinational force
NATO	North Atlantic Treaty Organization
NFU	no first use
不首先使用核武器政策	no-first-use policy
NGO	nongovernmental organization
核反击/核报复战役	nuclear counterattack campaign
核反击 or 核报复	nuclear counterstrike or nuclear retaliation
核威慑	nuclear deterrence
PLA	People's Liberation Army
PLAAF	People's Liberation Army Air Force
PLO	Palestinian Liberation Organization

QRF	quick-reaction force
被动	reactive, passive, or defensive (posture)
ROE	rules of engagement
ROK	Republic of Korea
RPG	rocket-propelled grenade
SNA	Somali National Alliance
重点突击	striking with focus
TF	task force
TLAM	Tomahawk Land Attack Missile
UNFIL	UN Interim Force in Lebanon
UNITAF	Unified Task Force
UNOSOM	UN Operation in Somalia
USFORSOM	U.S. Forces in Somalia
严密防护	*yanmi fanghu* [close defense or self-protection]
战争控制	war control
战争手段	warfighting techniques
重点反击	*zhongdian fanji* [key-point counterstrikes]
综合国力	*zonghe guoli* [comprehensive national power]

CHAPTER ONE

Introduction

Background

Escalation, in broad military terms, is an increase in the intensity or scope of conflict. It is a fundamental dynamic in which adversaries engaged in a contest for limited objectives increase the force or breadth of their attacks to gain advantage or avoid defeat. Escalation can be unilateral, but actions perceived as escalatory often provoke other combatants to increase their own efforts, either to punish the earlier escalation or to counter its advantages. Left unchecked, cycles of provocation and counterprovocation can intensify until the cost that each combatant incurs exceeds the value of its original stakes in the conflict.

This dynamic was identified in Western thought as early as the beginning of the 19th century, when Prussian military theorist Carl von Clausewitz proposed that war, being a contest between interacting human beings, will, in theory, culminate in each opponent's maximum exertion of strength.[1] However, systematic thought about escalation and theories on how to manage it did not crystallize until the Cold War, when the nuclear capabilities of the United States and the Soviet Union made the potential costs of uncontrolled escalation horrific.

Cold War–era thinking about escalation focused on the dynamics of bipolar, superpower confrontation, and theories on how to manage it emerged as a branch of nuclear-deterrence literature. Escalation-management constructs offered approaches for manipulating mutual

---
[1] Carl von Clausewitz, *On War*, Michael Howard and Peter Paret, eds. and trans., Princeton, N.J.: Princeton University Press, 1976, p. 77.

risk in the hopes that confrontations or limited wars would not ascend a metaphorical escalation ladder toward a nuclear exchange.[2] A substantial body of thought emerged on "brinkmanship" and similar methods of risk management, and one can find apparent examples of their mechanisms at work in the Berlin crises and in the Cuban missile crisis.[3] However, as the Cold War progressed, U.S. and Soviet leaders became increasingly chary about the dangers of risk manipulation, and the principal means of preventing escalation in both camps became avoiding direct superpower confrontation.

With the end of the Cold War, the specter of nuclear confrontation receded and concerns about escalation management diminished in U.S. strategic thought. The U.S. military's performance in the first Gulf War and in several subsequent operations demonstrated its overwhelming superiority in joint, high-speed conventional warfare. Cold War–era theories on escalation management would suggest that such superiority, buttressed by the United States' immense nuclear capability, should create sufficient risk for potential adversaries that they would be deterred from escalating limited conflicts in ways that would cause them to incur potentially catastrophic costs. However, differences between the contemporary strategic environment and that of the Cold War are significant enough to warrant a reexamination of the assumptions and logic that underpin existing theory.

---

[2] Herman Kahn introduced the escalation ladder metaphor in 1965, and it quickly became the predominant lens through which U.S. leaders and security analysts envisioned the dynamics of escalation. See Herman Kahn, *On Escalation: Metaphors and Scenarios*, Baltimore, Md.: Penguin, 1965.

[3] Thomas C. Schelling coined the term *brinkmanship* and was probably the most influential writer on risk-manipulation approaches to escalation management. See Thomas C. Schelling, *The Strategy of Conflict*, Cambridge, Mass.: Harvard University Press, 1960, and especially, *Arms and Influence*, New Haven, Conn.: Yale University Press, 1966.

Contemporary Challenges

During the Cold War, U.S. leaders focused their attention on one principal adversary: the Soviet Union.[4] While the prospect of war with a nuclear superpower was frightening, anticipating and managing confrontations with Moscow were, in many ways, easier tasks than those that U.S. leaders face today. The current security environment—one that some analysts now refer to as the *post post–Cold War* world–is complicated by a wide range of threats that fall into three interrelated but relatively distinct categories.[5]

First, the United States must remain prepared to manage potential confrontations with other large nuclear powers such as Russia and, particularly, China. China is the most populous country on the planet, and with the world's second-largest economy, Beijing is modernizing its military, building capabilities to project force beyond its borders in East Asia. Because the United States has key allies and important interests in the region, U.S. leaders must be prepared to manage escalation in any potential confrontation with this rising power.

Second is the emergence of several new nuclear powers in regions in which the United States has important interests. This development increases risks of escalation in regional crises and challenges efforts to manage those risks should U.S. leaders choose to intervene. Risks of escalation are inherently greater in confrontations with states whose nuclear forces are immature and whose leaders are inexperienced in nuclear stewardship. Today, matters are made worse by the fact that all of the new and soon-to-be nuclear powers have bitter animosities with their neighbors, and some are embroiled in ongoing conflicts. Some of

---

[4] This is not to say that U.S. leaders did not take seriously other adversaries, actual and potential, such as China, North Korea, North Vietnam, Cuba, Libya, and a host of other actors around the world. But in terms of escalation risk, the Soviet Union was always seen as the principal threat, and it absorbed the lion's share of attention in U.S. strategic thought.

[5] In 2005, several independent studies at RAND and in the U.S. Department of Defense grouped threats in the contemporary strategic environment into roughly the same three categories. See, for example, Andrew R. Hoehn, Adam Grissom, David Ochmanek, David A. Shlapak, and Alan J. Vick, *A New Division of Labor: Meeting America's Security Challenges Beyond Iraq*, Santa Monica, Calif.: RAND Corporation, MG-499-AF, 2007, pp. 11–14.

these regimes are hostile to the United States and, like Saddam Hussein's Iraq, have been singled out as rogue states or members of an axis of evil. In addition, several of these states have domestic problems that threaten their stability, and factions within them have known links to terrorist groups.

The third category is comprised of a wide range of irregular warfare threats generated by several coincident trends. First, the decline or failure of state authority in several strategically important regions of the world has created breeding grounds for terrorists and other dangerous nonstate actors. Second, the rise of a violent, transnational Islamist movement has challenged Western interests in the Muslim world and the security of the United States and its citizens, in particular. Finally, advances in information networks have enabled an international nexus of insurgent, terrorist, and criminal groups, some with unrelated or even divergent goals but all with a common adversary: the United States.

The transition of the global strategic environment from one of relative bipolar stability to this complex mélange of threats has generated uncertainty and frequent conflict. The United States has repeatedly led efforts to defuse crises, stabilize ungoverned or undergoverned regions, and defeat those who threaten U.S. citizens, interests, and allies. By all indications, such challenges will persist for the foreseeable future.

Purpose of This Monograph

This monograph seeks to help the U.S. Air Force anticipate and manage escalation risks in the early 21st century. It examines the dynamics of escalation and assesses the implications for air- and spacepower strategy in limited conflicts against adversaries armed with nuclear weapons and other asymmetric capabilities. The need to defend U.S. interests and provide stability in such a complex and dangerous environment raises several important questions that this monograph seeks to answer:

1. What is the fundamental nature of escalation? That is, removed from the historical and, perhaps, artificial context of bipolar,

superpower competition, what are the motives and mechanisms that drive escalation in military conflict?
2. What escalation risks result when those motives and mechanisms engage during confrontations with adversaries in the three categories of threat that characterize the current security environment?
3. What can U.S. military and civilian leaders do to manage those risks?

Organization and Approach

To answer these questions, this monograph surveys a wide assortment of information sources, ranging from Cold War–era theory and historical cases to records of more recent confrontations and the writings of contemporary adversaries, actual and potential. Chapter Two explores the nature of escalation and identifies its fundamental mechanisms and the motives that drive them, laying the groundwork for understanding how to manage the dynamic relationships between opponents that typify limited war.

Chapter Three examines contemporary Chinese thinking about escalation and war control. It assesses and interprets relevant writings by Chinese security analysts to determine potential escalation risks stemming from Beijing's strategic doctrines on nuclear weapons, conventional missile operations, and space warfare.

Chapter Four explores the escalation dynamics that new regional nuclear powers generate. It first identifies the risks that attend all states with emerging nuclear capabilities, regardless of their ideologies or forms of governance. The chapter then examines the escalation dynamics that might emerge in interstate wars or state failures in Northeast Asia, South Asia, and Southwest Asia.

Chapter Five takes on the thorny problem of how to manage escalation in conflicts with irregular adversaries. It identifies the diverse and often poorly understood escalation pressures that attend operations nominally placed at the low end of what some analysts refer to as the *spectrum of conflict*. Then, it examines more closely two cases that we believe are particularly instructive for the current security environment: Beirut, Lebanon, in 1982–1984 and Mogadishu, Somalia, in 1992–1994. Drawing lessons from those cases, the chapter examines the escalation dynamics of global jihad, the campaign of terrorist violence that militant Islamists have waged against the United States for more than a decade, and explains how escalation management should factor into any strategy to counter that threat.

Chapter Six synthesizes lessons from the foregoing chapters, considers what they suggest for managing escalation in the early 21st century, and offers recommendations for the U.S. Air Force.

This monograph includes three appendixes that provide additional analysis supporting selected portions of the text. Appendix A examines China's use of force since 1949, illustrating the continuities between China's historical propensity for escalation and the contemporary writings assessed in Chapter Three. Appendix B provides more detailed accounts of the Beirut and Mogadishu case studies summarized in Chapter Five. Appendix C explains the modified Delphi analysis methodology used to assess escalation dynamics in two scenarios: one involving a Sino-U.S. confrontation over the status of Taiwan and one involving nuclear powers and nonstate actors in a hypothetical collapse of the government of Pakistan.

CHAPTER TWO
The Nature of Escalation

During the Cold War, the subject of escalation attracted great attention from policymakers, strategists, and scholars. Their concerns centered primarily on the possibility of crises between the United States and the Soviet Union escalating into war; of limited, conventional wars escalating into world wars; and, especially, the use of nuclear weapons.[1] Escalation was by no means a new problem in international politics, as the July crisis triggering World War I in 1914 demonstrates,[2] but the nuclear and airpower revolutions greatly increased the possibility that escalation might quickly lead to catastrophic results, even as

---

[1] Among the most prominent studies of escalation during the Cold War are Kahn, 1965; Bernard Brodie, *Escalation and the Nuclear Option*, Princeton, N.J.: Princeton University Press, 1966; Richard Smoke, *War: Controlling Escalation*, Cambridge, Mass.: Harvard University Press, 1977; and Barry R. Posen, *Inadvertent Escalation: Conventional War and Nuclear Risks*, Ithaca, N.Y.: Cornell University Press, 1991.

However, escalation was a prominent concern in practically every analysis of nuclear strategy and deterrence. See Schelling 1960, 1966. For an overview of nuclear escalation issues, see Karl P. Mueller, "Strategic Airpower and Nuclear Strategy: New Theory for a Not-Quite-So-New Apocalypse," in Phillip S. Meilinger, ed., *The Paths of Heaven: The Evolution of Airpower Theory*, Maxwell AFB, Ala.: Air University Press, 1997.

[2] On the outbreak of World War I, see James Joll, *The Origins of the First World War*, 2nd ed., New York: Longman, 1992; Luigi Albertini, *The Origins of the War of 1914*, three vols., Isabelle M. Massey, ed. and trans., Oxford, UK: Oxford University Press, 1952–1957; Barbara W. Tuchman, *The Guns of August*, New York: Dell, 1962; L. C. F. Turner, *Origins of the First World War*, New York: W. W. Norton, 1970; Steven E. Miller, Sean M. Lynn-Jones, and Stephen Van Evera, eds., *Military Strategy and the Origins of the First World War*, rev. ed., Princeton, N.J.: Princeton University Press, 1991.

leaders sought to control it.[3] Once under way, wars often escalate into forms quite different from those anticipated by the people who began them;[4] among conflicts involving the United States, this has been true of, among others, the Revolutionary War, the War of 1812, the U.S. Civil War, the occupation of the Philippines, both World Wars, the wars in Korea and Vietnam, the interventions in Lebanon in 1983 and in Somalia in the early 1990s, and the 2003 invasion of Iraq.[5]

Thus, the problem of escalation has not disappeared as the potential for U.S.-Soviet nuclear confrontation has vanished, even though the attention devoted to studying escalation has waned over the past 15 years. Today, U.S. leaders must still consider escalation an important issue, not only in potential crises or conflicts with regional powers, including ones that possess or may soon possess nuclear weapons, but also when dealing with virtually any adversary in a situation in which the United States has an interest in keeping the conflict limited.

Understanding Escalation

Escalation can usefully be defined as *an increase in the intensity or scope of conflict that crosses threshold(s) considered significant by one or more of the participants.* Conflicts can intensify or expand in many ways, such as through attacks on targets previously considered to be off-limits, opening new theaters of operations against an enemy, or employing weapons not previously used in the conflict—a subject to which this discussion will return shortly. However, not every increase or expansion of violence is escalatory: Escalation occurs only when at least one of the parties involved believes that there has been a significant qualitative change in the conflict as a result of the new development. As will be discussed later, escalation can be a deliberate policy objective, an unintended side effect of policy, or purely accidental. Thus, it should

---

[3] Indeed, the development of airpower in World War I and of nuclear weapons in World War II were escalatory actions in their own right.

[4] See Geoffrey Blainey, *The Causes of War*, 3rd ed., New York: Free Press, 1988.

[5] U.S. experiences with escalation in Lebanon and Somalia are analyzed in Chapter Six.

be considered both as a strategic tool to be wielded or deterred and as a potential problem to be managed.

Escalation often occurs—and is usually envisioned—as an interactive process between two or more competitors, each escalating its threats or use of force in response to the actions of the other. But it can also be unilateral, with one combatant escalating to increase pressure against the other, independent of the enemy's actions. For example, during the air war that constituted most of Operation Desert Storm, Iraq repeatedly sought to escalate the conflict, including by firing ballistic missiles at Israel, in an effort to improve its situation in response to the frustratingly unchanging nature of the U.S.-led coalition's sustained air attacks. This was unsuccessful, as Israel did not intervene and the coalition refused to be drawn into a premature ground war. In contrast, the German initiation of unrestricted submarine warfare in World War I was intended to produce a decisive military advantage in the stalemate of that conflict without provoking a countervailing escalatory response. It was a strategic failure in both respects, as Britain soldiered on while the United States was drawn into the war on the side of the Allies far more quickly than Germany had anticipated.[6]

In general, when one side in a conflict violates an escalatory threshold, it will expect the enemy to follow suit. Thus, once Germany introduced gas warfare in World War I, it was natural for the Allies to conduct similar attacks, and this did not appear to either side to represent significant additional escalation.[7] In some cases, however, such a symmetrical response will be unavailable to or irrelevant for the adversary when the combatants' capabilities or vulnerabilities do not parallel each other. Responding in kind may also be unattractive even when it is possible because of the costs associated with doing so, espe-

---

[6] John Keegan, *The First World War*, New York: Vintage, 2000, pp. 265, 351–353; John Terraine, *The U-Boat Wars, 1916–1945*, New York: Putnam, 1989, pp. 8–16.

[7] This is not always the case, however. For example, during the Vietnam War, North Vietnamese forces made extensive use of neutral Laotian and Cambodian territory for their operations in South Vietnam before U.S. forces launched major operations in those states, yet the latter actions were widely perceived, including by the United States, as significant escalation.

cially when this would require a state to violate principles of conduct or morality to which it is attached.

Whether it occurs as the result of two parties responding, in turn, to each other's actions or through the unilateral actions of one side, escalation can occur quickly or slowly, in dramatic steps that are visible to almost any observer or in many incremental ones that may go unrecognized as constituting significant escalation until after the fact, even by those doing the escalating. In 1945, the U.S. strategic bombing campaign against Japan featured two profoundly escalatory developments: the initiation of devastating urban-area attacks with the firebombing of Tokyo on March 9–10 and the beginning of the nuclear era when Hiroshima was destroyed by an atomic bomb on August 6.[8] In contrast, the campaign against Japanese maritime commerce, primarily conducted by U.S. Navy submarines, escalated from near insignificance early in the war to the point of annihilating the Japanese economy without any individual action along the way amounting to a fundamental change in the terms of conflict.

In a general sense, escalation can occur in a host of different situations, including wars, crises (either with or without the possibility of armed conflict), trade disputes, and arms races, to say nothing of escalation in realms other than international politics. In this study, we focused on escalation in confrontations that involve or might come to involve the use of military force, though many of the features discussed here also apply to escalation in other arenas or circumstances. We do not address arms races in this analysis, even though they are military in nature, because, in most cases, they occur over prolonged periods during which the states engaging in them have ample time to make deliberate decisions that are usually executed in a centralized way. While some of the escalation dynamics discussed here also apply to the way in which arms races play out, other factors are involved that are not relevant to this study.

---

[8] It is noteworthy that the Hiroshima raid did not represent an unprecedented level of destruction; the first Tokyo raid caused far more death and damage than did any subsequent air attack. However, both U.S. and Japanese leaders perceived it as the beginning of a significant new phase in the conflict.

Thresholds and the Subjectivity of Escalation

Escalation thresholds come in many forms, and their diverse variety is one of the reasons that escalation can be more difficult to control, manage, or exploit successfully than optimists initially expect.[9] Some escalation thresholds are symmetric; that is, either side in a conflict might act to cross a threshold that is viewed more or less similarly by both, for example, by being the first to initiate hostilities in a crisis, to cross recognized international territorial boundaries, or to employ nuclear weapons in a war.[10] In other cases, a threshold may loom large for one side but may be obscure or invisible to the other. All thresholds are socially constructed and, ultimately, exist in the minds of the actors rather than in objective reality.[11] If one party knows that another considers a particular threshold to be important—say, for example, Beijing's great sensitivity to the possibility of a Taiwanese declaration of independence from China—the threshold is likely to be significant in its own eyes as a result. However, the adversary's perspective is not always well known or understood, nor is it always clear how accurate an enemy's understanding of its own concerns is. This issue is discussed further in this chapter and throughout this monograph.

In general, the thresholds that will be the easiest to anticipate are those that are well established in prewar or precrisis strategy and policy. These may be thresholds that apply across a range of adversaries and contingencies, such as the threshold of nuclear-weapon use, or may be

---

[9] See Schelling, 1966, pp. 153–168 and 283–286.

[10] Although employment of nuclear weapons is, perhaps, the most unambiguously escalatory action that a state can take in a war, even it might not be clearly recognizable. During the Cold War, there were concerns that some uses of very powerful conventional munitions, such as fuel-air explosives, might initially be mistaken for low-yield nuclear attacks. Moreover, some uses of nuclear weapons, such as a detonation in space to attack satellites or to create damaging but mostly nonlethal electromagnetic pulse effects against terrestrial targets, might represent something less than an unambiguous violation of the nuclear threshold as it is most commonly conceived. Whether hostilities have begun in a crisis can also be unclear, if forces on one or both sides launch attacks or commit territorial violations on a very limited scale.

[11] Opportunities for escalation can also be asymmetric, of course, such as when one party in a conflict possesses capabilities or suffers vulnerabilities that its opponent does not. In contrast, asymmetries in thresholds are conceptual rather than physical.

particular to specific cases, such as the prospect of Taiwan asserting its independence. Such thresholds may be viewed differently when their violation becomes an imminent possibility or when violation actually occurs, however, so assuming that they will work as previously advertised entails a significant risk of surprise for aspiring managers or practitioners of escalation. Even more challenging is the problem of anticipating thresholds that emerge during a conflict, typically in response to events or capabilities that were not foreseen or considered seriously as possibilities beforehand, as repeatedly occurred during the Cuban missile crisis.

States may also attempt to create or reinforce escalation thresholds to deter an enemy from crossing them. This may involve rhetorical or other political means, such as demonizing or formally outlawing the use of certain weapons[12] or physically limiting their own policy options, such as by visibly adopting war plans or force structures that will permit only large-scale warfare to deny the enemy the prospect of being able to start a limited war.[13] Most such measures will also constrain a state's own actions, however, which often weighs against the decision to employ them, or contribute to governments resisting efforts by outsiders to make escalation more difficult or expensive. Conversely, states may try to reduce the significance of a threshold to make crossing it easier, though altering an opponent's belief that something is important will often be more difficult than making a threshold appear more significant than it previously appeared to be.

Although some acts, such as using nuclear weapons in a war previously fought only with conventional arms, will appear escalatory to virtually any observer, in many cases, actions are perceived to represent significant escalation by one side in a conflict but not by another. The subjective nature of escalation thresholds has been an enduring problem for those seeking to control escalation, either to prevent it from

---

[12] The widely accepted declaration that chemical, biological, and nuclear weapons collectively constitute a single category of weapons of mass destruction, in spite of the enormous difference in the magnitude of their effects, is a particularly significant example of this pattern.

[13] Schelling, 1966, Chapters 2 and 3.

occurring or to use the prospect of potential escalation as a coercive lever. Cold War–era nuclear theorists and Kremlinologists wrestled with the problems of predicting Soviet escalation thresholds at great and ultimately inconclusive length. Would Moscow consider the use of chemical weapons on the battlefield to be a major escalation of conventional war, as Western leaders would? Would it view tactical nuclear attacks at sea or against targets in East Germany as more escalatory than conventional air strikes against the western USSR? Would Soviet leaders feel more threatened by nuclear attacks against their nuclear forces or against the Russian economic infrastructure? U.S. strategists also debated how the Soviets would respond to various forms of escalation: Would they be intimidated into backing down, or would anger or fear prompt them to respond in kind or with further escalation? But the problem of anticipating the enemy's perceptions was, in some ways, even more fundamental.

The opponents that the United States faces—or may yet face—in the 21st century generally have less spectacular escalation options than the Soviet Union did a generation ago, but predicting how they will perceive U.S. actions is not dramatically easier and, in some cases, can be even more challenging. For example, late in Operation Deliberate Force, NATO's 1995 air campaign against the Bosnian Serb Army, cruise missiles were employed for the first time in the conflict when U.S. Navy Tomahawk Land Attack Missiles (TLAMs) attacked an air-defense target in western Bosnia. Alliance air planners selected TLAMs for the mission purely for reasons of operational utility, but Serbian and Bosnian Serb leaders interpreted the use of cruise missiles as a major escalation in NATO's prosecution of the war.[14] Such surprises can result from having imperfect intelligence about the enemy, but in many cases, the problem is not that the enemy's attitude toward

---

[14] Similarly, the Serbs interpreted the expansion of NATO's air defense–suppression effort from eastern to western Bosnia, which occurred as a matter of course when sufficient aircraft became available to conduct the operation, as a deliberately and significantly escalatory step in NATO's campaign. During the same conflict, Italy rejected U.S. plans to base F-117 stealth fighters in its territory, considering this to be highly escalatory, to the consternation of U.S. military leaders who saw little political difference between dropping 2,000-pound bombs from F-117s and doing the same with F-16s.

one or another potentially escalatory action is unknown, but rather that the relevant beliefs and decisions are actually unformed until the event occurs. Subsequent chapters in this monograph illustrate this in the case of contemporary Chinese thinking about escalation, which is still in an early developmental state. Even after decades of deliberation about escalation, U.S. analysts cannot predict with certainty how their own government would be likely to react to many sorts of potential attacks, such as the deliberate destruction of U.S. satellites. Nor, in many cases, can U.S. leaders themselves know how they would respond until they are actually presented with such contingencies.

Limited War

To describe escalation as the expansion or intensification of conflict is equivalent to saying that it is the relaxation or erosion of limits on the use of force that are recognized, either formally or informally, by one or more of the combatants. Although the *limited war* label is most commonly associated with small conflicts fought in peripheral corners of the world, nearly all wars are limited to one degree or another. Even in the most desperate periods of World War II, certain rules of conduct were respected by most of the belligerents: The violation of neutral territory was the exception rather than the rule, some types of targets were typically exempted from attack, and certain weapons were not employed.[15] Such limits constrain the conduct of some wars and the actions of some combatants more than others, of course, with civil wars more often approaching the unrestrained ideal of "absolute war" than interstate wars over relatively low stakes. Yet, even in the most extreme conflicts, there are usually formal or tacit escalatory thresholds that can either be respected or violated by the participants.

Escalation Dominance

It is common to describe the process of escalation in terms of a metaphorical ladder for any given crisis or conflict, with each rung representing a different level of intensity in the confrontation. In a very simple

---

[15] See Jeffrey W. Legro, *Cooperation Under Fire: Anglo-German Restraint During World War II*, Ithaca, N.Y.: Cornell University Press, 1995.

formulation typical of the Cold War, the lowest escalatory rung might be normal peacetime conditions, with higher rungs corresponding, in turn, to shows of force, limited conventional conflict, full-blown conventional war, limited nuclear warfare, and—at the top of the ladder—an all-out strategic nuclear exchange. However, such a ladder could include a far greater number of distinct levels of escalation. Herman Kahn organized his book *On Escalation* (1965) around a hypothetical ladder of escalation in a confrontation between nuclear-armed superpowers comprising no fewer than 44 rungs, more than half of which involved at least some use of nuclear weapons.[16]

The ideal situation for a participant in a conflict or confrontation would be having the ability to win at any possible level of escalation and to be able to choose the rung on the ladder at which the issue would be resolved, since the goal is not merely to prevail but to achieve the most favorable outcome at the lowest possible cost, and costs and risks tend to rise as escalation occurs. A more plausible aspiration is to achieve a position of *escalation dominance*, a condition in which a combatant has the ability to escalate a conflict in ways that will be disadvantageous or costly to the adversary while the adversary cannot do the same in return, either because it has no escalation options or because the available options would not improve the adversary's situation.[17] If a combatant enjoys escalation dominance—and only to the extent that

---

[16] Kahn's ladder could, in fact, have been considerably larger, as it included few rungs involving purely conventional uses of force and none featuring the use of chemical or biological but not nuclear weapons.

[17] Escalation dominance was a central concern of Cold War–era strategists, who worried, for example, about facing situations in which the Soviets might possess the ability to fight a European war at a level of escalation that would be disadvantageous to the West, leaving NATO with a grim choice between losing the war or raising the level of violence and, subsequently, raising the costs of such a conflict to still-higher levels. Current U.S. Air Force doctrine defines escalation dominance as "the ability to increase the enemy's costs of defiance while denying them the opportunity to neutralize those costs or counter-escalate" (Headquarters, U.S. Air Force Doctrine Center, *Strategic Attack*, Air Force Doctrine Document 2-1.2, September 30, 2003, p. 33).

the enemy realizes this (a crucial additional consideration)—threats of escalation should be particularly powerful coercive instruments.[18]

True escalation dominance is rarely attainable in any challenging confrontation, however. Most enemies, even those dramatically inferior to the United States, will have some ability to escalate, even when few military options are available to them. High stakes and limited options can inspire desperate measures, such as resorting to irregular warfare or using one's own citizens as human shields. Therefore, it is more useful to treat escalation dominance as a philosophical aspiration than as a feasible policy objective. Moreover, when doing this, it is important to consider that invoking the *escalation dominance* label provides no real information about a situation beyond that which one must already possess to know whether, or to what extent, it applies. NATO gradually achieved something approaching escalation dominance during the course of Operation Allied Force, the 1999 coercive air campaign against Serbia, and this was ultimately recognized by Belgrade. But this observation does not explain what happened—that the Serbs gradually saw one potentially escalatory measure or event after another, ranging from largely ineffective air-defense efforts to serious alliance bombing errors to hopes for external assistance, fail to weaken NATO's growing resolve to see the campaign through to successful completion.[19]

One approach for seeking a measure of dominance in escalation is to cultivate asymmetries in which the enemy is unable to respond in kind to an escalatory act, for example, by acquiring a class of weapons that the opponent does not possess. If these are employed in a conflict, and the opponent cannot respond symmetrically, it may create an escalation dilemma for the adversary in the form of a choice between not countering the escalation or crossing other escalation thresholds, with all the risks and costs of doing so. Thus, during the Cold War, many Western strategists feared that not being able to respond effectively in

---

[18] Daniel L. Byman, Matthew C. Waxman, and Eric V. Larson, *Air Power as a Coercive Instrument*, Santa Monica, Calif.: RAND Corporation, MR-1061-AF, 1999, pp. 30–36.

[19] See Benjamin S. Lambeth, *NATO's Air War for Kosovo: A Strategic and Operational Assessment*, Santa Monica, Calif.: RAND Corporation, MR-1365-AF, 2001.

kind to a limited Soviet nuclear attack would weaken U.S. deterrence if threats of massive retaliation lacked credibility in Moscow and, for this as well as other reasons, advocated developing and maintaining extensive counterforce capabilities in the U.S. nuclear arsenal.[20] However, escalation dominance often has more to do with exploiting the enemy's asymmetric vulnerabilities than with developing unique means of attack: For example, U.S. aversion to killing large numbers of civilians often gives an escalatory advantage to insurgent enemies that has nothing to do with a lack of U.S. combat capability.[21]

Although it provides a handy first-cut image of the escalation concept, the escalation ladder metaphor can be seriously misleading if taken too seriously, in at least two respects. First, it offers a linear model of a phenomenon that is actually far more complex and ambiguous. There are a host of directions in which a conflict or confrontation can escalate, and, unlike the rungs on a ladder, it is not always clear whether the opponent or a third-party audience will consider one step to be more or less extreme than another, especially when the steps involve dissimilar measures. Will the first bombardment of a city using conventional explosives appear more or less escalatory than the first poison gas attack against a military target? Is attempting to kill a nation's leader more or less provocative than gravely insulting the national religion? Answering such questions is not only often difficult but also frequently unimportant.

The other serious problem with this metaphor is that you cannot fall up a ladder. Climbing a ladder requires purposeful effort, while escalation can happen unintentionally and—especially in armed conflicts and often in prewar crises—it is usually easier to escalate than to deescalate. Thus, instead of analogizing escalation to climbing a ladder, a more apt metaphor would be traversing a treacherous ravine face or mountainside, with the *bottom* of the slope representing the most

---

[20] Charles L. Glaser, *Analyzing Strategic Nuclear Policy*, Princeton, N.J.: Princeton University Press, 1990, Chapters 2 and 7.

[21] Similarly, if the United States possessed an arsenal of biological or chemical weapons, it would do little or nothing to ameliorate the potential threat of enemies using such weapons against U.S. targets.

extreme level of escalation.[22] Depending on the location of hand- and footholds, descending to greater degrees of escalation may assist one's progress, or may even be essential to it, but the challenge is to maintain control over this escalatory descent.

Dimensions of Escalation: Vertical, Horizontal, and Political

Escalation may take many different forms. Escalation that involves an increase in the intensity of armed conflict or confrontation, such as employing types of weapons not previously used in the conflict or attacking new categories of targets, is often collectively described as *vertical escalation*, in contrast to *horizontal escalation*, which refers to expanding the geographic scope of a conflict (for example, by conducting operations into or through territory previously treated as neutral by the combatants).[23] Escalation can also occur along lines that do not easily fit into either category, particularly when states adopt more extreme or unlimited objectives in conflicts or crises, but also through measures such as relaxing behavioral constraints that protect civilians[24] or causing deliberate environmental damage; we might reasonably group these other forms of escalation into a third dimension under the label *political escalation*.

Distinguishing between, say, vertical and horizontal escalation sometimes helps to clarify strategic discussions. For example, in the early 1980s, the Reagan administration floated the idea of threatening to respond to a Warsaw Pact attack against Western Europe with horizontal escalation—by attacking the Soviets or their allies in regions in

---

[22] How treacherous the slope is would depend on many factors, including leaders' understanding of escalation. In July 1914, European policymakers might be said to have been attempting to negotiate the mountainside at night, in the rain, while wearing sunglasses.

[23] Kahn, 1965, pp. 4–6, defined three dimensions of escalation: "increasing intensity," "widening the area," and "compounding escalation," the last being escalation that is both vertical and horizontal, as described here.

[24] See Alexander B. Downes, "Desperate Times, Desperate Measures: The Causes of Civilian Victimization in War," *International Security*, Vol. 30, No. 4, Spring 2006.

which the United States enjoyed clear conventional military supremacy, such as Cuba or the Far East—as an alternative to vertical escalation to the use of nuclear weapons in Europe.[25] Talking about horizontal escalation is also useful in its own right because it serves as a reminder that escalation can take forms other than the more vertical ones that are most commonly associated with the escalation concept, such as escalating from conventional to nuclear war.

In practice, however, the lines separating vertical, horizontal, and political escalation are often far from clear. Dropping bombs closer to the previously untouched enemy capital, for example, as the United States did gradually during Operation Rolling Thunder in Vietnam and abruptly in the 1942 Doolittle Raid against Japan, might reasonably be described as vertical or horizontal escalation or both. Blockading the enemy's homeland during a limited regional conflict might simultaneously constitute escalation on all three dimensions, as could initiating antisatellite warfare or computer-network attacks. Thus, in practice, it is more realistic to picture the three dimensions as defining a multidimensional escalation space rather than being exclusive policy categories into which particular acts of escalation can be sorted (see Figure 2.1). Moreover, labeling an action as vertical or horizontal escalation usually does not reveal or explain very much about it even, when doing so is relatively straightforward. For all of these reasons, discussing the dimensions of escalation tends to be less useful analytically, and less relevant for policymaking, than examining two other characteristics of escalatory actions that often receive less attention: the mechanisms of escalation, and the motives for it.

Escalation Mechanisms

In seeking to understand, rather than merely enumerate, the forms that escalation can take, particularly with respect to the goal of managing

---

[25] This idea foundered on the realization that Moscow might consider the loss of its peripheral interests relatively unimportant in comparison to the prospect of victory over NATO. See Joshua M. Epstein, "Horizontal Escalation: Sour Notes on a Recurrent Theme," *International Security*, Vol. 8, No. 3, Winter 1983–1984.

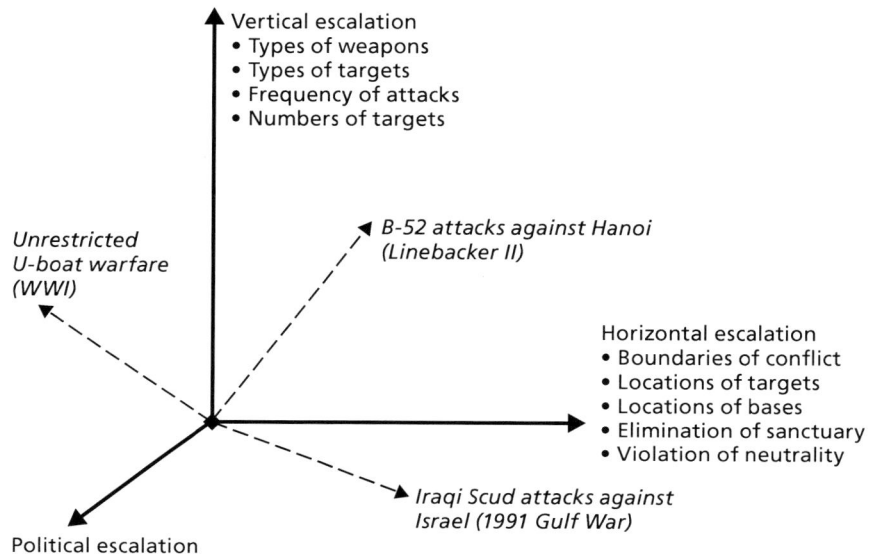

Figure 2.1
Dimensions of Escalation

Vertical escalation
- Types of weapons
- Types of targets
- Frequency of attacks
- Numbers of targets

Unrestricted U-boat warfare (WWI)

B-52 attacks against Hanoi (Linebacker II)

Horizontal escalation
- Boundaries of conflict
- Locations of targets
- Locations of bases
- Elimination of sanctuary
- Violation of neutrality

Iraqi Scud attacks against Israel (1991 Gulf War)

Political escalation
- Changes in objectives, demands, rhetoric, and other characteristics
- Relaxing or abandoning behavioral constraints or rules of engagement (ROE)

RAND MG614-2.1

or controlling escalation, two sets of properties loom large: the *mechanisms* by which escalation can occur (discussed here) and the *motives* that cause actors to pursue escalatory behavior (examined later in this chapter). Three different but not always separate types of mechanisms may lead to escalation, which we label as *deliberate, inadvertent,* and *accidental* escalation.

Deliberate Escalation

As its name indicates, deliberate escalation occurs when the actions of a state (or other actor) cross an escalatory threshold in a conflict or a confrontation more or less intentionally. The results may not be precisely as expected, but, at least in broad terms, the decision includes recognizing that the action under consideration could or will be escalatory and deciding that, in spite of—or because of—this, it is worth doing. There is a variety of possible motives for deliberate escalation, as the next section will discuss, but whatever these are, the action is taken in the expectation, or at least the hope, that doing so will make the escalating actor better off as a result. The most obvious form for this anticipated advantage to take would be a greater prospect of achieving success in the conflict or confrontation, or a reduced chance of losing.

This is the escalation mechanism most naturally associated with the metaphor of climbing a ladder of escalation: A state finds itself faring poorly in a conflict and calculates that, by escalating to the use of additional types of weapons, the less constrained use of force, or the widening of the war, it stands to improve its fortunes. Classic examples include Germany in World War I beginning unrestricted submarine warfare in the hopes of strangling the British war economy and introducing gas warfare in an effort to break the deadlock of trench warfare on the Western front, the British coastal mining and subsequent German invasion of Norway in 1940, and the German bombardment of England with V-1 and V-2 missiles in 1944–1945. Later, the Vietnam War was punctuated by repeated U.S. efforts to gain the upper hand through escalatory actions, including the bombing of North Vietnam, the invasion of Cambodia, the mining of Haiphong harbor, and the use of B-52 strategic bombers against Hanoi in December 1972.

In some cases, such as the air war against North Vietnam and the V-weapon attacks, deliberate escalation is attractive, at least in part precisely because it is escalatory and may have a particular psychological impact. Insurgents and terrorists often deliberately employ escalatory strategies to call attention to their actions or to provoke their enemies into overreacting in ways that will garner sympathy and generate additional recruits for their cause.[26] However, deliberate escalation can also occur in cases, as in the World War I submarine blockade of Great Britain, in which the escalatory nature of the policy is incidental to its value or is even a drawback if there is a dangerous risk of counter-escalation, such as encouraging aggrieved neutral states to support the enemy. Indeed, escalatory considerations may weigh both in favor of and against a measure. When the United States began bombing North

---

[26] See also Chaim Kaufmann, "Possible and Impossible Solutions to Ethnic Civil Wars," *International Security,* Vol. 20, No. 4, Spring 1996, on escalation effects in ethnic conflicts.

Vietnam, it also imposed many constraints on the air campaign to minimize international opprobrium and, especially, to avoid provoking Chinese or Soviet intervention in the war. Similarly, escalating rhetoric or taking up expanded war aims may bolster popular support for a conflict or reassure allies, but such actions may also intensify enemy hostility or suspicion.[27]

Averting deliberate escalation by an opponent is a matter of deterrence: that is, convincing the adversary that taking action will leave it worse off than it would be if it did not act. As when seeking to deter a potential belligerent from starting a war—which often is itself escalation of a prewar crisis—deterrence may be achieved through threats of punishment or of denial or through rewards for not violating the status quo.[28] In the context of escalation, punitive deterrence is based on making the costs of escalation high enough to outweigh its anticipated benefits, while deterrence by denial involves making the prospects that escalation will be beneficial appear low enough to render it less attractive than the alternative of not escalating. Reward or reassurance strategies seek to make the costs of not escalating appear low enough, or the benefits of restraint appear sufficiently high, to make it preferable to taking the escalatory action being contemplated.[29] Deterring deliberate escalation through either punishment or denial is likely to involve threats of counterescalation in response to the adversary's potential action. In some relatively easy cases, merely threatening to match the escalation symmetrically may be sufficient to deter it; more challenging are situations in which greater or different escalatory responses would be required to offset the advantage provided by the enemy's escalation. Deterrence also tends to be particularly challenging when the deterring

---

[27] See for example Anne Armstrong, *Unconditional Surrender: The Impact of the Casablanca Policy upon World War II*, New Brunswick, N.J.: Rutgers University Press, 1961.

[28] See, for example, Thomas W. Milburn, "What Constitutes Effective Deterrence?" *Journal of Conflict Resolution*, Vol. 3, No. 2, June 1959, and David E. Johnson, Karl P. Mueller, and William H. Taft V, *Conventional Coercion Across the Spectrum of Operations: The Utility of Military Force in the Emerging Security Environment*, Santa Monica, Calif.: RAND Corporation, MR-1494-A, 2002, pp. 7–18.

[29] David A. Baldwin, "The Power of Positive Sanctions," *World Politics*, Vol. 24, No. 1, October 1971.

party has not actually decided how it would want to respond to a given escalatory possibility.

Deterrence is often a difficult problem (and one to which this discussion will return shortly), but it is relatively well understood following decades of theoretical and historical scholarship far too extensive to summarize here.[30] If managing escalation were merely a question of deterrence, it would be a relatively straightforward challenge in principle, however complicated deterring specific actors from escalating under certain circumstances might be. However, escalation can also occur as a result of mechanisms that present a very different set of problems for strategists.

Inadvertent Escalation

Inadvertent escalation occurs when a combatant's intentional actions are unintentionally escalatory, usually because they cross a threshold of intensity or scope in the conflict or confrontation that matters to the adversary but appears insignificant or is invisible to the party taking the action. Such a failure to anticipate the escalatory effects of an action can result from a lack of understanding of how the opponent will view the action, it may result from incorrectly anticipating the second- or third-order consequences of the action in question, or both.

In the preeminent examination of this subject, Barry Posen predicted in the 1980s that in the event of a conventional war in Europe between NATO and the Warsaw Pact, alliance military operations, including suppression of Soviet air-defense radars and attacks against Soviet ballistic missile submarines in the Arctic Ocean, could quickly place Moscow in a position in which it might fear being disabled by a U.S. nuclear first strike, with a crippled early warning system and its survivable nuclear retaliatory capability eroded. Posen argued that, in this event, nervous Soviet leaders might be encouraged to employ nuclear weapons in the fear that an opening window of vulnerability

---

[30] Although deterrence is relatively well understood in the strategic context in which it was contemplated, namely, bipolar competition, this monograph will illustrate that the conditions in which it will need to be applied for escalation management in the current security environment are vastly different and yet to be fully explored.

to attack by U.S. strategic and theater nuclear forces would soon leave them helpless.[31]

One of the most significant cases in which inadvertent escalation actually did occur was China's entry into the Korean War in late 1950. As UN forces drove into North Korea after expelling the North Korean invasion force from the south, the possibility that this might provoke Chinese intervention was raised and dismissed. However, Chinese leaders deemed the situation to be unacceptably threatening and, as UN forces approached the Yalu, sent the People's Liberation Army (PLA) into Korea, turning the tide and resulting in two additional years of attrition warfare on the peninsula.[32] The July crisis of 1914 was riddled with inadvertent and deliberate escalation, including the German chancellor ordering his army to carry out its inflexible mobilization plan that depended on sending a German force across the Belgian border to seize the key transportation nexus of Liège, which would activate Great Britain's treaty commitment to defend Belgium, while averting British involvement in the coming war remained a central goal of German diplomacy.[33]

Inadvertent escalation cannot be deterred (though the actions that could lead to it might be), because it is not the result of decisionmakers choosing to escalate but, rather, failing to realize that there is a choice to be made. Thus, to reduce the risk of inadvertent escalation, the adversary does not need to be frightened but, instead, enlightened—or, more accurately, it must *first* be enlightened, after which deterrence

---

[31] Barry R. Posen, "Inadvertent Nuclear War? Escalation and NATO's Northern Flank," *International Security*, Vol. 7, No. 2, Autumn 1982; Posen, 1991.

[32] Historians and security analysts long assumed that the UN forces' approach to the Yalu was what provoked Chinese intervention. However, more recent scholarship based on Chinese records suggests that Beijing's escalation threshold was actually the 38th parallel (Thomas J. Christensen, "Threats, Assurances, and the Last Chance for Peace: The Lesson's of Mao's Korean War Telegrams," *International Security*, Vol. 17, No. 1, Summer 1992). This is a classic example of the difficulties of divining an adversary's thresholds and the associated risks of inadvertent escalation.

[33] Stephen Van Evera, "The Cult of the Offensive and the Origins of the First World War," in Miller, Lynn-Jones, and Van Evera, eds., 1991, especially pp. 93–95; see also Marc Trachtenberg, "The Meaning of Mobilization in 1914," in Miller, Lynn-Jones, and Van Evera, eds., 1991, pp. 208–219.

may or may not still be required, depending on whether the action still holds appeal once its escalatory potential is made clear.

Several factors make this more problematic in practice than it may appear at first glance, however. One is that an inadvertent escalation risk may not be recognized in advance by any party in a conflict. In 1950, the United States did not recognize the likelihood that China would intervene in Korea if UN forces continued advancing north; but Beijing, which had tried, too subtly as it turned out, to communicate its intention to enter the war, did not realize that the situation was not understood in Washington. In 1914, no one other than the German army could have explained to Chancellor Theobald von Bethmann-Hollweg that mobilizing to invade France meant that its troops would march into Belgium. In other cases, no one at all on either side may realize that a course of action (COA) is potentially escalatory until it is carried out, especially if it is a less-than-obvious possibility beforehand.

Another common obstacle to such strategic explanation is that it may appear to be risky to announce or acknowledge one's political or military vulnerabilities. It was a relatively straightforward matter for a U.S. political scientist to warn that conventional war in Europe might leave the Soviet Union vulnerable to a nuclear first strike to a degree that could make Moscow dangerously insecure. However, it would have been unthinkable for Soviet leaders to make the same suggestion.

Given these challenges, minimizing the risks of inadvertent escalation as a result both of one's own actions and those of the adversary potentially involves several elements. One is working to recognize in advance the paths by which inadvertent escalation might occur in a particular situation, which depends on collecting and, especially, analyzing intelligence about the adversary's capabilities and possible behavior, as well as analyzing one's own possible actions with attention to their potentially escalatory effects. Another is sensitizing leaders, strategists, and planners to the possibility and nature of inadvertent escalation in general and its potential risks in specific contingencies so that they will take these considerations into account when making decisions and plans. Finally, there is the problem of warning adversaries about inadvertent escalation risks they may not have recognized.

Accidental Escalation

Like inadvertent escalation, accidental escalation is unintended, but instead of being the unforeseen result of intentional action, it is the consequence of events that were not intended in the first place. These actions might be pure accidents, such as a bombing raid attacking the wrong target due to a navigation error or a mechanical failure or an attack striking the wrong target due to its misidentification. Among the most significant examples of such events occurred in 1940, when, on August 24, a small force of German bombers accidentally attacked London. In response, the Royal Air Force launched its first raid against Berlin on the following night, which, in turn, contributed to the German decision to begin the Blitz, the 1940–1941 urban bombing campaign against London and other British cities.

Scott Sagan has documented a number of accidents involving U.S. nuclear capabilities during the Cold War that either created the potential for escalatory results or could have done so if they had occurred during a crisis; that they did not spin out of control is encouraging for those who seek to manage escalation, but the fact that the accidents occurred at all in light of U.S. concerns about nuclear safety serves as a reminder about the incomplete extent to which even heroic efforts can reduce the likelihood of potentially significant accidents in military operations.[34] In a very different setting, the U.S. Revolutionary War began with (though it was not caused by) an act of accidental escalation: Who fired "the shot heard 'round the world" when British and colonial militia troops faced each other on the village green of Lexington, Massachusetts, on April 19, 1775, remains a mystery, but the shot was not fired at the order of either commander. The general exchange of fire that ensued marked the beginning of armed combat that continued for the next six-and-a-half years.[35]

---

[34] Scott D. Sagan, *The Limits of Safety: Organizations, Accidents, and Nuclear Weapons*, Princeton, N.J.: Princeton University Press, 1993.

[35] To this list of significant or potentially significant cases of accidental escalation could be added the Gulf of Tonkin incident. Two days after an attack by North Vietnamese patrol boats against the destroyer USS *Maddox* on August 2, 1964, *Maddox* and USS *Turner Joy* defended themselves for hours against what they mistakenly believed to be a series of attacks that is now recognized never to have occurred. In response to these events, the United States

Accidental escalation can also result from military forces intentionally taking actions that are not intended by national leaders because the former do not understand the intent of the latter (due to a failure either to give or to receive relevant orders and guidance clearly) or because they disregard it and act on their own. Several potential paths to accidental escalation during the Cuban missile crisis as a result of U.S. military operations being conducted according to standard operating procedures unfamiliar to national leaders have become enduring cautionary tales in escalation scholarship.[36] Certainly, the most significant case of accidental escalation in recent U.S. military operations was the highly publicized abuse of Iraqi prisoners at the Abu Ghraib prison in 2003, which caused far-reaching damage to U.S. efforts to achieve strategic success in the occupation and stabilization of Iraq by increasing hostility and resistance to U.S. forces in the country.

Like inadvertent escalation, accidental escalation is something to be managed rather than deterred. The sources of accidental escalation usually reside at the front line rather than in the centers of command, however, so policy responses to the mechanisms will look quite different. Prescriptions for minimizing the risks of accidental escalatory events depend on the nature of the accident. The chances of accidents occurring due to failures of mechanical systems (either literally or figuratively) can be reduced (but not eliminated) by designing these systems in such a way that allows for a high degree of reliability and by creating procedures, including ROE for armed forces, designed to minimize such risks. Accidental events that result from human error or indifference can be addressed by measures to improve operators' competence and their attention to minimizing the risks in question.[37] However, accidents that result from those implementing policy while

---

launched air attacks against North Vietnamese naval facilities and, three days later, Congress passed the Gulf of Tonkin Resolution authorizing President Johnson to use U.S. military force to defend South Vietnam.

[36] Graham T. Allison, *Essence of Decision: Explaining the Cuban Missile Crisis*, Boston: Little, Brown, 1971.

[37] On U.S. efforts to maximize nuclear weapons safety and the limits of what such measures can be expected to achieve, see Sagan, 1993.

unaware of their commanders' intent with regard to potentially escalatory actions have to be addressed in ways that reduce such shortfalls in knowledge, to which both military and bureaucratic habit and concerns about operational security often pose obstacles.

Complexity in Escalation

As this discussion indicates, controlling or preventing escalation calls for very different approaches, depending on the escalatory mechanism involved—approaches that may, in fact, conflict with each other. For example, measures to deter an enemy from seeking military advantage through deliberate escalation may increase the chances that escalation-provoking accidents will occur, or confidence-building measures to prevent inadvertent escalation may encourage the adversary to engage in deliberate escalation by signaling a reluctance to risk fighting with higher levels of violence.[38] However, the problem is further complicated by the fact that the three mechanisms do not operate in isolation of each other: The path that leads from the beginning of a crisis or conflict to its final form often involves more than one of these mechanisms, for example, when an inadvertently or accidentally escalatory reaction triggers a deliberately escalatory response.

It is also important to note that the three mechanisms of escalation described here are ideal types, and individual events can combine aspects of more than one of them, with correspondingly mixed implications for escalation management. For example, deliberately escalating in response to incorrect information about an adversary's actions—such as a false report that the enemy has attacked—resembles accidental escalation in some ways. The distinctions between these categories can also be straddled when decisionmakers consider the possibility that their actions will be escalatory but are so mistaken about

---

[38] The latter is known as the *stability-instability paradox*, the possibility that if both combatants expect nuclear war, for example, to be prohibitively costly, one of them might be emboldened to take military actions just short of the nuclear threshold, secure in the knowledge that the opponent will not be willing to escalate. See Glenn Snyder, *Deterrence and Defense*, Princeton, N.J.: Princeton University Press, 1961.

the nature or severity of these risks that their actions might be said to constitute inadvertent escalation, or when policies that are not directly escalatory nevertheless deliberately or inadvertently create conditions in which escalatory accidents become more likely. Figure 2.2 illustrates the primary categories of escalation in relation to these mechanisms and motives, which are discussed in the following section.

Motives for Escalation

Unlike inadvertent and accidental escalation, deliberate escalation is motivated, and, as with most deliberate behavior, understanding the

Figure 2.2
Key Escalation Categories

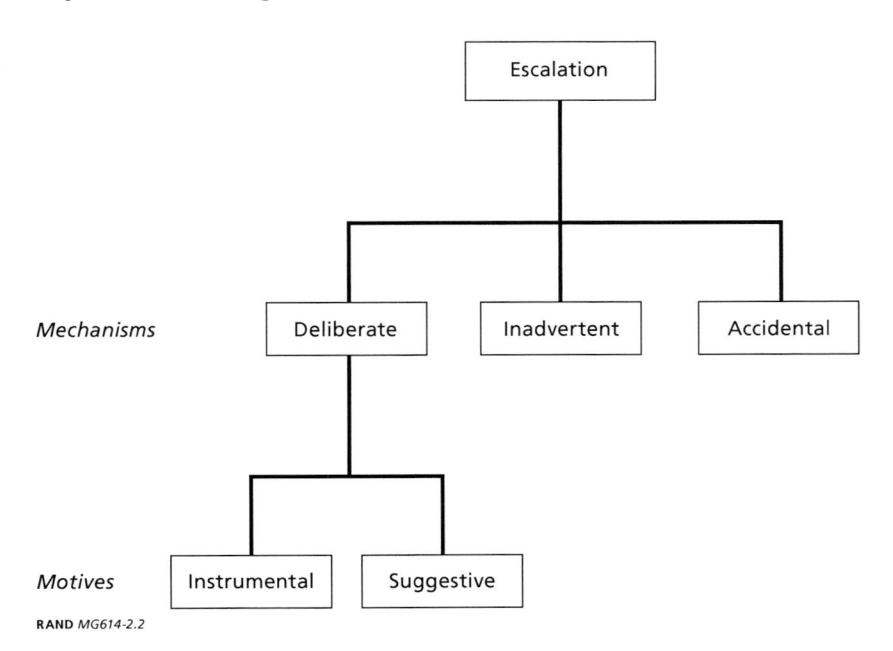

```
                        Escalation
                            |
         ┌──────────────────┼──────────────────┐
Mechanisms   Deliberate        Inadvertent        Accidental
                 |
         ┌───────┴───────┐
Motives  Instrumental   Suggestive
```

RAND MG614-2.2

motive for the action is central to deterring it.[39] There are, of course, many possible reasons that a participant may choose to escalate a conflict or confrontation, but at the most general level, it is useful to distinguish between two broad categories: *instrumental* and *suggestive* goals of escalation.

Instrumental Escalation

The most common reasons for escalation, and the motivations for most of the examples of deliberate escalation cited so far in this chapter, are instrumental ones. Instrumental motives for escalation are relatively direct: taking action that crosses an escalatory threshold because of the expectation, or at least the hope, that doing so will improve one's situation in the conflict, such as by making victory more likely or ending the conflict more quickly. Instrumental escalation often involves initiating the use of force in a crisis, such as launching an attack to rescue hostages whose release does not appear achievable through continued negotiation with their captors, or using force on a larger or more extreme scale during a conflict, such as invading an enemy's territory if blockade or coercive bombing alone seems likely to be ineffective or switching to suicide attack tactics in a terrorist campaign. It can also take the form of a desperate roll of the dice in the hopes of staving off defeat, as in the German V-weapon attacks against Britain or the Japanese kamikaze attacks against U.S. ships during the latter stages of World War II.

---

[39] *Motives*, as discussed here, refers to the objectives of the escalation action or strategy, rather than the actor's deeper, underlying motivation. Thus, for example, we would describe the introduction of gas warfare on the Western front in World War I as having been motivated by Germany's desire to break the deadlock of trench warfare and defeat the Allied armies, rather than by Germany's desire to become the dominant power in Europe and to achieve its "place in the sun," though the latter is also true in a more indirect sense. We do not distinguish greatly between, say, revisionist and status quo states' escalation behaviors, since either might employ or blunder into any of the escalation types described in this chapter. However, for discussions of the importance and effects of understanding such fundamental motivations, see Robert Jervis, "Cooperation Under the Security Dilemma," *World Politics*, Vol. 30, No. 2, January 1978, and Charles L. Glaser, "Political Consequences of Military Strategy: Expanding and Refining the Spiral and Deterrence Models," *World Politics*, Vol. 44, No. 4, July 1992.

The advantage anticipated from escalating is often essentially physical: Escalation promises to defeat the enemy, to halt an attacker, to present the adversary with a fait accompli that will be difficult to reverse. However, in some cases, escalation seeks to produce an effect that is more or less purely psychological or political, such as when Iraq began firing Scud missiles at Israel during the 1991 Gulf War.

Suggestive Escalation
In some cases, deliberately escalatory actions are taken not because of the direct results expected from them but, rather, to send a signal to the opponent (or to a third party) about what further escalation will or might occur in the future. This is suggestive escalation, a strategic approach most famously (and, after 40 years, still most elegantly) described by Thomas Schelling in *Arms and Influence* (1966). The essence of suggestive escalation is to communicate to the opponent that costly escalation will occur in the future in response to the potential behavior to be deterred or in the event that the adversary does not comply with certain demands. Sometimes, merely issuing an explicit threat is escalatory;[40] in other cases, suggestive escalation involves taking physical action, which may include using armed force, even on a substantial scale. In short, whatever its form, suggestive escalation hinges on creating the expectation or fear that the intensity or scope of a conflict will increase in the future.

The best-known example of suggestive escalation is, of course, Operation Rolling Thunder, the 1965–1967 bombing campaign in which U.S. leaders sought to coerce North Vietnam to abandon its support for the insurgency in South Vietnam through the prospect of an increasingly destructive series of air attacks. In this operation, U.S. planners hoped that gradually increasing the importance of the targets being attacked, striking targets progressively closer to the enemy capital, and increasing the number of sorties flown and the amount of munitions being dropped would make clear to Hanoi that the conflict

---

[40] Not all threats are escalatory, however. Threatening to harm an opponent is an act of escalation only if the act of making the threat itself crosses a significant threshold in the confrontation, whether or not actually carrying out the threat would constitute escalation.

would eventually escalate to a prohibitively costly level, so it would be sensible to comply with U.S. demands before suffering more serious losses. This message was not conveyed as clearly as Washington intended for a variety of reasons,[41] and even had it been, in retrospect, there was little prospect that the levels of destruction that the United States was ultimately willing to inflict would be sufficient to alter the North Vietnamese commitment to the war in the south.[42] The failure of gradual escalation in Operation Rolling Thunder gave the approach an exaggerated reputation for ineffectiveness, especially within the U.S. armed forces, that began to wane only with the success of the unintentionally gradual escalation of coercive air attacks against Serbia in Operation Allied Force some three decades later.

The use of force for suggestive escalation can also take forms other than gradual escalation. One of the most important is the demonstration attack, such as the detonation of a single nuclear weapon to signal that more may be used against more important targets if a conflict continues.[43] Perhaps the most famous such attack, though rarely cited as an example of escalation, was the 1942 Doolittle raid against Japan by carrier-launched U.S. Army Air Force bombers, which not only bolstered U.S. morale in the dark, early days of the Pacific war with the promise of more attacks on Japan to come, but also prompted the Japanese to divert significant forces to defend its home islands long before there was a serious threat of such attacks being mounted on a militarily significant level.

Another variation on the suggestive escalation theme that was particularly prominent in a number of crises between the superpowers during the first half of the Cold War is brinkmanship. In this strategy, one participant deliberately takes actions that create an existen-

---

[41] Wallace J. Thies, *When Governments Collide: Coercion and Diplomacy in the Vietnam Conflict, 1964–1968*, Berkeley, Calif.: University of California Press, 1980.

[42] Mark Clodfelter, *The Limits of Air Power: The American Bombing of North Vietnam*, New York: Free Press, 1989; Robert A. Pape, *Bombing to Win: Air Power and Coercion in War*, Ithaca, N.Y.: Cornell University Press, 1996, Chapter 6.

[43] Some other limited nuclear options would employ gradual escalation for suggestive purposes; see Glaser, 1990, pp. 41–44, 216–222.

tial shared risk of disaster: the possibility that further escalation that would be damaging to both sides will occur, regardless of whether either desires it, if the confrontation were to continue.[44]

Other Motives for Escalation

There are other possible, though less common, motives for deliberate escalation. For example, escalating the level of violence being used against an opponent can occasionally be attractive to a belligerent simply because of a desire to inflict damage for its own sake.[45] Deliberately escalating to set an example or to establish a reputation that may be coercively useful in future conflicts might also be considered a motivation separate from escalation, designed to alter the terms of the current conflict.[46]

In practice, these various motivations often overlap, particularly when a particular action both is instrumentally escalatory and signals the possibility of more escalation to come. Nevertheless, the distinction between instrumental and suggestive motives is significant when seeking to deter deliberate escalation, since different countermeasures will be relevant to making the enemy believe that escalation will be fruitless or counterproductive, depending on the results that the action under consideration is intended to achieve.

---

[44] Schelling, 1966, pp. 99–125.

[45] For example, the Iraqi decision to begin pumping Kuwaiti oil into the Persian Gulf in the final days of the 1991 Gulf War or, on an incomparably greater scale, the escalating Nazi extermination campaign against Jews and other genocidal target groups during World War II.

[46] See Jonathan Mercer, *Reputation and International Politics*, Ithaca, N.Y.: Cornell University Press, 1996, and Daryl G. Press, *Calculating Credibility: How Leaders Assess Military Threats*, Ithaca, N.Y.: Cornell University Press, 2005. Escalatory actions can also have reputational effects in a more immediate sense, such as when they make the escalating state appear more aggressive or dangerous, which may increase the adversary's determination to prevail and make concessions or make negotiation riskier. See Robert Jervis, *Perception and Misperception in International Politics*, Princeton, N.J.: Princeton University Press, 1976, Chapter 3.

Dynamics of Escalation

Most of the preceding discussion focused on the causes of individual escalatory acts or policies, but the most distinctive aspect of escalation is how a number of such actions can aggregate into a larger pattern, leading to an escalatory outcome that may not have been envisioned or desired by any of the actors when the process began. Thus, escalation is often more than the sum of its parts.

The intrinsic tendency of wars to escalate is due to several interconnected factors. The most obvious of these is that some escalatory actions are, by their nature, essentially irreversible. Once the use of a certain type of weapon, attacks on a particular class of targets, or the violation of a previously neutral state's territory has occurred and has been accepted as part of the evolving landscape of the conflict, reversing the change, short of ending the conflict itself, is usually infeasible and even unimaginable. These genies cannot be put back into their bottles, at least not while the war continues. Similarly, escalation can occur by accident, while accidental deescalation is essentially unheard of.

This directional tendency is less pronounced for some other forms of escalation, particularly those that involve rhetoric more than actions. A state can moderate the terms of its surrender demands against an enemy, for example. But even this type of action tends to be more difficult than its escalatory opposite; although wars are often ended through compromise or peace settlements, declaratory war aims are rarely reduced except under extreme duress.

This is a manifestation of a more general phenomenon: As wartime losses mount, victory tends to become more and more imperative for the combatants.[47] This makes it increasingly attractive to consider costly, risky, or even desperate measures, many of them escalatory, that

---

[47] See Pape, 1996, pp. 32–35. Similarly, the higher the stakes in a conflict appear to be, the more determined the adversaries will be to prevail and the more willing they will be to incur costs and take risks. See Richard K. Betts, *Nuclear Blackmail and Nuclear Balance*, Washington, D.C.: Brookings Institution Press, 1987, and Alexander L. George and William E. Simons, eds., *The Limits of Coercive Diplomacy*, 2nd ed., Boulder, Colo.: Westview Press, 1994.

seem to offer the possibility of success if the current trajectory of events does not appear to be leading toward a satisfactory outcome. After all, most escalatory actions will appear potentially beneficial to one side in the conflict, at least in terms of the likelihood or timing of victory or defeat. Thus, as a conflict proceeds, and especially as losses mount, once-forbidding escalation thresholds often become easier to cross, as the associated costs and risks begin to pale in comparison to those already being incurred. This is particularly true when one (or more) of the belligerents fails to achieve success and grows increasingly desperate.[48]

Barriers to escalation can also erode from one conflict to the next, or even disappear as precedent strips them of their significance. For example, Germany's initiation of unrestricted submarine warfare against British shipping in World War I was an action of sensational escalatory significance; by the outbreak of World War II, the world no longer expected submarines to follow rules that had evolved to govern commerce raiding in previous conflicts, and neither the German nor the U.S. submarine warfare campaigns in that war appeared to be dramatically escalatory.

Yet other escalation thresholds have grown in significance over the years. Under the grim shadow of experience, nuclear escalation became a much more daunting prospect in the years that followed World War II than it had been for U.S. decisionmakers in 1945, much as the possible use of poison gas as an instrument of war had previously given greater pause to leaders during and after the interwar years than it had during World War I. Technological progress also creates new escalation thresholds by increasing the potential for warfare to be more discriminate and humane.[49] During World War II, efforts to destroy enemy war-industry facilities almost invariably resulted in heavy attacks on

---

[48] For discussions of domestic politics and other factors affecting war aims, see H. E. Goemans, *War and Punishment: The Causes of War Termination and the First World War*, Princeton, N.J.: Princeton University Press, 2000, and Eric J. Labs, "Beyond Victory: Offensive Realism and the Expansion of War Aims," *Security Studies*, Vol. 6, No. 4, Summer 1997.

[49] On shifting expectations about the nature and the appropriate destructiveness of warfare, see John Mueller, *Retreat from Doomsday: The Obsolescence of Major War*, New York: Basic Books, 1989.

urban population centers due to limitations in bombing accuracy; the situation is very different today with the widespread use of precision-guided munitions. Wartime actions can also gain political significance due to unfavorable associations. For example, ethnic cleansing was once a routine part of European warfare, but, in the wake of Hitler, Stalin, the Yugoslav wars of the 1990s, and generally rising expectations about obedience to the spirit of the laws of armed conflict, it is now considered a war crime, giving it considerable escalatory significance, as was demonstrated in 1999 when Serbian ethnic cleansing in Kosovo did much to solidify NATO's commitment to Operation Allied Force.[50]

This discussion of the natural tendency toward escalation has focused on escalation once warfare begins. In crises that have not yet escalated to war, many of these tendencies are less powerful or absent altogether. When blood has not yet been spilled, the imperative for victory does not loom over policy in the same way, and unintended escalation is less likely to occur as well. However, even in prewar crises, escalation tends to be easier than deescalation; even without concern that the dead should not have died in vain, political reputations and national honor are often perceived to be at stake, and reversing the arrow of escalation requires deliberate decisionmaking by the leaders involved.

Constraints on Escalation

Given all the ways in which escalation can intentionally or unintentionally occur and the tendency for any change in the terms of a conflict to offer the promise of benefits to one side or another, why does escalation not run amok more often, making limited wars rare instead of commonplace? Why, in other words, do we typically speak of escala-

---

[50] Why do some escalation thresholds lose their power while others become more forbidding over time? A threshold is likely to lose its power as its crossing becomes commonplace in politics or conflict and, perhaps, when the escalatory action appears to be one that was forced on an actor by circumstances not of its own making (a perception that will, of course, vary from one observer to another). Thresholds are more likely to gain political weight when the opposite is true, and when the escalatory actions are particularly horrifying (which, again, is both highly subjective and prone to erosion). Note the extent to which suicide terrorism has lost some of its initial shock value in the West as the practice has spread from Sri Lanka through the Middle East.

tion ladders (or mountainsides) instead of an "escalation ripcord" that, once pulled, triggers a rapid chain of events, leading inexorably to all-out conflict?

In the simplest of terms, there are two general factors that tend to restrain escalation. The first is that, although changing the characteristics of a conflict or confrontation usually does make victory for one side more likely (or more certain) in any situation in which success for one participant is roughly equivalent to failure for the other and there is some doubt about the eventual outcome, such improvements in the prospects for victory usually come only at a cost. The direct cost of escalation can take many forms, ranging from intensified fighting leading to heavier casualties on the battlefield to costs denominated in hostile international opinion, damage to expected postwar relations with the enemy, or moral qualms about one's own behavior.[51] Coupled with the fact that victory often appears simultaneously to be attainable to both sides in a conflict and that escalatory measures may offer only very marginal improvement in these prospects, it is often the case that a belligerent will have escalatory options available that would work to its advantage in the pursuit of victory (or the avoidance of defeat) but that nevertheless appear not to be worthwhile. Thus, for example, neither side in World War II opted to escalate to the use of chemical warfare as had happened some 25 years earlier, even though the major combatants had all invested heavily in preparations for such escalation.

The other common disincentive for escalation is the risk that an escalatory action that appears advantageous in its own right will trigger a chain of further escalatory events that will lead to a result that is less appealing than the status quo—that is, the risk that escalation will in fact amount to pulling a ripcord that would be better left untouched. Thus, U.S. escalation in the Vietnam War was frequently constrained not only by humanitarian concerns but also, more significantly, by an intense desire to avoid actions that might lead to direct Chinese or Soviet intervention in the conflict, as the UN offensive into North Korea did in 1950. Because this can be such a powerful deterrent to

---

[51] Richard Ned Lebow, "Windows of Opportunity: Do States Jump Through Them?" *International Security*, Vol. 9, No. 1, Summer 1984.

escalation, including the initiation of war itself, especially when nuclear weapons or other factors make uncontrolled escalation a potentially catastrophic possibility, deterrence strategies often include measures to increase the apparent likelihood that escalation could spin out of control.

Escalation and Instability in the 21st Century

The security environment of the post post–Cold War world differs in many respects from the one that existed during the three decades of the middle and late Cold War, when escalation theory was a matter of central concern for scholars and policymakers, and also from that of the 1990s, when the subject of escalation was largely neglected. As the preceding discussion suggests, the fundamental issues involved in understanding escalation have remained essentially the same from one era to the next over the past century, but changing conditions do affect how these enduring principles manifest themselves. Looking ahead at the likely national security landscape of the early 21st century, there are several broad features that will challenge U.S. strategists seeking to manage escalation risks in ways that may not be entirely familiar to them.

New Escalation Options

The most obvious developments likely to present escalatory problems for U.S. leaders are those that give adversaries new or expanded capabilities to escalate in conflicts or confrontations with the United States. Nuclear weapons or accurate, conventionally armed ballistic or cruise missiles can enable states that, in the face of U.S. military superiority, otherwise would have little ability to mount attacks substantially beyond their own borders to threaten serious escalation against U.S. forces or allies before or during a conflict. Serious escalatory options may also be produced by developing capabilities to launch attacks with biological or chemical weapons, deploy special operations forces or other covert agents to strike behind enemy lines, or perpetrate computer-network attacks, all of which may be both difficult to defend against and sufficiently destructive to give pause to national leaders considering the use of force against weaker opponents.[52] Moreover, states developing such capabilities, especially if they perceive themselves to be weak or vulnerable, may do so in ways designed to increase the chances of accidental escalation in the event that they are attacked in order to magnify this deterrent effect.

Of all these threats, nuclear weapons are in a class by themselves, able to inflict genuinely massive destruction and thus potentially able to raise the specter of escalation to a literally catastrophic degree.[53] Nuclear proliferation is by no means a new development—it has proceeded steadily and perplexingly for more than half a century—but we may soon enter a period in which the only states willing to engage in traditional, as opposed to irregular, military conflicts with the United States will be nuclear armed. As discussed in Chapter Five, the escalatory considerations that would face the United States in a confrontation with a nuclear-armed North Korea or Iran would not simply mirror those in a crisis between the Cold War nuclear superpowers, but they would be fundamentally different from those related to the possibility of a purely conventional regional conflict. Actually employing nuclear weapons, especially against the United States, is, of course, a desperately dangerous step that no adversary would be likely to undertake lightly. However, unless the possibility of their use is vanishingly remote, experience indicates that the shadow of nuclear escalation will loom darkly over U.S. decisionmakers.

At the other end of the spectrum, less apocalyptic escalatory options, such as cyber attacks against Western computer networks,

---

[52] See Daniel Byman and Matthew Waxman, *The Dynamics of Coercion: American Foreign Policy and the Limits of Military Might*, Cambridge, UK: Cambridge University Press, 2002, Chapter 8.

[53] In comparison to their nuclear counterparts, biological, chemical, and radiological weapons hardly merit the overused weapons of mass destruction label, though many biological and some chemical weapons would, if deliverable, pose very significant escalatory threats in their own right. See John Mueller and Karl P. Mueller, "The Methodology of Mass Destruction: Assessing Threats in the New World Order," *Journal of Strategic Studies*, Vol. 23, No. 1, March 2000; and W. Seth Carus, *Defining "Weapons of Mass Destruction,"* Center for the Study of Weapons of Mass Destruction Occasional Paper 4, Washington, D.C.: National Defense University Press, February 2006.

may be attractive because the costs of carrying them out are likely to be small, assuming that the opponent's vulnerability to a symmetric U.S. response in kind would be relatively low.

Perceived Political Fragility

U.S. adversaries may also increasingly have, or believe that they have, powerful escalation options that derive not from new capabilities but from real or imagined contemporary U.S. strategic vulnerabilities. Notable among these are aversion to U.S. military casualties, sensitivity to civilian deaths, and the fragility of the alliances or coalitions with which the United States conducts military operations. The magnitude of each of these vulnerabilities is often exaggerated, sometimes to an extreme degree.[54] However, it is clear that many enemies or potential enemies of the United States believe that inflicting losses against U.S. or allied forces is a promising path to eventual success, based on events since the 1960s in Vietnam, Lebanon (for both Israel and the United States), Soviet-occupied Afghanistan, Somalia, and now Iraq. This belief contributes to the attractiveness of escalatory actions that promise to cause such losses or to increase the impression that U.S.-led forces are engaged in efforts that hold little prospect for victory.

Windows of Opportunity and Vulnerability

In past conflicts, one of the key factors influencing escalation decisions was the perceived existence of windows of opportunity: circumstances in which an actor believes it has a significant but temporary ability to attack, escalate, or take some other action and that if it does not do so, the opportunity will diminish or disappear.[55] Such windows can exist on time scales ranging from fleeting opportunities to disarm an opponent in the hours or days before it can mobilize its forces to long-term

---

[54] See, for example, Eric V. Larson, *Casualties and Consensus: The Historical Role of Casualties in Domestic Support for U.S. Military Operations*, Santa Monica, Calif.: RAND Corporation, MR-726-RC, 1996.

[55] Conversely, a window of vulnerability is an anticipated period during which the adversary will enjoy a significant advantage, creating an incentive for it to attack and for the other party to implement countermeasures against this threat before the window opens.

opportunities for successful preventive war that are expected to close in years or decades as a rival builds its economic power or alliances.[56]

In the context of escalation during crisis or conflict, windows of opportunity will often result from the expected future loss of the military capabilities required for the escalation or from the expectation that a window for escalation will close when the adversary takes some step to reduce its vulnerability. Having weapons that are vulnerable to an enemy attack or relying on command, control, and communication systems that are fragile if attacked, will tend to generate windows for their owners by creating incentives to "use it or lose it." Such concerns were central to efforts to improve nuclear stability between the superpowers during the Cold War, contributing to incentives to develop and deploy weapons such as submarine-launched ballistic missiles that would be invulnerable to an enemy first strike—and to strategic analysts' warnings that making the Soviet Union feel vulnerable might increase the risk of nuclear escalation in a crisis. Some measures to deter the enemy from exploiting windows of opportunity, such as hair-trigger defensive postures or predelegating decision authority for attacks to subordinate commanders as a bulwark against strategic decapitation, can also increase the possibility that accidental escalation will occur.

Such stability concerns remain important in the post post–Cold War world, especially when dealing with smaller or relatively new nuclear powers. But they are perhaps most striking when contemplating the relationship between escalation and space power, a subject whose importance in U.S. national security seems certain to grow. Current U.S. military reliance on space systems for myriad essential functions is likely to create significant incentives for adversaries to attack systems that are both critical and vulnerable.[57] These are likely to grow in the

---

[56] Stephen Van Evera, *Causes of War: Power and the Roots of Conflict*, Ithaca, N.Y.: Cornell University Press, 1999, especially Chapters 3 and 4.

[57] The criticality of a space system is a function not only of how much its users rely on it, but also of the backup options available to substitute for the loss of its services and the costs associated with making such an adjustment. Vulnerability depends on many factors, including the number and fragility of satellites in a constellation (some systems are more robust or redundant than are others or can be made more so), their orbits (satellites in low-earth orbit are far easier to attack than those at higher orbital altitudes), and the ability to overcome

future as the United States invests in new military force structures that depend increasingly on a network backbone of space-based communication, surveillance, and targeting systems. Deploying space-based systems for ballistic missile defense or antisatellite attack would add to these incentives to the extent (likely to be considerable) that the orbital weapons were vulnerable to enemy attack; if multiple potential adversaries deployed systems along the lines of currently hypothesized space-based laser constellations,[58] intense escalatory pressures would be created by the resulting combination of first-strike vulnerability and opportunity.[59] Even terrestrial antisatellite weapons, such as ground-based lasers, could encourage escalation, as attacking these might require striking targets deep inside and enemy's territory, far removed from the scene of a limited regional dispute, and the damage they could do would be limited most effectively by striking them very early in the conflict.

Indifference to Escalation Risks

A final set of considerations is particularly relevant to risks of inadvertent escalation: the potential effects of a party's disregard for the escalatory ramifications of its strategic and operational doctrine. For example, in an era in which the United States has achieved unprecedented military preeminence, it is seductively easy to regard escalation as a problem of the past and to focus on escalation as a potential coercive lever but not a dangerous possibility requiring attentive management. However, as noted earlier, U.S. adversaries often have a variety of sig-

---

interference with its operations or to replace satellite losses. See, for example, Barry D. Watts, *The Military Use of Space: A Diagnostic Assessment*, Washington, D.C.: Center for Strategic and Budgetary Assessments, 2001.

[58] See Bob Preston, Dana J. Johnson, Sean J. A. Edwards, Michael Miller, and Calvin Shipbaugh, *Space Weapons, Earth Wars*, Santa Monica: RAND Corporation, MR-1209-AF, 2002, and William L. Spacy II, "Assessing the Military Utility of Space-Based Weapons," *Astropolitics*, Vol. 1, No. 3, Winter 2003.

[59] For an overview of these and other issues in space weapon policy, see Karl P. Mueller, "Totem and Taboo: Depolarizing the Space Weaponization Debate," *Astropolitics*, Vol. 1, No. 1, Spring 2003.

nificant escalatory tools at their disposal, some of them very dangerous indeed.

In this environment, a number of elements of U.S. policy and doctrine may create perverse enemy incentives for escalation to an extent that is frequently overlooked. Strategic and operational concepts, such as rapid, decisive operations and strategic attack designed to produce paralytic effects against enemy command-and-control capabilities, are highly valued in U.S. military doctrine but may create escalation instability by producing windows of vulnerability as adversaries face the possibility of losing key military capabilities before they might otherwise be used. U.S. emphasis on the possibility of launching preemptive first strikes against potentially dangerous states armed with nuclear, biological, or chemical weapons may also encourage preemption or other escalation by adversaries seeking to avoid or disrupt an anticipated U.S. attack.[60] Similarly, when regime change becomes a central objective, targets of this policy have weaker incentives for escalatory restraint, especially if the end of their regime is tantamount to their incarceration or execution: Enemies with nothing to lose have nothing to lose in taking extreme risks.

These factors do not mean that the United States should necessarily eschew seeking quick, decisive victories or the removal of toxic governments, though an operational and survivable enemy nuclear arsenal will tend to remove some U.S. policy options from serious consideration under most circumstances. However, these factors do reinforce the importance of devoting considerable attention to avoiding or minimizing the possibility of undesirable escalation—deliberate, inadvertent, or accidental—when designing military or diplomatic strategies, planning operations, or developing concepts of operations.

Anticipating and Managing Escalation

It is, above all, the possibility that escalation will lead to disaster—which might range from a strategic nuclear exchange in a conflict

---

[60] K. Mueller et al., 2006.

between superpowers to infinitely smaller local policy disasters, such as those that ended the U.S. interventions in Lebanon and Somalia, discussed in Chapter Six—that makes escalation management a matter of such compelling importance for strategy makers. Later chapters in this monograph address escalation management in far greater detail, but a few observations about the subject bear reiterating here.

The first is that the escalation-management rubric encompasses or, at least, should encompass a wide range of countermeasures in keeping with the variety of mechanisms that can lead to escalation. Avoiding deliberate escalation means deterring it, while preventing inadvertent and accidental escalation requires policies that tend to look very different. This is not merely a matter of needing to do several things at once, however: It is not unusual for policies to counter one type of escalation to increase the risk that escalation will occur by some other route. In particular, there tends to be a trade-off between making war appear less attractive in an effort to deter it and making it less likely to escalate in the event that deterrence fails. For example, during the Cold War, NATO's tactical nuclear weapons made deliberate nuclear escalation against a Warsaw Pact attack easier, and probably increased the chances of accidental escalation as well, to make war in Europe appear less appealing in Moscow. Today, rogue states face a similar dilemma, as developing nuclear weapons to deter U.S. threats to national or regime survival could also provoke a U.S. attack.

A second general principle for strategists to recognize is that escalation control or management is an inherently imperfect business. It can be done well or poorly, but it is extremely rare for any set of policies to eliminate the risk of significant escalation altogether. Most adversaries will retain some troubling capability for escalation, whether they are strong or weak according to traditional measures of military and political power. Although the chances of inadvertent or accidental escalation can be reduced, it would be naïve to imagine that they can be eliminated altogether. Although strategists can aspire to achieve escalation dominance, they should be modest in their hopes of succeeding and even more modest about the likelihood that they will both achieve it and know with confidence that they have done so.

Finally, anticipating and controlling the risks of escalation depends heavily on an astute understanding of how the adversary will perceive and interpret events that have not yet occurred—not only in a general sense, but also under the specific and often difficult-to-predict conditions that will shape the opponent's perceptions and responses when a particular event occurs.[61] The importance of being able to see the world through the enemy's eyes has long been extolled in deterrence theory. It is likewise central to managing the risks of inadvertent and accidental, as well as deliberate, escalation.[62]

---

[61] Schelling, 1966, Chapter 4; Jervis, 1976. Some of the ways in which escalatory actions intended to send clear signals could be perceived differently by the opponent are described in Thies, 1980.

[62] Smoke, 1977, Chapter 10, identifies understanding the adversary's expectations, and how these differ from one's own, as the most important single challenge in escalation management.

CHAPTER THREE
China's Thinking on Escalation: Evidence from Chinese Military Writings

Introduction

The modernization of the Chinese military is one of the most consequential challenges that U.S. national security planners now face. In the past five to 10 years, the PLA has been engaged in a dedicated and deliberate effort to improve all aspects of its capabilities in order to deter a range of potential adversaries and, if necessary, to prosecute limited military conflicts in Asia. The PLA's current modernization efforts—in stark contrast to past activities—have been uniquely comprehensive, covering doctrine, force structure, and training and education. For the first time since the reform era began, the PLA is undergoing a complete makeover. A defining aspect of this process has been the renovation of PLA doctrine, which has focused on developing a joint operation doctrine for fighting limited, high-intensity conflicts using high-tech weapons.[1]

This evolution in the PLA's operational doctrine and capabilities raises numerous questions relevant to this study's examination of escalation and escalation management: How does the Chinese military think and write about escalation before and during conflict? How would the PLA's actions in a conflict affect the risk of escalation? Does the PLA's new doctrine predispose Chinese leaders to favor or reject deliberate escalation (either instrumental or suggestive) as a conflict-

---

[1] James Mulvenon and David Finkelstein, eds., *China's Revolution in Doctrinal Affairs: Emerging Trends in the Operational Art of the Chinese People's Liberation Army*, Alexandria, Va.: CNA Corporation, 2005.

management tool? How concerned is the PLA about causing inadvertent or accidental escalation? And what risks do PLA views on escalation pose for conflict management with the United States?[2]

This chapter aims to illuminate these issues by examining the PLA's professional military writings about its new and evolving doctrine for possible insights into Chinese views on escalation and escalation management. We assess three categories of PLA writings: those that address the concept of war control, those on Second Artillery operations (i.e., China's nuclear and conventional missile forces), and those on space operations and space warfare.[3] These three groups were chosen because they offer one of the best unclassified data sets on the concepts and beliefs that inform how the PLA will organize, train, equip, and operate itself in this time of dynamic modernization.

Assessing such material is important, as doctrine is the codification of what military institutions hold as fundamental principles for guiding their actions in pursuit of national objectives.[4] Military doctrine may offer only limited insights into the specific escalation-related decisions that Chinese leaders might make during a crisis, but it does reveal the range of options that have received prior consideration and suggests which actions military commanders will likely urge their leaders to authorize. Just as importantly, as doctrine guides how military forces are trained and employed, it describes *how* they will operate in a conflict, thus revealing potential pitfalls for accidental or inadvertent

---

[2] To date, there is almost no Western literature on Chinese escalation behavior. A prominent and notable exception is Lonnie D. Henley, "War Control: Chinese Concepts of Escalation Management," in Andrew Scobell and Larry M. Wortzel, eds., *Shaping China's Security Environment: The Role of the People's Liberation Army*, Carlisle, Pa.: U.S. Army War College, October 2006.

[3] This chapter's findings are also informed by a Delphi analysis conducted in RAND's Washington Office on June 1, 2005. See Appendix C for a description of the modified Delphi method of analysis used in that exercise.

[4] See the definition of doctrine in U.S. Joint Chiefs of Staff, *DoD Dictionary of Military and Associated Terms*, Joint Publication 1-02, April 12, 2001, as amended through June 13, 2007, p. 166.

escalation should their operations be poorly managed or go unchecked by national leaders.[5]

Chinese publications on PLA doctrine and operations can be considered *authoritative* but not necessarily *definitive* sources. The documents examined for this study are authoritative in the sense that many are teaching materials produced by the PLA for use in educating PLA officers about various aspects of its new joint operations doctrine. Such writings incorporate beliefs and concepts that we believe reflect those more thoroughly explained in classified military documents. In other words, they are part of the picture but not the entire portrait. Classified PLA contingency plans and war plans would presumably reveal, in far greater detail, specific PLA operations and, thus, the PLA's relative propensity for escalation.[6]

Moreover, the PLA's policies and practices on military operations are evolving as the PLA continues to develop its doctrine and capabilities. In this regard, one of the principle findings of this chapter is that Chinese military writings on escalation and escalation management appear to be undertheorized and still under development. To date, PLA strategists have apparently devoted limited research to analyzing the general issue of escalation in warfare and, more specifically, the effect of the PLA's new doctrine on the risks of inadvertent or accidental escalation. This chapter is intended to shed some light on how Chinese military strategists conceive the relationship between PLA doctrine and operations and escalation and escalation management. This relationship does not appear to have received extensive treatment in PLA circles.[7]

---

[5] Other important insights regarding China's propensities for escalation can be gained by examining historical patterns in Beijing's use of force and in assessing those patterns for continuity with Chinese contemporary writings. We provide such an assessment in Appendix A.

[6] A related limitation of these sources is that it is unclear whether they reflect the views of the military and political leadership at the national level. Answers to such questions are better pursued through interview research. On this point, see Henley, 2006, p. 91.

[7] To be sure, these claims about PLA research and publications are derived from openly available, public writings about escalation and escalation management. For additional analysis of Chinese military writings, see Evan S. Medeiros, "Undressing the Dragon: Researching the PLA Through Open Source Exploitation," in James C. Mulvenon and Andrew N. D.

Background and Conceptual Issues

One cannot appreciate contemporary Chinese views on escalation without considering how those ideas have developed over time. Chinese strategists write about escalation in terms of the Chinese concepts of war control [战争控制] and containment of war [遏制战争]. While preventing unnecessary and violent escalation is inherent in China's current military thought (as it is in most countries), PLA strategists have written very little in the public realm specifically about these issues. Compared to U.S. and Soviet treatments of escalation during the Cold War, Chinese work on escalation and escalation management is far less extensive and systematic. However, interest in these topics appears to be growing in the PLA.

The subject of war control did not appear in the seminal 1987 version of the Academy of Military Science's *The Science of Military Strategy*.[8] More recently, escalation was not addressed in two prominent PLA studies released in 1999 and 2000 (*The Science of Military Strategy* and *The Science of Military Campaigns*);[9] yet, the Academy of Military Sciences devoted a chapter to the topic in its 2001 edition of *The Science of Military Strategy*.[10] These books are widely seen as authoritative and a reflection of the new doctrinal concepts adopted in the late 1990s. Other public writings include a few journal articles and one doctoral dissertation from the National Defense University.

Recent Chinese interest in and writings about war control and related doctrinal issues has likely resulted from efforts to renovate the PLA's operational doctrine. After several years of research and experimentation on new doctrinal concepts in the early 1990s (during the

---

Yang, eds., *A Poverty of Riches: New Challenges and Opportunities in PLA Research*, Santa Monica, Calif.: RAND Corporation, CF-189-NSRD, 2003.

[8] Gao Rui, ed., *Zhanluexue* [*The Science of Military Strategy*], Beijing: Junshi Kexue Chubanshe, 1987.

[9] Wang Wenrong, ed., *Zhanluexue* [*The Science of Military Strategy*], Beijing: Guofang Daxue Chubanshe, 1999; Wang Houqing and Zhang Xingye, eds., *Zhanyixue* [*The Science of Military Campaigns*], Beijing, China: Guofang Daxue, May 2000b.

[10] Peng Guangqian and Yao Youzhi, eds., *Zhanluexue* [*The Science of Military Strategy*], Beijing: Junshi Kexue Chubanshe, 2001, especially Chapters 8 and 19.

eighth Five-Year Plan), by the late 1990s (at the end of the ninth Five-Year Plan), the PLA issued a series of new guidelines governing the operation of all branches of its armed forces, which aimed to facilitate joint combat operations. During the same period, a small number of military strategists also began to study and write about war control. The existing PLA writings on war control tend to be very general and discursive in nature and provide limited insights into actual PLA behavior during conflict. It is not clear from them how the PLA applies the concept of war control to actual military operations. As the PLA seeks to operationalize its new doctrine in the coming years, more PLA writings on war control and escalation may appear.

When examining these writings, escalation should be seen as entwined within a trinity of related concepts: (1) deterrence, (2) escalation and war control, and (3) war termination. These three ideas collectively represent, for China, the multitude of strategic and tactical policy choices in times of crisis or conflict. Separating one from the others can obscure the policy goal(s) that a military seeks to achieve through its various operations during both crisis periods (i.e., prewar) and wartime. In the context of Chinese military thought, analyzing escalation in isolation of the other two concepts may confound understanding of the manner in which China seeks to use its forces in a conflict. Viewed through the lens of this conceptual trinity, some of the PLA's military goals, and its possible use of escalation to achieve them, come into clearer focus. Moreover, these three concepts are particularly relevant to PLA missile operations because they help delineate the distinct aims that China seeks to accomplish with the deployment and posturing of nuclear and conventional missile forces.

Understanding Chinese Views on Escalation and War Control

Chinese definitions of *war control* and *war containment* are quite general and all-encompassing. They note that *war control* encompasses the employment of all aspects of "comprehensive national power" [*zonghe guoli*, 综合国力] to avoid being put on the defensive or losing the initiative in conflict.[11] For China, war control is a doctrinal tool for putting the adversary on the defensive at the start of or during conflict—a goal that is universal in Chinese writings about military operations. According to the 2001 version of *The Science of Military Strategy*,

> War control is the deliberate action of war leaders to limit or restrain the outbreak, development, scale, intensity, and aftermath of war. The objective of war control is to forestall the outbreak of war or, when war cannot be avoided, to control its vertical and horizontal escalation, to strive to minimize the consequences of war, or to strive to achieve the greatest victory for the smallest cost. War control includes arms control, crisis control, control of armed conflict, and so on, and is a major component of contemporary strategic research and strategic guidance.[12]

The breadth of this definition is further indication that these concepts have not been extensively developed in PLA doctrinal circles; numerous operational activities could be subsumed by this definition. It also provides little indication about how escalation can be limited or how PLA doctrine specifically seeks to do this.

The Conceptual Foundation of War Control

The conceptual foundation of war control in Chinese military thought has several components. Chinese strategists argue that the era of unlimited war is over, as most nations now possess the military tools to accomplish their political objectives. In the past, unlimited war resulted from insufficient military means to pursue political objectives. Moreover, Chinese strategists argue that the current global political, social, and economic context of warfare is completely different from that in the past, creating conditions that both enable and con-

---

[11] This section draws on numerous Chinese sources as well as on the impressive essay on Chinese views of war control by Lonnie D. Henley, 2006. Henley's analysis draws on the previously mentioned editions of *The Science of Military Strategy* and a small and explorative PLA study on war control (Xiao Tianliang, *Zhanzheng Kongzhi Wenti Yanjiu* [*Research on War Control*], Beijing: Guofang Daxue Chubanshe, 2002).

[12] Peng and Yao, 2001, p. 213.

strain the use of war control during conflict. Chinese military thinkers note several changes in the global context for armed conflict. The advent of war under high-technology conditions facilitates the ability to direct large military operations from afar in real time. Also, among nuclear-armed states, unlimited warfare is far too dangerous, and no major power faces such a grave threat to its existence that it would be willing to escalate uncontrollably. A prominent argument in Chinese writings about war control is that conflict is far more transparent in a globalized world, and, thus, it is subject to national and international limits—some of which constrain China and others that China would seek to use to its advantage during conflict. Chinese strategists also argue that most nations possess the material ability and political will to control warfare; in other words, there is no ipso facto reason that warfare cannot be controlled.

Chinese writings also discuss the various components of war control. Chinese conceptions of war control include not only military operations but also economic, political, and diplomatic instruments of national power to avoid being put on the defensive and losing the initiative. These include steps to shape the international security environment, peacefully resolve disputes, and reduce the threat of war; measures to manage crises and prevent or postpone the outbreak of war (i.e., crisis management that includes intimidation or bargaining approaches); and actions taken during war to control the scale, pace, scope, or intensity of the conflict. The general nature of current Chinese thinking about the concept of war control is further underscored in these broad ideas.

The political dimensions of warfare are a particularly prominent part of war control theory. In other words, war control is embedded in a broader approach to warfare that stresses far more than accomplishing solely military objectives. Chinese writings strongly emphasize that military operations are meant to achieve a political aim and, thus, that military operations are subordinate to the Chinese leadership's political objectives. The former should not guide the latter. In this context, war control can be used to modulate the pace or intensity of military operations in the pursuit of specific political ends. War control, in essence, is about how to moderate the use of force to pursue political ends. This can involve raising or lowering the intensity of conflict: The intensity can be lowered to avoid being put on the defensive politically (in a highly transparent international system in which public opinion plays an important role); the intensity can be raised to accomplish a rapid and decisive victory—or to make limited gains to terminate the war. Additionally, Chinese writings on warfare and war control stress that military operations are but one part of a strategy in which the Chinese government would also use coordinated political, economic, and diplomatic means to shape the outcome of a conflict in China's favor. Moreover, Chinese strategists pay close attention to the international context for warfare because it affects China's ability to prevail at limited cost in a conflict. Chinese strategists emphasize avoiding actions that would lead to China's international isolation during warfare and using international public opinion during a conflict to pressure the adversary in pursuit of Chinese war aims.[13]

Operationalizing War Control: Military Measures to Contain Warfare

Beyond the theoretical generalities about war control, Chinese writings also discuss certain military actions that pertain to containing warfare and creating favorable conditions for China to prevail.[14] Chinese writings note that war control includes a wide range of military actions that seek to shape the overall situation in China's favor, and such shaping is encapsulated in a concept called *zaoshi* [造势]. While war control for China includes the application of military, political, economic, and diplomatic capabilities, the military aspects of war control are heavily focused on *zaoshi*. Chinese writings highlight eight such military actions.

First, the positioning and posturing of military force for military intimidation and deterrence is critical to war control. Such displays of capabilities and overt deployments seek to demonstrate China's capability and will to pressure an opponent, help China attain the initiative, and assist it in controlling the development of a situation. These kinds

---

[13] Peng and Yao, 2001, Chapter 19.

[14] See Henley, 2006, and Xiao, 2002. See also Peng and Yao, 2001, Chapter 8.

of military actions are also seen as critical to effective crisis management insofar as they could prevent the outbreak of conflict by signaling China's resolve. Such overt deployments can involve either nuclear or conventional forces and are often combined with covert deployments in case the conflict escalates.

In the Chinese literature on war control, a second military step involves controlling the overall objective of the conflict to ensure that military actions are subordinate to the political objective. Preventing unintended escalation, for China, is a matter of maintaining the right balance between military and political objectives. The importance of delineating the political objectives of a conflict, and of subordinating military operations to them, is a pervasive theme in Chinese writings on war control.

Appropriately choosing military targets is a third element of war control. Chinese strategists write about balancing the need to strike vital targets for a decisive effect against avoiding targets that will prompt the adversary to launch an incessant and vengeful counterattack. Target choice is also critical to shaping international perceptions and to avoiding external intervention that would raise the probability of unwanted escalation and could precipitate China's loss of the initiative.

Fourth, Chinese strategists highlight the value of carefully manipulating the parameters of military operations, which has a significant impact on the ability to control conflict and the possibility of unintended escalation. This has several dimensions. Determining such parameters involves choosing the right form of warfare [战争形式]: offensive or defensive. These forms of warfare are then further expressed as forms of operations [作战形式]. Another important element of determining the appropriate parameters of conflict is the commander's determination [指挥员的决定] of the overall military situation, which includes the military requirements and objectives of a conflict, the primary and secondary operational directions of a conflict, and the selection of the size and capabilities of the forces to be used.

A fifth military element of war control is controlling the warfighting techniques [战争手段]. Chinese military analysts argue that, given that modern weapons are highly destructive and modern battlefields are highly transparent, China's warfighting techniques need to be carefully calibrated to overall political objectives. Chinese writings stress the importance of avoiding excessive civilian casualties to prevent the situation from spinning out of control or enraging an adversary. Chinese writings do not rule out "extreme measures" but note that they should be used sparingly.

Controlling the pace, rhythm, and intensity of a conflict is the sixth aspect of war control in Chinese writings. Chinese military thinkers argue that the deliberate management of the pace and intensity of a conflict can create conditions favorable to Chinese political aims. Chinese strategists stress that this task is especially important to ensuring that China gains and maintains military and political initiative during a conflict. A key aspect of this task is coordinating military operations with the political, economic, and diplomatic dimensions of conflict to collectively provide China with initiative and advantage.

The seventh and eighth military measures for war control involve controlling the end of warfare and controlling the postconflict situation. The former involves a political determination (not a military one) regarding whether China's political aims have been achieved, and military operations may by terminated even if they have not yet played out to fruition. Military operations, too, can assist in war termination. For example, the 2001 edition of *The Science of Military Strategy* notes that if the overall military situation is not in China's favor, it can pursue local military gains to create conditions for ending the conflict in a manner favorable to China.[15] More generally, Chinese writings argue that pausing the fight, intensifying it, or using special "assassin's mace weapons" can help China to *zaoshi* or influence the situation in a manner conducive to ending the conflict on China's terms.[16] PLA writ-

---

[15] Peng and Yao, 2001.

[16] Assassin's mace weapons [*shashoujian*] is a vague expression the Chinese use when referring to a category of weapons, entire weapon systems, or simply critical weapon technologies that provide the PLA with the capability to decisively turn the tide of a conflict in China's favor, especially during conflict with a larger and more technologically sophisticated adversary. The precise nature of this type of weapon system is unclear. In general terms, such weapons may function as force multipliers for the PLA or allow the PLA to exploit specific weaknesses of stronger military adversaries. This term is widely used in Chinese contexts other than that of military operations, such as professional sports or even romantic relation-

ings note that the military has excelled at this task in all major Chinese armed conflicts since 1949. With regard to postconflict situations, the eighth aspect of war control, PLA writings highlight that the military's role does not end when the conflict stops. Military posturing is still needed to ensure that an adversary abides by the terms of the postwar agreement; such posturing can include the threat or consummation of renewed operations to force compliance or to punish violations.

By far, the most prominent theme in Chinese writings about the military measures to contain war (as well as most other aspects of PLA operations) is the importance of seizing and retaining initiative. For PLA strategists, this is central to China's ability to prevail in a conflict. Chinese writings emphasize the importance of gaining the political and military initiative [争取主动] and avoiding situations that could put China in a reactive, passive, or defensive [被动] posture. PLA writings highlight how difficult and costly such control is to regain once lost and specify a series of steps to achieve and maintain initiative, including rapid reaction to incipient crises, quick deployments, strong standing forces, solid contingency planning, rapid mobilization of societal forces, a resolute political stance, rapid generation to wartime postures, and avoiding outsider intervention and the internationalization of the situation.

In the context of the persistent emphasis on the initiative in PLA writings on war control, a noticeable and worrisome omission is any recognition that the PLA's efforts to seize the initiative during a crisis could directly accelerate the outbreak of conflict by signaling imminent Chinese aggression. Further, such actions during a conflict could elicit escalatory reactions in response to the intensity of Chinese military efforts to gain the initiative. In other words, China's commitment to gaining the initiative as part of war control could precipitate the very opposite outcome: uncontrolled and rapid escalation. Moreover, it is unclear from available documents whether the Chinese recognize the risks of inadvertent or accidental escalation or have considered any means to mitigate those risks. As noted earlier, there is some discussion

---

ships. See Alastair Iain Johnston, "Toward Conceptualizing the Chinese Concept of a *Shashoujian* (Assassin's Mace)," unpublished manuscript, August 2002.

in PLA literature about modulating the pace, scope, and intensity of warfare to avoid disadvantageous outcomes, but it is unclear how, in a crisis, Chinese leaders will resolve the inherent tension between war control and the PLA's broader commitment to gaining the initiative.

Assessing Chinese Escalation Behavior Through the Lens of the Second Artillery Doctrine

This section is intended to develop further insights about Chinese approaches to escalation by looking beyond Chinese writings about war control, which are very general and theoretical in nature. It does so by assessing Chinese writings on Second Artillery operations to evaluate whether they reveal more specific escalation preferences or proclivities. The Second Artillery was chosen because the PLA has placed significant emphasis on it in recent modernization efforts; in particular, the Second Artillery's conventional missile forces will likely be used in future contingencies such as those over Taiwan. In addition, the Second Artillery's doctrine has only recently come to light in terms of its position on both nuclear and conventional missile operations. The PLA's renovation of its entire military doctrine in the late 1990s led to the articulation of a distinct set of concepts that define both nuclear and conventional missile campaigns. These were likely expressed in 1999 in a classified planning document called a *gangyao* [纲要] for the Second Artillery.[17]

Before proceeding, two methodological points must be made. First, in assessing Chinese writings about the Second Artillery's operations, this analysis sharply differentiates between the Second Artillery's nuclear and conventional missile operations. This distinction is par-

---

[17] A *gangyao* is a type of highly classified Chinese document that outlines core military concepts for a service branch. In 1999, *gangyao*s were also issued for the army, navy, and air force and for joint military operations. The full name of the *gangyao* for the Second Artillery is Zhongguo Renmin Jiefangjun Dierpaobing Zhanyi Gangyao. A general articulation of these new ideas can be found in *Zhanyixue* [*The Science of Military Campaigns*] (Wang and Zhang, 2000b) and in Xue Xinglin, ed., *Zhanyi Lilun Xuexi Zhinan* [*Campaign Theory Study Guide*], Beijing: Guofang Daxue Chubanshe, 2001, pp. 384–393, 636.

ticularly relevant to assessing Chinese views on escalation and escalation management. PLA publications about the goals and missions of its nuclear and conventional missile forces differ—starkly, at times—and this distinction is directly relevant to assessing the role of Second Artillery operations in escalation during a Taiwan conflict. Chinese writings about Second Artillery operations highlight distinct sets of concepts for nuclear and conventional missile strikes, and each set of ideas raises distinct implications for escalation. These differences are not merely conceptual; they also bear on questions of deterrence and war termination. Key differences in operational requirements include basing and deployment modes, command-and-control arrangements, coordination with other PLA forces in a joint campaign, and force protection and safeguarding. In this sense, this chapter argues that it is not accurate to draw strong linkages between the concepts driving the Second Artillery's nuclear and conventional missile force operations—at least not yet. PLA writings highlight the differences between the conceptual and operational dimensions of Second Artillery nuclear and conventional operations, and, thus, our analysis of escalation should be sensitive to these very distinctions.[18]

Second, Chinese writings and thinking about nuclear and conventional missile operations possess a limited, albeit growing, institutional basis. In other words, there seems to be more and more of it, as the Second Artillery develops its new doctrine. This underscores the relevance of using this literature to assess possible escalation preferences and proclivities. The PLA arrived late to the study of nuclear strategy, and, as a result, the military's thinking appears to be catching up with the international state of the art regarding nuclear strategy and doctrine. For decades after 1964, when China first tested a nuclear device, Chinese thinking about nuclear weapons was undertheorized and underinstitutionalized. It was not until 1985, according to *The Science of Military Campaigns* and other sources, that the PLA and the

---

[18] We make this point because some analysts have argued that the more aggressive, first-strike–oriented aspects of China's conventional missile forces could affect or bleed over into the operations of China's nuclear forces. This argument seems to be essentially pure speculation and is inconsistent with the PLA's own conceptualizations of nuclear and conventional missile operations.

Second Artillery began to actively engage in the study of nuclear strategy questions.[19] Similarly, because the Second Artillery's conventional missile forces were first deployed in the mid-1990s, doctrine for conventional missile operations is even newer than that governing nuclear missile operations. According to *The Science of Military Campaigns*,

> In April 1998, the Second Artillery established the concept of "regular missile attacking campaigns" and compiled the textbook, *Regular Missile Attacking Campaign of the Second Artillery*, further enriching and developing the various forms of the Second Artillery campaign.[20]

More recent PLA sources on doctrinal development indicate that the PLA has yet to complete a full set of doctrinal concepts governing conventional missile operations.[21] Given the relative newness of the ideas guiding conventional missile strikes, the Second Artillery has likely had minimal experience operationalizing such concepts—and no real combat experience. This immediately raises questions about the risks of inadvertent and, especially, accidental escalation; it also suggests further doctrinal evolution in the future as operational realities become more apparent via exercises or other practical tests. Thus, any conclusions about existing Second Artillery conventional missile operations and escalation should be treated as necessarily tentative.

---

[19] Wang and Zhang, 2000b; "Dier Paobing Junshi Xueshu" ["Second Artillery Military Studies"], in *Junshixue Yanjiu Huigu yu Zhanwang* [*Military Academic Research Review and Prospects*], Beijing: Academy of Military Sciences Press, 1995, pp. 358–371.

[20] Wang and Zhang, 2000a, p. 369.

[21] See "Ershiyi Shiji Chu Erpao Junshi Lilun Fazhan yu Chuangxin" ["The Development and Innovation of 2nd Artillery Military Theory in the 21st Century"], in National Military Philosophy and Social Science Planning Office, ed., *Ershiyi Shiji Chu Junshi Xue Xueke Jianshe yu Chuangxin* [*Development and Innovation of Military Science in the 21st Century*], Beijing: Junshi Kexue Chubanshe, 2004.

These ideas are addressed at greater length in Evan S. Medeiros, "Minding the Gap: Assessing the Trajectory of the PLA's Strategic Missile Forces," paper presented at Exploring the "Right Size" for China's Military: PLA Missions, Functions, and Organization, U.S. Army War College, Carlisle, Pa., October 6–8, 2006.

Second Artillery Nuclear Operations and Escalation

Chinese writings about Second Artillery nuclear operations have increased in scope and specificity in recent years.[22] This development is an extension of the PLA's renovation of its operational doctrine in the late 1990s and is part of what is referred to as *the revolution in doctrinal affairs*.[23] This process led to a much more formal thinking and articulation of the concepts guiding Second Artillery operations. Analysis of the new writings about Second Artillery campaigns reveals a collection of specific beliefs and policies within the PLA about nuclear weapons, missile warfare, escalation, and escalation management.

These writings indicate that the PLA would not likely resort to nuclear weapons, even when faced with probable defeat in a limited conventional conflict. While the possibility of deliberate nuclear escalation by the PLA should never be ruled out (especially if the line between conventional and nuclear operations becomes blurred), the current and dominant focus of Chinese writings about Second Artillery nuclear operations is not on such discrete, instrumental uses of nuclear weapons. Rather, this reading of PLA publications suggests that the Second Artillery's nuclear forces are postured, first and foremost, for deterring nuclear attacks on China and preventing deterrence failures. For decades, this has been the main preoccupation of the Second Artillery: possessing a credible capability to deter nuclear aggression against China. However, if deterrence fails, PLA writings clearly indicate that the Second Artillery would conduct retaliatory strikes. It would do so, ironically, for the purpose of deescalation and, perhaps, war termina-

---

[22] This section draws on the following Chinese sources: Xue, 2001; Wang and Zhang, 2001; Wang Wenrong, 1999; Peng and Yao, 2001; *Zhanyixue Yanjiu* [*Campaign Studies Research*], Beijing: Guofang Daxue Chubanshe, 1997, pp. 278–286; Gu Dexin and Niu Yongjun, *Heyouling De Zhengdong: Ershishiji Hewenti Huihu Yu Sikao* [*Rumblings of the Nuclear Specter: Looking Back at and Considering the Nuclear Problem in the 20th Century*], Beijing: Guofang Daxue Chubanshe, 1999, pp. 274–288; Hu Guangzheng, *Zhongwai Junshi Zuzhi Tizhi Bijiao Jiaocheng* [*Teaching Materials on a Comparison of Chinese and Foreign Military Organizational Systems*], Beijing: Junshi Kexue Chubanshe, 1999, p. 223.

[23] David Finkelstein, "Thinking About the PLA's 'Revolution in Doctrinal Affairs,'" in James Mulvenon and David Finkelstein, *The Revolution in Chinese Military Doctrinal Affairs*, Santa Monica, Calif.: RAND Corporation, forthcoming.

tion. Chinese actions might not be deliberately escalatory, insofar as China might seek to simply retaliate, but PLA writings suggest that the Chinese believe they can do so in ways that will inflict enough shock and pain that an adversary will put an end to the nuclear phase of the conflict or even the entire conflict.

We base this assessment on several observations. First, a collection of Chinese military books (including instructional and teaching materials for officers) argue that China's nuclear weapons serve only two goals: nuclear deterrence [核威慑] and nuclear counterstrike or nuclear retaliation [核反击/核报复]. These dual ideas are repeatedly raised in internal and public military writings. The frequency of the use of these twin ideas, especially in internal military writings, suggests a wide degree of formal acceptance—not merely propaganda for external consumption. In these books, there is seldom a direct discussion of contingencies in which nuclear weapons are used for more than deterrence or retaliation. PLA doctrinal writings specifically state that the sole campaign of Second Artillery nuclear forces is a nuclear *counterattack* campaign [核反击/核报复战役] in which China responds to a nuclear first strike from an adversary. The use of this specific terminology (as opposed to a nuclear *strike* campaign) is a consistent feature of Chinese writings about Second Artillery nuclear operations, and, unlike other branches of the military, only one campaign (as opposed to multiple campaigns) is identified for the nuclear forces.

Furthermore, the description of the goals of a nuclear counterattack campaign suggest that such strikes would not be used for deliberate escalation but, rather, in retaliation and to catalyze an end to either the nuclear phase of a conflict or the entire conflict. *The Science of Military Campaigns*, for example, makes the following statement:

> The main task of the nuclear retaliation campaign of the Second Artillery is to launch a nuclear attack on key enemy strategic and campaign targets, paralyzing its command system, reducing its war potential, sabotaging its strategic intention, wavering its war will, and stopping the escalation of nuclear war.[24]

---

[24] Wang and Zhang, 2000b, Chapter 14, p. 369.

Key Nuclear Doctrine Concepts

The use of nuclear weapons for deterrence and retaliation (and not escalation) is codified in specific doctrinal concepts as well. These concepts further elucidate Chinese views on using Second Artillery nuclear strikes for deescalation and war termination as well as for signaling during a crisis. Drawing on PLA writings, there are four main concepts that collectively form Second Artillery nuclear doctrine.[25]

The first concept is *houfa zhiren* [后发制人], or gaining mastery by striking after the enemy has struck. This is a strategic-level concept that serves as a guiding principle [原则立场] for the Second Artillery's nuclear missile operations. *Houfa zhiren* is an expression of China's long-standing no-first-use (NFU) policy [不首先使用核武器政策] and the PLA's consistent reliance on a secure second-strike capability as the basis for credibly deterring nuclear aggression against China. China's articulation of this principle is meant to codify that China's nuclear forces are for deterrence, based on a survivable retaliatory capability. As one important indication of China's interpretation of NFU, many PLA texts about Second Artillery nuclear operations are based on the assumption that China has already been hit with nuclear weapons, and some explicitly state that the Second Artillery is operating under "grim" nuclear conditions. While most Western analysts of nuclear affairs regularly and, to some extent, rightly, dismiss NFU pledges as unreliable confidence-building measures, there are numerous indications in Chinese writings that such a commitment is taken seriously by PLA strategists as well as by operators in the Second Artillery. A key question for Western analysts pertains to identifying the thresholds that, once crossed, equate to enemy first use in the minds of Chinese leaders, thereby justifying a nuclear retaliation without violating their NFU principle. Chinese writings are intentionally ambiguous on this issue, but they suggest that such thresholds may include early warning of an impending nuclear attack or even conventional missile strikes on China's nuclear assets.[26]

---

[25] These four concepts are drawn from Wang and Zhang, 2000b, and Xue, 2001.

[26] For a further treatment of these issues see, Medeiros, 2006, pp. 3–10.

A second core concept in Second Artillery nuclear operations is *yanmi fanghu* [严密防护], which means *close defense* or *self-protection*. This principle captures the PLA's top priority of ensuring the survivability of Chinese nuclear forces so that they can launch a counterattack. This emphasis on surviving a first strike is likely one of the reasons that *yanmi fanghu* has been articulated by the Second Artillery since the earliest days of nuclear campaign planning. China's continued emphasis on this concept is a further indication that China envisions using its nuclear weapons for retaliatory purposes. Unlike the general principle of *houfa zhiren*, this one is a campaign-level concept that directly informs operational planning.

A third principle in Chinese nuclear doctrine is the key-point counterstrike, or *zhongdian fanji* [重点反击]. This concept, like that of close defense, has been a longtime cornerstone idea informing Second Artillery operations over the past two decades; to be sure, the PLA's interpretation of it appears to have evolved over the years. This concept is central to understanding China's use of nuclear counterstrikes for deescalation or war-termination purposes, and it raises questions about China's inclinations to risk inadvertent escalation.

The current meaning behind *key-point counterstrikes* in a nuclear context is that the Second Artillery, in targeting an adversary's "key points," will bolster the credibility of China's nuclear deterrent and, thus, help to deter nuclear attacks on China. PLA writings also indicate that, if deterrence fails, counterstriking an adversary's key points will accomplish two additional goals: It will heavily damage an enemy's ability to prosecute war against China and it will engender such a strong psychological blow that the adversary terminates nuclear operations. In this sense, key-point nuclear counterstrikes seek to cause shock and pain by hitting assets of value and by retarding an adversary's ability to conduct war against China; by doing this, China seeks to bring about deescalation of nuclear exchange and, possibly, of the entire military conflict. To be sure, whether Second Artillery nuclear counterstrikes would actually be able to bring about the desired effect of deescalation or war termination is an open question. One can envision multiple scenarios in which such retaliation would lead to further nuclear escalation. Current PLA writings about this key concept do not reflect an awareness of the high risks of precipitating inadvertent escalation.

A fourth principle informing Chinese nuclear doctrine is that of counter–nuclear deterrence or intimidation, or *fan heweishe* [反核威慑]. This is a distinctly Chinese term insofar as an analogous one does not exist in the Western strategic nuclear lexicon. This term's origin in Chinese strategic thought derives from the pejorative meaning associated with the term *deterrence* [威慑]. For many Chinese strategists, the Western concept of deterrence is seen as akin to using a significant threat, or *wei* [*might* or *power*], to intimidate and coerce an adversary. Thus, deterrence (and the intimidation inherent in it) is a specific policy objective that requires countering, especially for a country such as China, which acquired nuclear weapons to avoid nuclear "blackmail" and coercion from other nuclear-armed states.

Chinese texts discuss counterdeterrence as a military operation, usually a posturing of nuclear missile forces during a crisis, to demonstrate China's determination and will to use nuclear weapons, usually in response to an adversary's perceived efforts to coerce China with nuclear threats. In this sense, Chinese views of the role and function of counterdeterrence are roughly equivalent to one of the central pillars of Western nuclear deterrence theory: nuclear signaling. For the deterrence function of China's nuclear force to be credible, not only does it need to possess a capability to inflict unacceptable damage, but China must also communicate the resolve to use it. For China, counterdeterrence operations seem to be efforts to communicate China's willingness to respond to nuclear threats and attacks. In this sense, counterdeterrence for China is a form of signaling to an adversary, though Chinese sources seldom discuss in detail the types of signals that might be sent during a crisis.

Additional Questions About Second Artillery Nuclear Operations
Despite the availability of these new Chinese sources and their ability to shed light on PLA doctrine, many important and detailed questions remain unanswered. It is not clear how the PLA would effectively carry out nuclear retaliation strikes to actually achieve deescalation or war termination. The tensions between this goal and the risks

of inadvertent escalation are not addressed in PLA writings. Does the PLA distinguish between U.S. military bases in Japan, U.S. bases in Guam (U.S. territory), Hawaii (a U.S. state), or the continental United States in conducting nuclear retaliation strikes? These distinctions have direct implications for the risks of escalation. For instance, Chinese nuclear counterstrikes against U.S. bases in Japan and Guam might keep the conflict contained to the Asia-Pacific theater, but it is not clear whether they would cause enough damage and shock to bring about deescalation, as China intends. Moreover, the U.S. government considers bases in both locations to be U.S. territory, so it is far from certain that Washington would respect Beijing's restraint and not further escalate the conflict with nuclear strikes on the Chinese mainland. Chinese nuclear counterstrikes on the U.S. mainland would create such desired shock, but they would be so highly provocative that they would likely precipitate a devastating U.S. strike on China's home territory. While such theorizing is clearly macabre and somewhat detached from modern-day political and military realities, to some extent, it is important for China to understand the relative viability of its nuclear deescalation and war-termination strategy; this would help prevent miscalculation and inadvertent escalation during a crisis.

Furthermore, Chinese nuclear planners currently face two challenges that will influence the risk of escalation and the possibility of escalation management in a Taiwan conflict. First, China's continued reliance on large, retaliatory nuclear strikes for deterrence (as indicated by the current configuration of its nuclear forces) may not be credible in eliminating the coercive influence of nuclear threats or deterring nuclear strikes at lower levels of nuclear conflict, especially if an adversary does not threaten to strike the mainland. An adversary could, theoretically, threaten or use low-yield nuclear weapons against PLA naval formations in the belief that Beijing would not respond with its large megaton-sized warheads on the adversary's foreign bases or its homeland. In this sense, China may be facing the same problem the United States confronted in the late 1950s, when the massive retaliation doctrine was discarded because of its inability to offer proportionate response options for conventional or limited nuclear attacks. This ultimately led the United States to develop capabilities to facilitate a new doctrine of flexible response in which U.S. leaders sought to deter aggression on several levels of conflict by maintaining conventional, theater nuclear, and strategic nuclear forces.

A further challenge for the Second Artillery is how to respond to U.S. conventional missile attacks on Chinese nuclear weapon support facilities or actual nuclear-capable missiles. Under a narrow interpretation, such attacks would *not* constitute nuclear first use and, therefore, would not justify a Second Artillery nuclear counterattack campaign. Yet, the possibility of suffering a disarming first strike by conventional precision-guided weapons is clearly a source of concern for Chinese planners, one that is currently being debated in Beijing. This scenario directly calls into question the sustainability of China's current NFU policy in the face of advances in U.S. conventional weapon technology. This issue is also directly related to U.S. war planning and escalation management insofar as such conventional strikes on Chinese nuclear weapon assets may be a critical threshold for the PLA that would lead to either horizontal or vertical escalation of a conflict—including crossing the nuclear firebreak. Recent events and Chinese media reports suggest that the PLA may consider conventional attacks on any nuclear weapon–related facilities as crossing such a threshold, which could lead to nuclear retaliation by China.[27] In fact, Chinese officials, military officers, and scholars have been debating in recent years whether to abandon or condition their NFU pledge in light of these emerging challenges to it. To date, the stated public policy of China remains the continued support for NFU as a

---

[27] See Shang Yi, "Zhu Chenghu: Foreign News Agency 'Cites Out of Context,'" Ta Kung Pao (Hong Kong) Foreign Broadcast Information Service, trans., July 15, 2005. In this news report, Li Yunsheng, a military commentator, stated that

> at present, the Chinese military and society are considering how China should react at a critical juncture if national security comes under substantial threat. He added that *some countries' precision guided weapons have similar power to that of a small-scale nuclear weapon, thus if China's nuclear facilities are attacked by such weapons it actually implies the outbreak of a nuclear war, hence the country will consider the use of nuclear weapons under such circumstances.* At the same time, Li reminded us that, "We should be aware of the context when speaking." [Emphasis added.]

core element of Chinese nuclear weapon policy.[28] Nevertheless, the precise conditions under which NFU applies are still an open question that concerns China's current nuclear doctrine and policy. The manner in which China ultimately addresses this issue will inform our understanding of PLA views on escalation.

Second Artillery Conventional Missile Strike Campaigns

The Second Artillery's conventional missile strike campaigns [常规导弹打击战役] differ significantly from their nuclear counterparts and thus raise different issues regarding Chinese views on escalation and escalation management. In contrast to China's nuclear operations, conventional missile strikes are not just about deterrence and retaliation. These writings are far more offensively oriented. They emphasize preemptive missile strikes and follow-on missile attacks for the purposes of compelling the adversary, escalation control, and escalation dominance to elicit an adversary's early and rapid capitulation. PLA conventional missile doctrine clearly stresses striking first, aggressively, precisely, and rapidly to seize the initiative and to quickly gain campaign control. According to Xue Xinglin's *Campaign Theory Study Guide*, the Second Artillery will use conventional missile strikes to "smash or weaken the enemy's military strength, to politically shock the enemy, to shake the willpower of war, to check the escalation of war and to speed up the progress of war."[29] In this sense, China would seek to use such strikes for both instrumental and suggestive escalation, but with an emphasis on the former.

These goals are to be accomplished through the use of missile attacks in various campaigns, including a joint blockade campaign, a joint island-landing campaign, or a joint firepower campaign. *The Sci-*

---

[28] "A General of the People's Liberation Army and Arms Control Experts Discuss Chinas' Nuclear Policy in the New Period," *Liaowang Dongfang Zhoukan*, No. 32, August 11, 2005, in Foreign Broadcast Information Service, trans., as "PRC Arms Control Experts Discuss China's Nuclear Policy."

[29] Xue, 2001, p. 394.

ence of Military Campaigns details the multiple tasks of conventional missile strikes in their support of such campaigns:

> The main tasks of regular missile-attack campaigns are to conduct a combined ground campaign together with the army and air force campaign corps to attack key enemy targets in deep areas; to support the army, navy, and air force campaign corps in conducting a sea blockade, an island blockade, or a landing campaign to attack key enemy targets such as a naval base, an air force base, or a C4I [command, control, communication, computer, and intelligence] system and to seize local campaign control over the sea and sky; and to conduct a combined air attack campaign together with the air force campaign corps to attack an enemy airport, air defense system, C4I system, and other key targets to seize local campaign control over the sky. Additionally, it can carry out other special combat tasks when needed.[30]

The Science of Military Campaigns further specifies six main combat operations for the Second Artillery's conventional missiles in support of the these tasks. They are (1) missile deterrence combat, (2) missile-damaging attacks, (3) missile blockade attacks, (4) missile disturbance attacks, (5) missile force mobile combat, and (6) missile firepower combat.[31]

Chinese writings about Second Artillery conventional missile operations consistently emphasize two themes in the six types of operations: preemption (i.e., timing) and massively striking an adversary's critical targets (i.e., target selection.) These ideas are captured in the PLA's so-called guiding ideology for conventional missile campaigns as follows: forestalling the enemy [先机制敌] and striking with focus [重点突击]. This principle and its related concepts are repeatedly stressed in numerous PLA publications about the Second Artillery's conventional missile operations.[32]

---

[30] Wang and Zhang, 2000b, Chapter 14.

[31] Wang and Zhang, 2000b, Chapter 14.

[32] See Medeiros, 2006, pp. 12–15, and Wang and Zhang, 2000b, Chapter 14.

Implications for Chinese Escalation Behavior

PLA writings on offensive conventional missile strikes open the door to both vertical and horizontal escalation. In terms of the former, conventional missile campaign theory clearly calls for additional attacks of increasing intensity, depending on the outcome and efficacy of the initial strikes. In discussing the execution of a conventional missile campaign, PLA writings identify multiple waves of missile strikes of increasing intensity. The first is the initial strike, carried out by a basic strike group. After the initial strike, the Second Artillery can conduct follow-up strikes based on the needs of campaign development in the progress of a joint campaign. This type of strike could include the use of a reserve strike group, which would likely increase the intensity of the initial missile attack. The Second Artillery may then conduct supplementary strikes if the latter two types of missile strikes are not effective. Chinese texts also generally discuss the possibility of using warheads tailored to specific operational needs in conducting initial, follow-up, or supplemental conventional missile strikes. In characterizing one of the principles informing conventional strikes, a senior Second Artillery officer wrote, "'Strike ferociously' means that one must meticulously select key strategic targets and adopt a method, such as convergent strikes, sustained attacks, or multiwave attacks."[33] Indeed, the growing size and changing composition of the PLA's conventional missile forces further underscores its desire to use conventional strikes for these purposes.[34]

Second Artillery conventional missile operations may encompass and intentionally precipitate horizontal escalation during a conflict, especially in a Taiwan contingency. While the PLA's public writings do not explicitly raise this issue, cross-border missile strikes emerge as a strong possibility given the discussion of (1) the battlespace for conventional missile operations and (2) the target sets for conventional missile strikes. The Second Artillery conceives of the battlespace for conven-

---

[33] Li Tilin, "Dui Dier Paobing Xinxihua Jianshe de Sikao" ["Thoughts on the Development of Second Artillery Informationalization"], *Junshi Xueshu* [*Military Science*], December 2004, p. 55

[34] Medeiros, 2006, pp. 13–20.

tional operations as wide and spacious.[35] The Second Artillery's target sets for conventional missile strikes include "political and economic centers, important military bases, command centers, communication hubs, massive force groups, and rear-area targets in the enemy's strategic and campaign depth."[36] The latter types of targets, combined with the depiction of a wide battlespace, seem to suggest a strong possibility of missile strikes on U.S. bases in Japan, Guam, and even Hawaii. Indeed, Western analyses of such a conflict often note that China could significantly increase the probably of operational success of an amphibious landing operation by preemptively striking U.S. bases in Japan and Guam to disrupt mobilization and resupply operations and to prevent U.S. forces from maintaining combat air patrols over the Taiwan Strait.[37] Unfortunately, PLA writings about conventional strikes do not identify specific thresholds related to China's willingness to conduct various types of conventional missile strikes—either China's thresholds or its perception of U.S. thresholds.

Chinese Views on Space Warfare and Escalation

Over the past decade, China has been expanding its civilian space activities in an effort to become a major space power. In 2004, it launched 10 satellites into orbit, and by 2020, it hopes to have launched 100 remote sensing satellites.[38] In October 2003, it launched its first manned spacecraft (Shenzhou-5), and it aspires to operate a space station by 2020. As China's civilian space activities become increasingly sophisticated, U.S. defense officials worry that China may also be develop-

---

[35] This concept of the battlespace incorporates both the operational positions of missile forces as well as the target areas of the adversary.

[36] Xue, 2001, p. 393.

[37] David A. Shlapak, David T. Orletsky, and Barry Wilson, *Dire Strait? Military Aspects of the China-Taiwan Confrontation and Options for U.S. Policy,* Santa Monica, Calif.: RAND Corporation, MR-1217-SRF, 2000.

[38] "China Plans to Launch 100 Satellites Before 2020 to Form an Observation Network," Xinhua, November 16, 2004.

ing antisatellite weapons such as ground-based lasers and antisatellite satellites.[39] In fact, as the U.S. military's reliance on space has grown, and as U.S. military leaders have increasingly described space as necessary for achieving victory and have more publicly debated future space-based warfighting options, Chinese military writings have increasingly discussed the role of space in future military operations, including the need to achieve space control.[40]

For example, the *Science of Military Campaigns* recognizes that the modern battlefield has expanded and that space will play an increasingly important role in future operations.[41] *A Course on the Science of Campaigns*, published in 2001, expanded the discussion of space and clearly identified space as a battlefield that must be won:

> During campaigns in high-tech local wars, achieving information and air superiority is to win the operational initiative. The aerospace battlefield is the main area for achieving information and air superiority. At the same time, it is also an important area for effectively carrying out command-and-control and precision-guided firepower for ground and naval operations.[42]

Chinese strategists also note that space is key to transforming the PLA into an "informationalized" force capable of winning an infor-

---

[39] Office of the Secretary of Defense, *The Military Power of the People's Republic of China*, annual report to Congress, 2005, p. 36; Office of the Secretary of Defense, *The Military Power of the People's Republic of China*, annual report to Congress, 2004, p. 42.

[40] For U.S. strategists, the space-control mission is defined as providing freedom of action in space for friendly forces while, when necessary, denying it to an adversary. It includes offensive and defensive operations by friendly forces to gain and maintain space superiority and situational awareness of events that impact space operations. This conception of space control is based on that provided in U.S. Joint Chiefs of Staff, *Joint Doctrine for Space Operations*, Joint Publication 3-14, August 9, 2002, pp. x, IV-3, GL-6.

[41] Wang and Zhang, 2000b, pp. 24–25.

[42] He Diqing, ed., *Zhanyixue Jiaocheng* [*A Course on the Science of Campaigns*], Beijing: Military Sciences Press, 2001, p. 244.

mationalized war—a central thrust of current PLA modernization efforts.[43]

The PLA sees the U.S. military's use of space as a threat. The author of a *Liberation Army Daily* article writes that the United States "maintains that a space war is inevitable" and that through the use of space, the "United States can occupy a commanding height in issuing a threatening signal to opponents to make them stop their threat of armed force, and thus reach its goal of 'forcing the enemy to surrender without a fight.'" The author concludes,

> Space fighting is not far off. National security has already exceeded territory and territorial waters and airspace and territorial space should also be added. The modes of defense will no longer be to fight on our own territory and fight for marine rights and interests. We must also engage in space defense as well as air defense.[44]

The increasing importance of space to Chinese strategists and the threat posed by U.S. forces enabled by space assets has led some Chinese military writers to advocate the development of space weapons. According to a book published by the prestigious Military Science Press,

> Based on the needs of national security and our nation's space development, the planning of space weapon development can be divided into two stages, with the first stage covering from now until 2010 and the second stage from 2010 to 2025. In the first stage, we must strive to make our space weapon systems possess support and safeguard capabilities as well as a basic space combat capability. In addition, they can complement our operations on the ground, sea, and air and, at the same time, provide effective surveillance, monitoring, early warning, communication, naviga-

---

[43] Chang Xianqi, "Space Strength and New Revolution in Military Affairs," *Zhongguo Junshi Kexue* [*China Military Science*], March 2003.

[44] Teng Jianqun, "Thoughts Arising From The U.S. Military's Space War Exercise," *Liberation Army Daily*, February 7, 2001, in Foreign Broadcast Information Service as "*Jiefangjun Bao* Views U.S. Preparations for Space Warfare," February 7, 2001.

tion, and positioning support to our combat units. They should also have a certain combat capability in space, particularly with regard to defensive capability. In the second stage, we should build on the foundation of the first stage by further improving the offensive and defensive capability of space weapon systems. In particular, the offense capability in space should, if necessary, be capable of destroying or temporarily incapacitating all enemy space vehicles that fly in above our sovereign territory.[45]

Other authors echo these recommendations, writing,

A war may break out on our periphery that directly uses military space systems, including space support, attack, and defense spacecraft. To meet this threat, we must intensify research into ground-based and space-based (concentrating on ground-based) antisatellite systems and, as soon as possible, develop one or two antisatellite weapons that can threaten enemy space systems and allow the initiative to be taken in space.[46]

China's relative inferiority to the United States in both space and general conventional military capabilities may lead Beijing to consider offensive operations in space in an effort to counter the United States' comparative advantages. According to an article in a leading Chinese military journal, "The party with inferior military space forces will be unable to organize a comprehensive and effective defense. It should therefore concentrate its limited military space forces on the offensive."[47]

The relative balance in Chinese and U.S. reliance on space assets will affect escalation dynamics. China's current limited reliance on

---

[45] Li Daguang, *Hangtian Zhan* [*Space Warfare*], Beijing: Military Science Press, 2001, pp. 413–414.

[46] Xie Yonggao, Qin Zizeng, and Huang Haibing, "Junshi Hangtian Jishu de Huigu Zhanwang" ["Looking at the Past and Future of Military Space Technology"], *Zhongguo Hangtian* [*China Aerospace*], No. 6, 2002.

[47] Hong Bing and Liang Xiaoqiu, "Guanyu Kongjian Zhanlue Lilun de Jige Jiben Wenti" ["The Basics of Space Strategic Theory"], *Zhongguo Junshi Kexue* [*China Military Science*], Vol. 1, 2002, p. 31.

space capabilities (for either civilian or military tasks) may present difficulties in deterring Beijing from engaging in space warfare. China's large economy and growing technological prowess will almost certainly enable it to develop weapons capable of attacking U.S. space systems. At the same time, its focus on participating in conflicts on its periphery, most notably Taiwan, reduces Beijing's dependence on space. In such a conflict, China could rely on terrestrial-based communication equipment for command and control and on airborne platforms for intelligence, surveillance, and reconnaissance. This might give China the freedom to attack U.S. orbital assets, while the United States would be hard pressed to find comparable Chinese targets that it could threaten in the credible, proportionate way needed to deter initial Chinese attacks or subsequent attacks without escalating the conflict. This possible limitation in the United States' deterrent leverage, combined with the Chinese belief that controlling space is a prerequisite for gaining initiative and the emphasis on surprise and preemptive strikes, may provide China an incentive to strike first in space in a conflict against the United States.

The evolution of China's space program could also indicate how it may act in a conflict. If China's interest in numerous small satellites and a robust launch capability come to fruition, for example, it may gain confidence that it can fare better in a space war than the United States, whose space program is now characterized by smaller numbers of complicated satellites and a low launch capability. Of course, if the United States shifts its emphasis to smaller satellites, increases its launch capabilities, and develops ways to better defend its orbital assets, the incentives for Beijing to escalate a conflict by attacking U.S. space systems will lessen.

The few Chinese writings on space deterrence available in the open literature suggest that China is considering how to manage warfare in space, as China's space equities grow and as the United States develops space weapons. While space operations and nuclear deterrence are both strategic in nature, Chinese analysts observe that nations are reluctant to use the immense destructive power of nuclear weapons. Alternatively, they recognize that space weapons are not as destructive but can produce strategic effects; thus, Chinese strategists believe that space weapons are more likely to be used.[48] Moreover, there appears to be a universal belief among Chinese authors that the U.S. military advocates the development of space weapons; many Chinese strategists hold a corresponding view that if China is to deter other powers in space, it must not only be a significant space power, it must also develop its own space-control technologies.[49] They write that these technologies can range from "soft-kill" methods such as laser dazzling to "hard-kill" methods such as kinetic kill vehicles. While hard-kill methods are permanent, some analysts recognize that soft-kill methods are sometimes more suitable than hard-kill methods because they are less permanent and, thus, less escalatory.[50] One pair of Chinese authors has observed that the intensity of a space war may also need to be controlled to allow the participants opportunities to deescalate.[51] If these opinions are common in the PLA, they may form the basis for an international understanding on the conduct of space-control operations and related technology development programs.

Conclusion

This chapter reviewed contemporary Chinese military writings for information about PLA views on escalation and escalation management. Given the revision of Chinese military doctrine in the late 1990s and China's ongoing, ambitious force modernization programs, such

---

[48] Xu Wei and Chang Xianqi, "Shilun Kongjian Weishe" ["A Tentative Discussion of Space Deterrence"], *Zhuangbei Zhihui Jishu Xueyuan Xuebao* [*Journal of the Academy of Equipment Command and Technology*], February 2002, p. 11.

[49] See, for example, Zhang Ming and Li Suoku, "Kongjian Xinxi Zuozhan yu Guoji Kongjian Fa" ["Space Information Operations and International Space Law"] *Zhuangbei Zhihui Jishu Xueyuan Xuebao* [*Journal of the Academy of Equipment Command and Technology*], April 2003, and Li Daguang and Wan Shuixian, "Zhengduo Zhi Tian Quande Jiben Tezheng" ["The Fundamental Features of the Struggle for Space Dominance"], *Zhuangbei Zhihui Jishu Xueyuan Xuebao* [*Journal of the Academy of Equipment Command and Technology*], December 2003, p. 41.

[50] Li and Wan, 2003, p. 39.

[51] Xu and Chang, 2002, p. 12.

writings are an important starting point for understanding the relationship among PLA doctrine, operations, and escalation-related ideas and behaviors. This chapter examined three categories of open-source PLA writings: the general literature on war control and two groups of more specialized writings on Second Artillery operations and space warfare. These bodies of work yielded preliminary insights into the PLA's views on escalation.

Several themes stand out from the preceding analysis. First and foremost, PLA writings on escalation appear to be undertheorized insofar as they do not address a host of core issues related to how the PLA conceives escalation risks or intends to manage those risks. China's war control literature is so general that it suggests a lack of serious attention to these topics, at least in the open literature. In addition, PLA writings about the conduct of specific military operations, such as conventional missile strikes, provide little evidence of an awareness of the risks of inadvertent escalation.

That said, the war-control literature highlights some general themes that are helpful in deciphering Chinese views on escalation. First, it emphasizes the importance of subordinating military goals to political objectives and that war control involves finding the appropriate balance between the two. Second, Chinese strategists believe that the era of unlimited warfare is over and that there is no ipso facto reason that conventional conflict would escalate out of control. Third, they recognize that the political and diplomatic dimensions of warfare can be as important as the military dimensions, especially in a globalized world in which warfare is transparent. In this respect, Chinese writings highlight that international public opinion can both constrain and enable PLA operations. Fourth, a key element of war control is seizing and maintaining the initiative to control the scale and pace of a conflict; this theme is repeatedly emphasized in military writings. However, it is not accompanied by a corresponding recognition that actions to seize the initiative could also precipitate a harsh reaction, leading to inadvertent escalation.

PLA writings about Second Artillery operations provide a different set of insights about escalation and escalation management. First, the Second Artillery will likely play a central and defining role in escalation, given its ability to strike at long distances with increasingly destructive force. Chinese writings about Second Artillery operations implicitly affirm this argument, as does the continued investment in nuclear and conventional missile capabilities, especially the latter. Second, there is very little evidence that the PLA seeks to use *nuclear* missile strikes for the purposes of deliberate escalation or to achieve escalation dominance. PLA writings suggest that the Second Artillery is primarily postured to conduct retaliatory nuclear counterstrikes and not preemptive ones, though the latter possibility can never be ruled out. By contrast, the Second Artillery's specific goal in conducting such nuclear counterstrikes would be to catalyze deescalation of a nuclear exchange and, perhaps, complete war termination. Such goals may be highly unrealistic and inconsistent with the operational realities of both China's capabilities and the likely ways in which the United States and others would respond to Chinese retaliatory strikes. It is far from certain that a Second Artillery nuclear counterattack would precipitate such a response from the United States or other nuclear-armed adversaries.

The limited role of the PLA's nuclear missile forces contrasts with the far more offensive role of its conventional missile forces. The Second Artillery's conventional missile forces are postured for preemption and escalation dominance in support of PLA naval and air force operations in the Taiwan theater, such as amphibious-landing and naval blockade operations. PLA writings about conventional missile strikes stress the existence of a wide battlespace, the employment of numerous waves of missile attacks, and striking multiple types of targets, including an adversary's staging and mobilization centers. This raises the distinct possibility of both horizontal and vertical escalation, depending on the efficacy of the first wave of missile attacks. Indeed, Western analyses of a Taiwan conflict confirm the potential value of such escalation (both vertical and horizontal) in enabling the PLA to conduct an amphibious invasion of Taiwan. Therefore, in contrast to PLA views on nuclear counterstrike campaigns, the Second Artillery's doctrine for conventional missile strike operations is increasingly aligned with the capabilities needed to carry out a conventional campaign.

A final point of this chapter is to underscore the evolving nature of PLA thinking and writing on military doctrine and, specifically, its theories about war control. There are a great number of known unknowns about PLA escalation preferences. Chinese views on some of the most fundamental aspects of escalation are not clear from the available literature on war control or from open-source PLA writings about Second Artillery operations. Most basically, it is unclear whether Chinese strategists recognize the inherent tension between their concept of using nuclear counterstrikes for deescalation and war termination and the risks of inadvertent escalation. Nor can we fathom whether the Chinese recognize the risks of inadvertent and accidental escalation inherent in the Second Artillery's aggressive conventional missile campaign doctrine or emerging theories on space warfare. These issues constitute a significant gap in Western understanding about the PLA, and they highlight the risks associated with armed conflict with China. Additional questions about Chinese perspectives conclude this chapter. These questions should guide further research on the PLA, as they can help analysts to systematically examine PLA literature for answers to questions about escalation and escalation management.

First, it is not clear how strategic thinkers in China view the dynamics of escalation. Do they think about escalation in a manner similar to the categories outlined in this volume—as deliberate, inadvertent, and accidental—or do they envision escalation as moving up a series of rungs on a ladder? If it is the second, how do they define each rung? Do the Chinese think about conflict as occurring in levels, stages, or states, and, if so, how do military planners identify those categories? More specifically, how does the PLA conceive of the mechanisms for moving among the various rungs of a notional escalation ladder or moving among the various levels, stages, or states of a conflict? And what are the forces that motivate moving among the various levels of escalation?

Second, and perhaps more importantly, what might Chinese leaders consider critical escalation thresholds during a conflict? While it is fairly clear that they recognize that a significant threshold exists between nuclear and conventional warfare, the existence of other thresholds are not explicit in military writings. How would Beijing react to attacks on Second Artillery units or space warfare–related facilities on the Chinese mainland? At this point, we do not know, but there are indications that Chinese military leaders would consider conventional strikes on Second Artillery nuclear assets as crossing the nuclear threshold, justifying nuclear strikes in retaliation.[52] This is a serious concern, as the distinction between nuclear and conventional targets in China could become blurred if the Second Artillery colocates any of its nuclear forces with space warfare assets or conventional forces or if they share command-and-control facilities.

Third, how does China think about vertical versus horizontal escalation? The Second Artillery would likely play a central role in either form of escalation, given the PLA's increasingly destructive conventional and nuclear capabilities and its ability to use missiles to strike far from the mainland at minimal cost for the military. Are Chinese leaders predisposed to one type of escalation over another? What U.S. actions would lead them to pursue one pathway over another? The Second Artillery's doctrine for conventional missile campaigns describes a wide and spacious battlespace; yet China's attention to the role of international public opinion in the conduct of warfare suggests that horizontal escalation (especially when it involves striking another country) may not be highly preferred.

Fourth, how might China signal during a crisis or war, and would the Second Artillery be used for such signaling? Might Beijing deploy the Second Artillery's mobile launchers to operational locations or mate warheads to missiles during a crisis to signal China's intentions or concerns? A particularly important issue is how such signaling might be linked to the issues of thresholds and vertical or horizontal escalation. Would China seek to signal the sanctity of certain thresholds in a conflict, such as counterforce attacks on nuclear missile brigades? While PLA writings suggest that the Second Artillery's missile forces (especially the nuclear forces) would be used for signaling during a crisis, it is not clear that the PLA has systematically developed a concept of operations for such activities.

---

[52] Shang, 2005.

Answers to these questions may remain mysteries rather than secrets that can be discerned through careful textual research, as some of them inevitably depend on the geopolitical circumstances of a specific conflict, and Chinese leaders themselves may not hold uniform and definitive views beforehand. Nevertheless, as PLA writings on escalation evolve, our understanding of these issues may come further to light. Therefore, these questions provide direction for future research.

CHAPTER FOUR
Regional Nuclear Powers

In recent years, several states in regions in which the United States has important interests have acquired nuclear weapons or are attempting to do so. These developments are not only disturbing in and of themselves, but they signal the end of a positive trend in efforts to contain nuclear proliferation. The end of the Cold War initially brought encouraging changes in membership to the international nuclear club: Aside from Russia, all of the former Soviet republics and the Republic of South Africa elected to give up their nuclear weapons and accede to the international Treaty on the Non-Proliferation of Nuclear Weapons as nonnuclear states. Moreover, several regional rivals previously attempting to develop nuclear weapons agreed to abandon their efforts, such as North and South Korea, which signed a joint declaration on the denuclearization of the Korean peninsula in 1991, and Argentina and Brazil, which began mutual inspections in 1992.[1] But the trend toward denuclearization was short-lived. India and Pakistan successfully tested nuclear devices in 1998. In February 2005, North Korea announced that it too had developed nuclear weapons, and it tested one with at least partial success in October 2006. Although Libya renounced its nuclear program in 2003 and Iran suspended efforts to develop nuclear weapons in the fall of that year, Iran has continued uranium enrichment activities. The U.S. National Intelligence Council estimates with

---

[1] For summaries of national nuclear capabilities and levels of compliance with international nonproliferation treaties and protocols, see Center for Nonproliferation Studies, "Country Profiles: What Are the Threats from Weapons of Mass Destruction?" Nuclear Threat Initiative, Web page, updated continuously.

moderate confidence that "Iran probably would be technically capable of producing enough [highly enriched uranium] for a weapon sometime during the 2010–2015 time frame."[2]

The emergence of new nuclear states increases risks of escalation in regional crises and challenges efforts to manage those risks should the United States need to intervene to protect its interests. While emergent nuclear states pose inherent escalation risks regardless of their ideologies or forms of government, matters are made worse by the fact that all of the new and soon-to-be nuclear powers share bitter animosities with their neighbors and some are embroiled in ongoing conflicts. Some of these regimes are revisionist states, eager to change the status quo in their regions. Some are hostile to the United States and, like Saddam Hussein's Iraq, have been singled out as rogue states or members of an axis of evil. Therefore, they may be anxious that Washington will attempt to impose regime change on them, raising risks of escalation should U.S. forces intervene in a crisis in their region. Finally, some of these states have domestic problems that threaten their stability, and factions within them have known links to terrorists.

This chapter examines the escalation risks that regional nuclear powers present. It illustrates some potential paths of escalation that could occur in military confrontations and other crises involving these states then draws implications from these examples for escalation management.[3]

---

[2] National Intelligence Council, *Iran: Nuclear Intentions and Capabilities, National Intelligence Estimate*, Washington, D.C.: Office of the Director of National Intelligence, November 2007, p. 7.

[3] In presenting potential paths of escalation, we do not attempt to cover every possible future scenario, nor do we predict that any of the notional scenarios we do examine will necessarily occur. We simply seek to illustrate the potentially volatile dynamics of confrontations with emergent regional nuclear powers. In addition to the research presented in this chapter, the findings are also informed by a Delphi analysis conducted on July 20, 2005. See Appendix C for a description of the modified Delphi method used in that exercise.

Escalation Risks Inherent in Emergent Nuclear Capability

States that develop nuclear weapons do not do so in a strategic vacuum. While there may be nonsecurity-related motives for acquiring nuclear capabilities, such as the belief that doing so will garner the state and its leaders prestige, regimes that seek nuclear weapons most often do so principally to improve their security and bolster their coercive leverage vis-à-vis regional or global rivals. Consequently, the imminent emergence of a new nuclear state alarms neighbors and other actors that have interests in the region, impelling them to consider what options they have to redress their own security in the face of this new threat. If they have the ability to do so, one or more may try to prevent an embryonic nuclear program from reaching fruition, as Israel did with its 1981 air raid on the Iraqi nuclear reactor at Osiraq.[4] More often, however, states in the race to develop nuclear weapons have cleared the final hurdle without suffering military intervention, creating or intensifying security dilemmas between them and their rivals and making subsequent confrontations more dangerous.

Confrontations with new nuclear states raise serious risks of escalation, not only because the state or coalition opposing the newly armed regime is threatened, but also because the emergent nuclear capability itself may be vulnerable. It takes time for emergent states to produce enough fissile material to build more than a handful of weapons. Early on, the weapons are not mated to delivery vehicles, are typically stored at a central location, and may even consist of unassembled components. All of this can make them inviting targets for adversaries in the event of a crisis. Emergent nuclear powers may lack sophisticated strategic warning and attack-assessment systems, adding to their vulnerability and feeding their leaders' sense of insecurity. Such vulnerability to a disarming first strike—or, in the parlance of nuclear deterrence, lack of a "survivable second-strike capability"—generates pressures to

---

[4] For a detailed examination of the Osiraq raid, as well as other cases in which states have considered taking military action to prevent the emergence of new nuclear powers, see K. Mueller et al., 2006. For seminal work on the security dilemma, see Kenneth N. Waltz, *Man, the State, and War: A Theoretical Analysis*, New York: Columbia University Press, 1959. See also Jervis, 1976.

escalate on both sides. Knowing that an adversary is tempted to strike the emergent state's nuclear capability preemptively puts pressure on that regime to use its weapons before they are lost. Conversely, the adversary, fearing the weapons and sensing that the enemy is pressured to use them, feels increasingly driven to preempt. These escalatory pressures are more severe, and the results potentially more catastrophic, if both sides are new nuclear states with similar vulnerabilities.

Assembling the weapons and dispersing them to fielded forces before or during a crisis presents other escalation risks. Policies may not have been developed detailing who in the national hierarchy has authority to order the use of nuclear weapons and under what circumstances.[5] Even if such details have been worked out, strategic command-and-control linkages may be vulnerable to interdiction, and the state's new nuclear forces may not have adequate procedures and technology (such as the permissive-action links used by the United States and Russia) to prohibit weapons from arming without authorization from designated authorities. Such conditions extend dangerous latitude to field commanders in control of the weapons, officers without experience in nuclear matters and probably without an established body of doctrine and training to guide their decisions. If conflict erupts and the tide of conventional battle turns against them, they may miscalculate the consequences of crossing the nuclear threshold and make reckless decisions. Once again, an adversary's anticipation of these risks intensifies the security dilemma, potentially prompting that state to attack locations and forces believed to be harboring weapons.

Making matters worse, leaders of states with new nuclear capabilities can aggravate regional instabilities by engaging in risky behaviors they would not otherwise have attempted. Such risk-taking was evi-

---

[5] Note, for example, that although the United States employed atomic weapons in 1945, the Truman administration did not develop a postwar policy regarding the authorization of their use until the first Berlin crisis forced them to address the issue. President Truman eventually signed a policy statement in September 1948. See K. Mueller et al., 2006, p. 120; David Alan Rosenberg, "American Atomic Strategy and the Hydrogen Bomb Decision," *Journal of American History*, Vol. 66, No. 1, June 1979, p. 69; and David Alan Rosenberg, "The Origins of Overkill: Nuclear Weapons and American Strategy, 1945–1960," *International Security*, Vol. 7, No. 4, Spring 1983, p. 13.

dent in the crises Moscow triggered in confrontations with the United States in Berlin and Cuba and in the border conflict Beijing provoked with the Soviet Union shortly after China acquired nuclear weapons. In none of these cases did the presence of nuclear weapons deter states from resisting conventional aggression. As Cold War leaders discovered, nuclear deterrence may reduce the probability of war at the highest level, but it is difficult to make nuclear threats, whether implicit or explicit, credible in lower-level conventional conflicts. In fact, the presence of nuclear weapons may make such conflicts more likely. Analysts have characterized this phenomenon as the *stability-instability paradox*, first elaborated by Glenn Snyder in 1965: "The greater the stability of the 'strategic' balance of terror, the lower the stability of the overall balance at its lower levels of violence."[6] The logic here is that if both sides possess a reliable and survivable nuclear deterrent, the strategic balance will be stable and each will feel freer to engage in conventional aggression. Conversely, if one or both states' nuclear forces are vulnerable to a disarming first strike, they will, theoretically, avoid conventional conflict for fear that impending defeat on either side might lead to nuclear preemption. This latter corollary better describes the condition in which emerging nuclear powers first find themselves, suggesting that they should avoid conventional provocation for fear of escalation to nuclear conflict.

Unfortunately, leaders of newly armed revisionist states may not always appreciate this danger. With little or no experience to guide their judgment, they may risk aggressive behavior, overestimating the ability of nuclear weapons to deter their adversaries from escalating in resistance to conventional incursions, while simultaneously underestimating the danger that their provocations might upset a not-yet-stable nuclear balance. Such miscalculations can lead to catastrophic esca-

---

[6] Glenn Snyder, "The Balance of Power and the Balance of Terror," in Paul Seabury, ed., *Balance of Power*, San Francisco, Calif.: Chandler, 1965. For more on the stability-instability paradox as it relates to new nuclear states, see Peter Lavoy, "The Strategic Consequences of Nuclear Proliferation," *Security Studies*, Vol. 4, No. 4, Summer 1995; Michael Krepon, "The Stability-Instability Paradox, Misperception, and Escalation Control in South Asia," in Michael Krepon, Rodney W. Jones, and Ziad Haider, eds., *Escalation Control and the Nuclear Option in South Asia*, Washington, D.C.: Henry L. Stimson Center, November 2004.

lation. Indeed, Robert Jervis argues that miscalculations and misperceptions can occur even when mature nuclear powers, whose strategic relationships are theoretically stable, engage each other in conventional conflict.[7] If he is correct, how much higher might the dangers be in crises involving states with immature nuclear capabilities and leaders inexperienced in nuclear stewardship?

All of this, of course, compels us to consider what constitutes a "mature nuclear power." While there is no formal definition, we submit that nuclear maturity exists when a state overcomes most or all of the deficiencies addressed here. That is, when it possesses a survivable second-strike capability, supported by reliable surveillance and warning systems and a sophisticated command-and-control system with safeguards comparable to the permissive-action links employed by the United States and Russia; when its custodial forces attain a high state of professionalism, having been thoroughly trained according to a nuclear doctrine emphasizing surety and national authority over weapon control and release; when military and civilian leaders are sufficiently educated and experienced in nuclear diplomacy to understand not only the coercive potential of nuclear weapons, but also the limitations of their utility and the grave responsibilities that come with possessing them. By these standards, the United States and Soviet Union probably did not reach nuclear maturity until sometime after the 1962 Cuban Missile Crisis.

Sources of Regional Instability

While the escalatory pressures noted here are present in any confrontation with an emergent nuclear power, regardless of its ideology or form of government, they are more severe when ideological conflicts or historical animosities create regional tensions, and conditions are most volatile when states are already embroiled in conflict. Domestic instabilities add to these concerns, particularly if the nuclear state (or

---

[7] Robert Jervis, *The Illogic of American Nuclear Strategy*, Ithaca, N.Y.: Cornell University Press, 1984, pp. 148–150.

factions within it) has close ties to other dangerous regimes or terrorist groups. Unfortunately, these conditions exist to varying degrees in all the regions in which states have recently acquired nuclear weapons or are likely to do so in the near future.

Instability and Risks of Escalation in Northeast Asia

Even before North Korea's nuclear test, the principal sources of instability in Northeast Asia were the unresolved issue of Korean unification and the repressive, xenophobic nature of the Pyongyang regime. The Democratic People's Republic of Korea (DPRK) commands the fourth-largest military establishment in the world, with about 70 percent of its forces deployed within 100 miles of the demilitarized zone (DMZ) that separates it from the Republic of Korea (ROK) in the south.[8] Though hobbled by a failed economy, Pyongyang continues to devote a major portion of its declining gross national product to maintaining its military forces and developing strategic weapons, even as its people starve. These conditions feed regional instability due to the risk of war that such a regime represents. Also, though the imminent danger of state failure in North Korea has receded since the late 1990s, the potential still exists that the Pyongyang regime could ultimately collapse under a growing burden of economic failure and social inequity.[9] A crisis caused by either eventuality would entail serious risks of escalation.

    Prospects for War and Escalation in Korea. Although Pyongyang's occasional diplomatic overtures to Seoul have encouraged some South Koreans to hope that North Korean leaders are willing to abandon their goal of forcefully reunifying the peninsula, North Korea's force dispositions tell a different story. By all indications, the DPRK's mili-

---

[8] When ranked by numbers of active-duty, uniformed troops, the top six nations are (1) China, with 2,250,000; (2) the United States, with 1,625,852; (3) India, with 1,325,000; (4) North Korea, with 1,075,000; (5) Russia, with 960,000; and (6) South Korea, with 685,000. See GlobalSecurity.org, "Active Duty Uniformed Troop Strength," updated January 25, 2006a.

[9] For a 1999 analysis of potential scenarios that Korea watchers posited for the DPRK's demise, see Jonathan D. Pollack and Chung Min Lee, *Preparing for Korean Unification: Scenarios and Implications*, Santa Monica, Calif.: RAND Corporation, MR-1040-A, 1999.

tary objectives remain focused on (1) achieving operational surprise in a crisis; (2) applying massive firepower to South Korean and U.S. forces with artillery, rockets, and surface-to-surface missiles; (3) neutralizing opposing air power; (4) capturing Seoul and closing all air and port facilities necessary for getting U.S. reinforcements onto the peninsula; and (5) causing widespread panic among the citizens of South Korea, thereby raising domestic pressure for a negotiated settlement.[10]

The ROK–U.S. Combined Forces Command (CFC) has successfully deterred North Korea from attacking the South for more than 50 years. As South Korea's economic strength grows and its democratic institutions continue to develop, North Korea's claims to legitimacy fade, as do its hopes of reunifying the peninsula by diplomatic stratagem or force of arms. Yet the availability of nuclear weapons could change the decision calculus, and if North Korea's economic plight takes another turn for the worse, Pyongyang may become desperate. Impoverished, isolated from the international community, and facing a closing window of opportunity, its leaders could conclude that they have little to lose in attacking the South while trusting their nuclear capability to deter or impair U.S. efforts to reinforce CFC defenses.[11]

Such an attack might not entail a major conventional assault at first, but geographical factors and the balance of forces on the peninsula suggest a high risk of rapid escalation to full-scale war. Pyongyang might begin with a series of small-scale incursions designed to test CFC reactions and undermine the armistice agreement, as they attempted in the submarine infiltration incidents in September 1996 and June 1998. If the results of such probes are encouraging, the DPRK might escalate to an open conflict with limited aims, hoping that some initial gain would result in a collapse of morale in the South, then offer to negotiate in an effort to undermine ROK-U.S. relations and commitment to resist. But with Seoul only about 30 miles south of the DMZ, any

---

[10] Pollack and Lee, 1999, pp. 67–68.

[11] In fact, when the DPRK was in the depths of economic crisis in 1997, a high-ranking North Korean defector told interviewers that the DPRK was close to launching a war on the South. See Kevin Sullivan, "Key Defector Warns Again of North Korean War Plans," *Washington Post*, July 10, 1997.

attack that would result in a DPRK breakthrough into ROK territory would likely result in rapid escalation due to Seoul's vulnerability and the urgency with which the CFC would need reinforcements.

To help deter Pyongyang from renewing its military aggression against the South, the United States currently maintains a force of about 25,000 military personnel in South Korea, with 47,000 more in Japan to provide logistical support and reinforcement.[12] The U.S. response to a DPRK breakthrough would likely entail intense air strikes against a wide range of targets in the North while rushing reinforcements to the peninsula. With the battle escalating, Pyongyang's chances of success would largely depend on closing South Korean airfields and ports to interdict the reinforcement effort. Achieving that objective would be a challenge, as the CFC would probably win air dominance over South Korea early in the conflict. But North Korea maintains a stockpile of chemical weapons and might employ them in such a mission, using surface-to-surface missiles. More seriously, as many U.S. air strikes would launch from Japanese bases, Pyongyang might feel impelled to target those locations with chemical weapons in an effort to shut them down. Indeed, in 1997, Hwan Jang Yop, the highest-ranking North Korean official ever to defect to the ROK, informed South Korean officials that, barring U.S. reinforcement, the North was confident that it could defeat South Korea with an all-out missile attack on Seoul. He said that the attack would last only a matter of minutes and that North Korean leader Kim Jong Il believed that he could keep the United States out of the conflict by threatening missile strikes on Tokyo and other Japanese cities.[13]

It is difficult to predict how Tokyo would react to such a development. An attack on bases in Japan would inevitably result in civilian casualties. Given the long history of U.S.-Japanese security coopera-

---

[12] Until recently, U.S. Forces, Korea, comprised approximately 37,500 military personnel. In 2004, Washington and Seoul agreed to transfer 10 selected military missions from U.S. to South Korean forces, allowing the withdrawal of approximately 12,500 U.S. troops over a three-year period. See General B. B. Bell, Commander, UN Command; Commander, Republic of Korea–U.S. Combined Forces Command; and Commander, U.S. Forces, Korea, statement before the Senate Armed Services Committee, March 7, 2006, p. 24.

[13] Sullivan, 1997.

tion and historical animosities between Japan and both Koreas, Tokyo could respond by entering the war against Pyongyang. Such a development would alarm Beijing, potentially increasing the chances of a Chinese intervention in the conflict.

Whether Japan or China enters the war at that juncture, other factors would exert ever-greater escalatory pressures on actors in the region. The campaign against the DPRK would have to be extremely intense, given the time-driven gravity of the crisis associated with Seoul's vulnerability. In addition to striking forces directly employed against the South, CFC air power would likely hammer North Korea's command-and-control system at every level (including attacks on leadership), its integrated air defense system, and missile, chemical, and nuclear weapon sites wherever they could be found. Such a concentrated attack might well threaten the continued viability of the Pyongyang regime, a development that would alarm China's leaders and might prompt Beijing to offer military assistance to forestall the collapse of a state that China has long regarded as an important buffer between it and U.S. forces in the south.[14]

Though unlikely, certain aspects of this scenario might persuade U.S. and ROK commanders to seek authority to conduct ground operations against North Korea above the DMZ. Given North Korea's mountainous terrain, the extensive tunneling and hidden fortifications built there over the decades, and the inherent difficulty of finding and targeting mobile missile launchers and artillery, it would be doubtful that the CFC could destroy enough launchers and storage sites with air power alone to reduce the threat of chemical and nuclear attack to levels that allied leaders consider acceptable. Ordinarily, one would expect South Korean leaders to oppose any U.S. proposal to invade North Korea, but, given the emergent nuclear threat, it is conceivable (however unlikely) that Seoul might conclude that it is time to remove the threat from the DPRK once and for all.

A CFC invasion of North Korea could have grave consequences in terms of escalation. If China's historical behavior offers any indica-

---

[14] See Appendix A for a summary of China's historical proclivity to intervene in conflicts on its borders.

tion, an overt effort to remove the Pyongyang regime, particularly one that entails U.S. forces moving up the peninsula, would likely prompt Beijing to intervene in the conflict. That would result in a more intense battle with more serious potential for further escalation between major nuclear powers. Beyond that, a concerted effort to impose regime change on North Korea would increase the probability that leaders in Pyongyang would conclude that they have little to lose in crossing the nuclear threshold. While one might question what a dying regime could gain from a brutal nuclear spasm, the use of one or two weapons on counterforce or minor countervalue targets, while holding Seoul and Tokyo at risk with the remaining arsenal, would be perfectly rational and would change the terms of the conflict dramatically.

Conflict and Escalation Resulting from Internal Collapse. Pyongyang need not mount a premeditated attack on South Korea to trigger something similar to the foregoing chain of events; conflict and escalation on the Korean peninsula could also result from an internal collapse of the DPRK. A precipitous decline in North Korea's economy in the 1990s led many Korea watchers late in the decade to predict the DPRK's imminent collapse. Conditions were so dire there that it seemed to many analysts that it was less a question of *if* the Northern regime would end, but *when* and whether the political demise would be violent. Yet, the DPRK managed to stay intact, largely due to the substantial quantities of economic aid it received from China, South Korea, and the United States.[15] Nevertheless, conditions remain austere in North Korea, and the possibility persists that some internal development could set in motion events that ultimately spin out of control, bringing down the current regime.

While the international community hopes that political change in Pyongyang will unfold as a nonviolent "soft landing," such as that witnessed in the dissolution of East Germany or, at worst, one in which violence is limited to the ruling elite, as was the case in the demise of Romania's Ceauscu, there is a significant risk that the DPRK will end

---

[15] For an empirically rich analysis of how the DPRK has managed to sustain itself and what its future prospects are, see Nicholas Eberstadt, "The Persistence of North Korea," *Policy Review*, No. 127, October–November 2004.

in bloody chaos. The pervasive nature of the control measures used to ensure loyalty to Kim Jung Il and his coterie make it difficult for any individual or group to challenge policy, much less power, and survive. Yet if economic conditions suffer another dramatic decline, Kim's circle of supporters may eventually fracture. A likely scenario for change might be one in which a clique of senior military officers becomes so dissatisfied that it carries out a coup against Kim and seizes the reins of government.[16] What it would do at that point is impossible to predict. The hope is that it would renounce the previous political and economic policies, declare its commitment to reform, and begin serious reunification talks with the South. However, it is just as likely, perhaps more so, that it would attempt to secure itself within a semblance of the DPRK's existing political structure. More dire possibilities include the emergence of contending claims to power, with rival military units controlling different parts of the country and different weapon systems, presaging a descent into civil war. In what is probably the worst-case scenario, either Kim or the new leaders could try to repair their hold on power by focusing attention on an external scapegoat and launching an attack on the South.

All of these possibilities entail significant risks of escalation. At the very least, the chaos ensuing from a political meltdown in North Korea would likely result in mass refugee flows into China and South Korea, creating serious economic and humanitarian problems in the border regions of those countries. Such a development might prompt China, South Korea, the United States, or some coalition of countries to intervene in the crisis in an effort to restore order and stem the human suffering. Any intervention on North Korean territory would raise risks of conflict with remnants of the DPRK army and confrontation with China, particularly if Beijing intervenes as well.

A fractured North Korean military establishment would raise questions regarding the control of chemical and nuclear weapons. The devolution of control of such weapons to individuals or rogue military units would raise serious concerns, as it may be more difficult to deter substate actors from using nuclear weapons or transferring them

---

[16] Pollack and Lee, 1999, pp. 58–59.

to other, more radical, entities than it has been to deter states from similar transgressions. The extreme economic deprivation present in a failed North Korean state would create severe risks that chemical or nuclear weapons, items that would fetch high prices on the international black market, might find their way into the hands of terrorists or state actors with interests inimical to the United States.[17] Acutely aware of these dangers, leaders in the United States and other countries might feel compelled to intervene in efforts to secure or destroy such weapons. Such operations would risk getting the United States more deeply embroiled in the North Korean crisis. They might also draw intervening states into confrontation with each other and, particularly, with China. Finally, a preemptive intervention against substate actors in North Korea might increase the probability that some group or individual might employ one or more of the weapons in an effort to defeat the operation or deter further intervention.

Instability and Escalation in South and Southwest Asia

South and Southwest Asia are contiguous regions in which the United States has important and enduring interests. The global war on terrorism (GWOT), the war in Iraq, Washington's commitment to the security of Israel, and the need to protect international access to fossil fuels are only the most prominent issues among many that necessitate U.S. commitment to security and stability in this part of the world. Yet significant sources of instability have plagued these regions since states there gained independence following World War II. Many of these problems have grown worse since the end of the Cold War, while other, more virulent ones have emerged.

Both regions are rife with conflict between states and within them. India and Pakistan have fought repeatedly since achieving statehood, and Islamabad has supported an insurgency in Kashmir, fought both by indigenous forces and foreign jihadists, since 1989. The Arab states have fought four major wars with Israel and several lower-level conflicts. Regional autocrats have launched wars against

---

[17] See George Jahn, "Experts Describe Tight-Knit Nuclear Black Market: Millions in Sales Motivated by 'Personal Greed and Ambition,'" *Washington Times*, February 3, 2004.

their neighbors to expand territorial control, seize economic resources, and enhance domestic power. The Palestinian Liberation Organization (PLO) and other Muslim groups sympathetic to the Palestinian cause have conducted guerrilla warfare and terrorist operations against Israel for decades. The Soviet Union invaded Afghanistan, resulting in a brutal 10-year struggle, and Western powers have intervened in several interstate and intrastate crises. Insurgencies are currently under way in Iraq, Afghanistan, Kashmir, and India. The long-term effects of these frequent and bitter conflicts include the aggravation of deep-seated ethnic, tribal, and religious rivalries within states, contributing to the collapse of Lebanon, repeated civil wars in Afghanistan, and the rise of Islamic extremism in Iran, Afghanistan, and elsewhere.

Adding to these sources of chronic instability are India's and Pakistan's emergence as nuclear powers and Iran's advance toward that threshold.[18] These developments create significant risks of escalation in conflicts between states. More ominously, the governments of Iran and Pakistan, or powerful groups within them, have known links to terrorist groups. India and Pakistan are plagued by domestic violence, and Pakistan, in particular, may be vulnerable to coup or insurrection. The collapse of central authority in Pakistan would create serious dangers that nuclear weapons could fall into the hands of terrorists, generating strong pressure for external intervention and raising the risks that violence would escalate, both within the ungoverned territory and between states.

---

[18] We must point out that India and Pakistan are, in some ways, more mature as nuclear powers than North Korea or Iran will likely be after achieving nuclear capabilities. Although India and Pakistan tested nuclear devices in 1998, both states were believed to be technically capable of doing so a decade or more earlier and, therefore, have likely given deterrence and stability issues considerable thought. Indian and Pakistani "defense intellectuals" have attended Western conferences on nuclear policy for decades. They are fluent in English and have been uninhibited in associating with Western strategists. Nevertheless, as this chapter shows, since becoming nuclear powers, both states have exhibited behaviors that have jeopardized stability in South Asia.

Risks of Escalation in the Ongoing Conflict Between India and Pakistan

One of the most serious sources of instability in South Asia is the long-standing rivalry between India and Pakistan. This rivalry focuses largely on the unresolved dispute over Kashmir, which dates back to the states' partition following liberation from British colonial rule.[19] While more than 60 percent of the residents of Kashmir are Muslim, India administers the region, and both states argue that it is important to their national identities. Islamabad claims that it is integral to Pakistan's identity as a Muslim state; New Delhi maintains that it is important for India's identity as a secular, multiethnic state. Both consider control of Kashmir a vital interest, one worth fighting for.[20]

The dispute over Kashmir escalated to conventional war in 1947 and again in 1965. In 1971, Pakistan attempted to take Kashmir for a third time when India's support for Bangladesh (then East Pakistan) in the Pakistani civil war provoked Islamabad to launch another conventional attack. India, the more powerful nation, prevailed in all of these conflicts, and the growing economic and military disparity between India and Pakistan has long been an aggravating factor in South Asian instability. As early as 1987, U.S. military observers in the region estimated that if full-scale conventional war broke out, India could defeat Pakistan within a month.[21]

Lately, the disparity has only worsened, as India's accelerating economic growth has enabled New Delhi to invest more than twice the money in defense as Islamabad almost every year since 1990. By 2000, India's defense budget was more than three times Pakistan's.[22] Consequently, Pakistan's military strategy, in the event of another con-

---

[19] For a thorough analysis of the sources of instability in South Asia, see Peters et al., 2006.

[20] Peters et al., 2006, p. 20.

[21] See Sunil Dasgupta, review of Kanti P. Bajpai, P. R. Chari, Pervaiz Iqbal Cheema, Stephen P. Cohen, and Sumit Ganguly, *Brasstacks and Beyond: Perception and Management of Crisis in South Asia*, New Delhi: Manohar, 1995, *Bulletin of the Atomic Scientists*, Vol. 52, No. 1, January–February 1996.

[22] Anthony H. Cordesman, *The Asian Military Balance: An Analytic Overview*, Washington, D.C.: Center for Strategic and International Studies, May 1, 2003, pp. 67–68.

ventional war, has long been to quickly seize enough territory to give Islamabad bargaining leverage then appeal to the international community to intervene before India has time to defeat Pakistani forces. India's strategy, in contrast, has been to promptly mobilize superior conventional forces at the onset of a crisis then defeat Pakistan before international pressure forces New Delhi to accept a cease-fire.[23] The time pressures inherent in these strategies create conditions for rapid escalation in a crisis.

Given India's conventional military superiority, Pakistan has resorted to other means for putting pressure on New Delhi in efforts to erode India's will to hold on to Kashmir. In 1989, Islamabad began supporting Kashmiri separatists in an insurgency, one joined by jihadists from Afghanistan following Soviet withdrawal from that region. Ten years later, Pakistan, then an emergent nuclear power, infiltrated a regiment-sized force of irregular combatants across the Indo-Pakistani line of control (LOC) to seize a ridgeline on Indian territory, precipitating the spring 1999 Kargil crisis.[24] And in December 2001, Kashmiri separatists, allegedly of Pakistani origin, attacked the Indian parliament, killing eight security guards and a gardener, triggering an Indo-Pakistani border crisis that lasted until October 2002.

Some analysts, both Western and South Asian, maintain that the latter two crises indicate that, once India and Pakistan acquired nuclear weapons, the stability-instability paradox became operative in South Asia.[25] If that were the case, despite the fact that both states were then very young nuclear powers, each must have been sufficiently confident in the stability of mutual deterrence to risk lower-level military operations. Alternatively, S. Paul Kapur argues that a different logic was at work. He maintains that the Indo-Pakistani strategic relationship was *unstable*, just as one would expect between emergent nuclear

---

[23] Peters et al., 2006, p. 30.

[24] For a thorough analysis of the Kargil crisis, see Ashley J. Tellis, C. Christine Fair, and Jamison Jo Medby, *Limited Conflicts Under the Nuclear Umbrella: Indian and Pakistani Lessons from the Kargil Crisis*, Santa Monica, Calif.: RAND Corporation, MR-1450-USCA, 2002.

[25] For a summary of these arguments, see Krepon, 2004.

powers, but that Islamabad, a revisionist power seeking to change the status quo in Kashmir, deliberately manipulated the risk of uncontrolled escalation to deter strong Indian resistance to its incursions.[26] As events will demonstrate, both arguments are supportable: Kapur's more so in the first episode, with the stability-instability paradox gaining strength later on. But regardless of which template one employs to interpret these crises, the fact remains that once they began, India and Pakistan both flirted with risks of uncontrolled escalation.

Although authorities in Islamabad and New Delhi assured the world following their 1998 nuclear tests that both countries saw nuclear weapons as instruments of deterrence only and that their attainment would, if anything, be a stabilizing influence in Indo-Pakistani relations, Pakistan clearly believed that its newly demonstrated nuclear capability would afford it greater latitude to take risks in Kashmir.[27]

Infiltrating a regiment-sized force of Pakistani irregulars across the LOC to seize territory in Kargil was a notable escalation from Pakistan's previous practice of supporting Kashmiri insurgents in a proxy war. This incursion caught New Delhi off guard, so closely following the February 1999 Lahore Declaration, a joint acknowledgement by the prime ministers of India and Pakistan that their nuclear capabilities imbued them with a mutual responsibility to avoid conflict. Nevertheless, the Indian military quickly responded with preponderant force, dealing the Pakistanis a sound defeat. Observers who did not know of Pakistan's direct involvement in the incident were shocked by the aggressiveness of India's response, which included the first use of air power in Kashmir since the 1971 war. Pakistani leaders were also alarmed, having failed to anticipate such a response from New Delhi.[28] In fact, the extent of India's mobilization was sufficiently threat-

---

[26] S. Paul Kapur, "India and Pakistan's Unstable Peace: Why Nuclear South Asia Is Not Like Cold War Europe," *International Security*, Vol. 2, No. 5, Fall 2005.

[27] V. R. Ragavan, "Limited War and Nuclear Escalation in South Asia," *Nonproliferation Review*, Vol. 8, No. 3, Fall–Winter 2001; Rodney W. Jones, "Nuclear Stability and Escalation Control in South Asia: Structural Factors," in Michael Krepon, Rodney W. Jones, and Ziad Haider, eds., *Escalation Control and the Nuclear Option in South Asia*, Washington, D.C.: Henry L. Stimson Center, November 2004b, pp. 25–26.

[28] Tellis, Fair, and Medby, 2002, p. 14.

ening to Islamabad that Pakistan put its nuclear forces on alert and Prime Minister Nawaz Sharif is purported to have threatened to use the "ultimate weapon" should India cross the LOC.[29] India alerted its nuclear forces, as well, adding to the tensions. Fortunately, the presence of nuclear weapons seems to have dampened escalation in this instance, as India, whose forces drove deep into Pakistan in previous conventional conflicts and clearly could have done so again, did not cross the LOC, despite the fact that doing so would have enabled them to flank the irregulars' high-ridge redoubts, thereby reducing Indian casualties.[30]

Although Islamabad's direct involvement in the December 13, 2001, terrorist attack on India's parliament is questionable (India claimed that the Kashmiri separatists who conducted the attack were from a group based in Pakistan and directed by the military's interservice intelligence directorate, but the evidence is inconclusive), the crisis that event triggered may well have pushed the two countries closer to the brink of major war than any since they acquired nuclear weapons.[31] The attack stirred outrage in India and prompted New Delhi to deploy the bulk of its armored and mechanized forces to the Pakistani border and begin moving its naval forces to the Arabian Sea opposite Karachi.[32] In response, Islamabad redeployed up to 70,000 troops to the eastern border region with India from Pakistan's northwest frontier, where they had been serving as an "anvil" against which U.S. forces were attempting to drive Taliban and al Qaeda fighters from Afghanistan.[33] By late December, both countries had put their nuclear forces

---

[29] Ragavan, 2001, p. 4.

[30] Ragavan, 2001, pp. 4, 11.

[31] Rama Lakshmi, "Indians Blame Attacks on Pakistan-Based Group," *Washington Post*, December 15, 2001; Steve Coll, "The Standoff: How Jihadi Groups Helped Provoke the Twenty-First Century's First Nuclear Crisis," *New Yorker*, February 13–20, 2006, p. 126.

[32] Rodney W. Jones, "America's War on Terrorism: Religious Radicalism and Nuclear Confrontation in South Asia," in Satu P. Limaye, Mohan Malik, and Robert G. Wirsing, eds., *Religious Radicalism and Security in South Asia*, Honolulu: Asia-Pacific Center for Security Studies, 2004a, p. 298.

[33] Coll, 2006, p. 126.

on alert, and India appeared to be readying for a drive into Pakistan, perhaps to seize the city of Lahore. This alarmed U.S officials, who worried that if India crossed Pakistan's "red line," Islamabad would resort to the use of nuclear weapons; Pakistani generals had said as much in informal discussions but were deliberately vague about just where that red line was. In an effort to forestall such a catastrophe, Washington engaged both governments, urging restraint.[34]

The diplomatic initiative was at least partially effective. On January 12, 2002, Pakistan's president and army chief, General Pervez Musharraf, denounced religious extremism in a speech on Pakistani television and condemned the attack on the Indian parliament as an act of terrorism. Encouraged but skeptical, India withheld its attack but kept its forces forward deployed, as did Pakistan.[35] Then conditions worsened. On May 14, a cell of suicide terrorists attacked an Indian army garrison near the city of Jammu, killing 34 people and wounding 50 others, many of them women and children. That event shoved India and Pakistan to the brink of war. The Indian army was outraged, and, based on the tenor of the Indian press and government contacts in New Delhi, U.S. and British officials concluded that an Indian offensive was imminent.[36] Worried once again that such an event might trigger a nuclear exchange, Washington and London evacuated their embassies in Islamabad and New Delhi of all but essential personnel on May 31.[37]

Fortunately, war was averted, largely due to the emergency round of shuttle diplomacy that U.S. Deputy Secretary of State Richard Armitage conducted between Islamabad and New Delhi. Assuring

---

[34] Coll, 2006, pp. 131–132.

[35] R. Jones, 2004a, p. 304.

[36] See for instance, "Exploring India's Options," *Indian Express*, May 16, 2002; "Government Opens Defence Umbrella in Pak Face," *Indian Express*, May 20, 2002; Ahmed Rashid and Toby Helm, "India Accused of Tyranny, 'War Hysteria': Pakistan's President Draws Ire with Talk of Hindu Terrorists," *National Post* (Canada), May 24, 2002.

[37] Coll, 2006, p. 134. See also Michael Evans and Phillip Webster, "Britain Fears Nuclear War Over Kashmir: Plans Being Drawn Up to Get Britons Out of India, Pakistan," *Ottawa Citizen*, May 24, 2002.

Indian Prime Minister Atal Vajpayee that Musharraf was sincere in his pledge to crack down on Kashmiri militants, he persuaded India to signal its willingness to deescalate the crisis by pulling its naval forces back from the Pakistani coast.[38] It worked. Tensions gradually eased, and in October 2002, Indian and Pakistani forces stood down from their wartime mobilization.

Some observers, particularly those in New Delhi and Islamabad, argue that the Kargil conflict and the 2002 border crisis offer evidence that, despite occasional flare-ups in the long-standing conflict, India and Pakistan are sufficiently responsible to resist pressures to escalate to the use of nuclear weapons. In fact, Indian and Pakistani officials have suggested that the border scare was South Asia's version of the Cuban missile crisis, a "confrontation that came so close to catastrophe that it shocked both sides into a new approach to nuclear deterrence, one that is grounded in military restraint, political patience, and negotiations about underlying grievances."[39] Similarly, some Western analysts conclude that the stability-instability paradox will persist in South Asia: India and Pakistan will continue to maintain a kind of ugly stability, avoiding major conventional conflict while engaging in irregular warfare and occasional, low-level skirmishes.[40]

Indeed, there is some evidence to support these conclusions. In neither crisis did India launch a conventional assault into Pakistan as it had done in all the major conflicts before 1998, suggesting that New Delhi was deterred by the risks of escalation. Both countries have declared moratoriums on further nuclear tests and implemented other confidence-building measures, such as prenotification of missile tests and an agreement not to attack each other's nuclear installations. India has a declared NFU policy. Since the 2002 confrontation, India and Pakistan have begun tentative efforts to normalize relations, restoring

---

[38] "U.S. Envoy Back for Talks," *St. John's Telegram* (Newfoundland), August 24, 2002.

[39] Coll, 2006, p. 139.

[40] The term *ugly stability* was coined by RAND analyst Ashley Tellis in 1997 and has since been used by several other writers. See Ashley Tellis, *Stability in South Asia*, Santa Monica, Calif.: RAND Corporation, DB-185-A, 1997. For a summary of arguments posited by the "deterrence optimists" regarding South Asia, see Krepon, 2004, pp. 3–6.

bus services between the two countries and engaging each other in cricket matches.

Yet there are reasons to worry about prospects for escalation in a future Indo-Pakistani confrontation. First is the accelerating growth of India's conventional military power, vis-à-vis Pakistan's, and the dilemma it creates for Islamabad. As India grows ever stronger, Islamabad may perceive a closing window of opportunity for forcing a favorable resolution to the Kashmir dispute. Seeing India's restraint in the previous two nuclear crises, Pakistani leaders might conclude that their nuclear capabilities are sufficiently threatening that they can afford to gamble—they can seize Kashmir and deter India from responding with overwhelming conventional force long enough for the international community to intervene and pressure New Delhi into accepting a negotiated settlement. Such a gamble would likely be a dangerous miscalculation, because Indian military leaders took their own lessons from Kargil and, particularly, the border crisis: namely, that Indian forces failed to respond to Pakistani provocation with sufficient speed and aggressiveness to punish Islamabad's adventurism before U.S. diplomacy intervened. Consequently, the Indian army has since developed a doctrine they call *Cold Start*, emphasizing quick mobilization and rapid combined arms assaults into Pakistan, stopping just short of what India believes to be Islamabad's red line for nuclear retaliation.[41] It is unclear whether Cold Start has been formally approved, but the Indian military has subjected it to extensive testing in joint exercises.[42] Employing such a doctrine would be a serious gamble for New Delhi, as Pakistani leaders, for obvious reasons, remain deliberately vague regarding the location of the supposed red line. Statements that Sharif allegedly made during the Kargil conflict and those that Musharraf

---

[41] R. Jones, 2004b, p. 35. For a hawkish Indian assessment of why Cold Start is required and admonitions to execute it aggressively, even if nuclear strikes are required, see Subhash Kapila, "India's New 'Cold Start' War Doctrine Strategically Reviewed," South Asia Analysis Group, No. 991, May 4, 2004.

[42] Muhammad Azam Khan, "Indian Army Doctrine and Pakistan," *The Nation* (Pakistan), September 5, 2005.

publicly made during the 2002 border crisis suggest that the red line might even be the LOC.[43]

Even if Islamabad does not attempt to overtly seize parts of Kashmir, continuing efforts to pressure New Delhi via irregular warfare could also result in escalation. As Pakistan's ability to take Kashmir via conventional arms grows ever more remote, Islamabad may feel compelled to turn up the heat on New Delhi using irregular warfare, lending greater support to insurgencies in Kashmir and northern India and possibly trying, once again, to infiltrate Pakistani soldiers across the LOC. Musharraf has disavowed Pakistan's further involvement in such operations and claims to be trying to rein in the jihadists in Kashmir. Whether his efforts are sincere, there are serious questions about how much control he has over these religious extremists, or even over certain elements within the Pakistani military and interservice intelligence directorate who may identify with the jihadist cause.[44] Groups committed to insurgency against India but whose members oppose Musharraf due to his stance on the GWOT may attempt to carry out spectacular terrorist strikes for the express purpose of drawing India and Pakistan into a major war.[45] Such events could have dire consequences. Although New Delhi has managed to restrain the Indian military during the past two nuclear crises, there is no guarantee it will do

---

[43] In a May 31, 2002, address to frontline troops, Musharraf said, "If there is any incursion, even by an inch, across the LOC this will unleash a storm which will sweep the enemy." Later in the speech, he said that he had confidence in the Pakistani military's ability to inflict "unbearable damage" on India. See Munir Ahmad, "Musharraf Fans Flames With Threat to Unleash a 'Storm,'" *The Advertiser* (South Australia), May 31, 2002; "Musharraf Warns India of Storm," *Herald Sun* (Melbourne, Australia) May 31, 2002.

[44] For an analysis of the complex relationships between religious extremists and state authorities in Pakistan and the potential impacts of those relationships on nuclear stability, see Mohan Malik, "The Stability of Nuclear Deterrence in South Asia: The Clash Between State and Anti-State Actors," in Satu P. Limaye, Mohan Malik, and Robert G. Wirsing, eds., *Religious Radicalism and Security in South Asia*, Honolulu: Asia-Pacific Center for Security Studies, 2004. Regarding relationships between jihadist groups and the Pakistani military and interservice intelligence directorate, see Hussein Haqqani, "Pakistan's Terrorist Dilemma," in Limaye et al., 2004.

[45] Coll, 2006, p. 138.

so in the future if a particularly violent terrorist attack inflames India's sense of outrage.

Moreover, India's adversaries, whether state or nonstate, were not the only actors who increased the risks of escalation in previous crises; taking a page from U.S. national security strategy, New Delhi has brandished threats of conventional preemption.[46] When the Indian military deployed at the onset of the 2002 border crisis, Indian leaders let it be known they were considering preemptive raids on suspected terrorist training camps in Pakistan, including some located near nuclear facilities. Some Indian officials privately conceded that New Delhi was not serious about launching such attacks—the preemption talk was part of a strategy designed to force Washington to apply pressure on Islamabad.[47] Nevertheless, such rhetorical brinkmanship is potentially escalatory in a crisis, particularly one with a conventionally inferior adversary who may feel that its nuclear capability is vulnerable to a disarming first strike.

An escalatory chain reaction between India and Pakistan would have serious impacts on U.S. interests in South Asia. Beyond the calamitous effects that a nuclear exchange would have on the global environment, the nuclear nonproliferation regime, and international relations more broadly, it would place the United States in a precarious position as a state both friendly to India and allied with Pakistan in the GWOT. Societal disruption and human suffering would be severe in both countries, and the United States would likely be called on to provide humanitarian assistance and support for such activities as damage assessment, plume and fallout plotting, and cleanup operations.[48]

Deploying U.S. forces into India and Pakistan for these missions could bring them into contact with local military units—some might be disorganized, confused, fearful, and perhaps even hostile—raising risks of confrontation and conflict. Refugees may flee the stricken

---

[46] Malik, 2004, p. 322.

[47] R. Jones, 2004a, pp. 298, 298 (fn23 and fn24), 307. See also Rajiv Chandrasekaran, "Pakistan, India Mass Troops: Tensions Escalate as New Delhi Considers Strike," *Washington Post*, December 24, 2001.

[48] Peters et al., 2006, p. 46.

areas en masse, complicating relief efforts and flooding across borders into neighboring states, creating severe economic and social problems there and raising prospects of additional foreign intervention. Ultimately, the disruptive impacts of a nuclear exchange might be so severe as to result in state collapse, particularly in Pakistan, potentially adding to the worldwide list of ungoverned territories, some of which provide breeding grounds for terrorists. Alternatively, if state authority in India and Pakistan did not collapse, the current leaders might be discredited and replaced with ones more radical—Hindu nationalists in India, Islamists in Pakistan. Such developments would increase the probability of further conflict and deal a severe blow to the U.S.-led GWOT.

Risks of Escalation Due to Domestic Instability in Pakistan

Domestic instability in Pakistan could generate serious risks of escalation even short of a catastrophic war with India. In stark contrast to Pakistani nationalist Muhammed Ali Jinnah's 1947 dream of seeing the emergence of a secular, democratic state, sectarian tensions have wracked the country throughout its history, resulting in violent internal conflicts and repeated military takeovers, hobbling the development of democracy.[49] Multiple forces have combined to polarize Pakistani society. The leading factors include uneven development; tribal and clan influences; chronic frustration over the Kashmir dispute; deliberate, politically motivated Islamization; backlash from the Iranian revolution and the U.S.-sponsored jihad in Afghanistan; the appeal of fundamentalist doctrines and other Arab influences; and the rising tide of global jihadism.[50] Musharraf, himself the beneficiary of a military coup, has been forced to balance his commitments to Washington in the GWOT with the ever-present need to control and mollify various radical factions in Pakistan, including those within his own military and intelligence services. At least three attempts have been made on his

---

[49] Jinnah expressed this aspiration in numerous settings, including a speech at the inaugural session of Pakistan's Constituent Assembly on August 11, 1947.

[50] For a detailed analysis of the causes of sectarian tension in Pakistan, see Suroosh Irfani, "Pakistan's Sectarian Violence: Between the 'Arabist Shift' and the Indo-Persian Culture," in Satu P. Limaye, Mohan Malik, and Robert G. Wirsing, eds., *Religious Radicalism and Security in South Asia*, Honolulu: Asia-Pacific Center for Security Studies, 2004.

life since September 11, 2001, and the potential for a change of government in Islamabad is always present to some extent.[51] If that potential is realized, it could bring radical Islamists to power. There is also a degree of danger that some event could intensify the centrifugal forces in Pakistan, ultimately pulling the country apart and resulting in civil war or anarchy. Either eventuality would be a disaster for U.S. interests and would create a crisis with multiple paths for potential escalation.[52]

The rise of a radical Islamist government in Pakistan would be a serious threat to regional stability and create escalatory pressures in the event of a conflict with India. Such a regime would likely intensify its efforts to wrest Kashmir from New Delhi and destabilize India more broadly by increasing support to Islamic insurgencies and terrorists. This would raise the risks of conflict in ways noted previously but with greater pressures on both states to escalate than in a similar conflict with Pakistan governed by a more moderate regime. Although Indian leaders have not permitted preemptive strikes or conventional military attacks on Pakistan in previous nuclear crises, they may conclude that the dangers of radical Islamists crossing the nuclear threshold are sufficient to warrant attempting a disarming first strike or a conventional attack aimed at changing the regime in Islamabad. Pakistani leaders, in turn, seeing the imminent danger of an Indian attack, would likely brandish nuclear weapons, intensifying the crisis. To make matters worse, U.S. leaders would have more difficulty defusing such a crisis than ever before, as Washington, with little or no influence in a radicalized Islamabad, would be hard pressed to constrain New Delhi.

---

[51] "Six Convicted for Role in Assassination Attempt," *Prince George Citizen* (British Columbia), October 5, 2005.

[52] Although this section focuses on domestic problems in Pakistan, we should acknowledge that India also suffers from similar sources of instability. India has a history of sectarian violence, and several of its leaders have fallen to assassins. Insurgencies are under way not only in Kashmir but also in several northern provinces. Terrorist attacks are not uncommon. Moreover, the rise of extreme Hindu nationalism, or as Suroosh Irfani calls it, "Vedic Talibanism," mirrors that of radical Islam in troubling ways. Nevertheless, given the resilience of India's secular democracy and the long-standing tradition of civilian control in India's highly professional military establishment, the dangers of escalation due to domestic instability in India do not compare to those of Pakistan. See Irfani, 2004, pp. 147–148, 165.

An Islamist government in Pakistan would also lead to escalation in the GWOT, as Islamabad would likely stop cooperating with U.S. efforts to defeat al Qaeda and Taliban forces along the Afghan border. Such a development would provide al Qaeda and the Taliban a sanctuary in northwest Pakistan from which they could continue insurgent warfare against Afghanistan and mount terrorist operations against Western interests globally. That would set conditions for conflict and escalation between the United States and Pakistan, as U.S. forces would be inclined to violate Pakistani sovereignty in hot pursuit of insurgents along the border, and Washington might authorize strikes on terrorist bases and training camps in Pakistan. A subsequent conflict between U.S. and Pakistani forces might result in nuclear threats from Islamabad, U.S. preemptive strikes and a military campaign to remove the Islamist regime, and Pakistan's resort to the use of one or more nuclear weapons, keeping most of its arsenal in reserve to hold U.S. forces, Kabul, and New Delhi at risk.

Dark as the foregoing scenario may seem, it is not as frightening as that if governing authority in Islamabad were to collapse, plunging Pakistan into civil war or anarchy. As in previous failed-state scenarios, such an event in Pakistan could create significant social disruption and human suffering, but that would not be the greatest immediate concern. A collapse of central authority in Islamabad would immediately elicit a series of anxious questions in Washington, New Delhi, and Tel Aviv: Who has control of Pakistan's nuclear weapons? What is their ideological orientation? Do they have sympathies for or, worse yet, relationships with insurgents or terrorists? Getting quick answers to these questions would likely be impossible in the confusion that would characterize this scenario—that is, unless the nuclear-armed faction or factions identified themselves by brandishing the weapons or using them on their enemies. Even without immediate threats or employment, there would be immense pressures in the above-named capitals to intervene to find and secure or preemptively destroy the nuclear weapons in order to preclude them falling into the hands of terrorists. That is because, while there may be reason to believe that even radical governments could be deterred from transferring nuclear weapons to terrorists, few analysts expect deterrent threats to carry much weight against substate or nonstate actors.[53] Yet the very lack of intelligence that makes this scenario so frightening would also hinder efforts to seize or destroy the weapons, and attempting to do so would risk sufficiently threatening their custodians that they might use one or more of them in an effort to defend themselves or deter further intervention. These dynamics would present a series of dark dilemmas in Washington, not the least of which might include how to dissuade New Delhi and Tel Aviv from taking rash actions that further escalate the crisis.[54]

The Risks of Escalation in a Conflict with Iran

As Tehran approaches the nuclear threshold, the risks of conflict in South and Southwest Asia increase significantly. Iran became an Islamic theocracy after overthrowing the U.S.-backed regime of Shah Reza Pahlavi in an Islamic revolution in 1979. Since that time, Tehran's policies, largely shaped by radical Shiite clerics, have been hostile to U.S. interests, advocating the overthrow of the state of Israel and sometimes attempting to spread Islamic revolution to other secular Muslim states. Tehran has supported, perhaps even directed, several leading Middle Eastern terrorist groups, and Iranian intelligence has been linked to major terrorist attacks throughout the region. For these reasons, the U.S. Department of State put Iran on the list of state sponsors of terrorism in 1984, the Clinton administration branded it a

---

[53] While some policymakers have expressed concern that state sponsors of terrorism such as North Korea, Pakistan, or Iran might transfer nuclear weapons to their terrorist clients, many analysts conclude that risks of that are not great. States with identifiable territory, infrastructure, and leaders to protect are not likely to trust their survival to the hands of undeterrable nonstate actors, thereby risking retribution should those terrorists detonate a weapon that might be forensically traced to the state of origin. See Coll, 2006, p. 138; Malik, 2004, pp. 335–345; Jasen J. Castillo, "Nuclear Terrorism: Why Deterrence Still Matters," *Current History*, Vol. 102, No. 668, December 2003; Judith S. Yaphe and Charles D. Lutes, *Reassessing the Implications of a Nuclear-Armed Iran*, McNair Paper No. 69, Washington, D.C.: Institute for National Strategic Studies, 2005, p. 41.

[54] This assessment benefits from a Delphi analysis led by Roger Cliff in July 2005. In that exercise, a team of RAND analysts (regional specialists, military strategists, and nuclear effects experts) and U.S. Air Force officers explored the many paths of escalation that might result from a state failure in Pakistan. See Appendix C for a description of the modified Delphi method of analysis used in that exercise.

"rogue state" in the mid-1990s, and the Bush administration declared it to be part of an "axis of evil" in 2002.

The risks of an escalatory confrontation with Iran are amplified by its geographical location vis-à-vis its potential adversaries and by regional demographics. Sharing a border with Iraq to the west and Afghanistan to the east, Iran sits between two Muslim states in which U.S. forces are conducting counterinsurgency operations and nation-building efforts. Tehran is suspected of supporting anti-U.S. movements in Iraq, and Iranian influence there is of particular concern, as about 60 percent of that state's citizens are Shiite.[55] In addition, Iran and Israel are within range of each other's ballistic missiles and strike aircraft, though conducting air strikes might be challenging due to aircraft range and overflight limitations.

Given its radical political orientation and links to terrorism, a great deal of concern has been expressed about whether Iran would be a responsible custodian of nuclear weapons. Consequently, when Tehran was seeking to develop nuclear weapons, a number of U.S. and Israeli security analysts advocated taking action to prevent the Iranian program from reaching fruition, envisioning, perhaps, a preventive strike similar to Israel's 1981 raid on the Iraqi reactor facility at Osiraq.[56] Such proposals are likely to resurface should intelligence estimates indicate that the Iranians are reconstituting their program. Whether successful, a raid of this nature might provoke a military conflict. At the very least, Muslims throughout South and Southwest Asia would likely be outraged, terrorism against U.S. and Israeli interests would escalate, and Shiites might obstruct or even violently oppose U.S. efforts in Iraq.[57]

Moreover, prospects for success in such a raid would be questionable, both in the short term and, especially, the long term. The Osiraq raid set back Iraq's nuclear program by several years, but the lesson Saddam Hussein took from that experience was that he needed to disperse his nuclear research and development facilities and hide them

---

[55] See Kenneth Katzman, *Iran's Influence in Iraq*, Washington, D.C.: Congressional Research Service, RS22323, updated February 2, 2007.

[56] Yaphe and Lutes, 2005, pp. 16–17.

[57] Katzman, 2007, p. 6.

underground. This made it all but impossible for outsiders to monitor the program's progress, much less destroy it from the air. Learning their own lesson from the Osiraq example, Tehran dispersed and hid the critical elements of the Iranian program, making it less likely that a preventive strike, or even a series of air raids, would set it back very much.[58] They would no doubt do so again.

Therefore, military action to prevent Iran from acquiring nuclear weapons would probably require a ground operation to find and destroy the facilities. Depending on the locations of those facilities, finding them all with confidence might not be possible without removing the Tehran regime and taking control of the country. Even if that were not among Washington's objectives, Iranian leaders would almost certainly assume that it was, given the precedent set in neighboring Iraq, and resist to the full extent of its military and paramilitary capabilities.

Alternatively, if military actions were not taken and if Iran were to develop nuclear weapons, the potential for confrontation and escalation would still exist. Once armed, Iranian leaders might decide to increase their support to terrorist and insurgent groups, believing that their nuclear capability would deter retribution.[59] Similarly, those groups might be more aggressive, believing that they share some degree of protection under Iran's nuclear umbrella. An escalation in terrorism against Israel would likely provoke retaliatory raids on terrorist camps in neighboring states. If attacks became sufficiently onerous and clear links were found between the attackers and Tehran, Tel Aviv could decide to take punitive action against Iran. This could lead to a conventional conflict that would potentially escalate into a nuclear crisis. At the same time, a nuclear-armed Iran would likely hearten some Iraqi Shiites, and Tehran might encourage them to assert greater dominance in Iraq, repressing Sunnis and thereby feeding the insurgency resisting the U.S.-led nation-building process.[60] Iranian-instigated trigger events

---

[58] Yaphe and Lutes, 2005, p. 38.

[59] Kenneth R. Timmerman, "The Day After Iran Gets the Bomb," in Henry Sokolski and Patrick Clawson, eds., *Getting Ready for a Nuclear-Ready Iran*, Carlisle, Pa.: Strategic Studies Institute, 2005.

[60] Katzman, 2005, pp. 3–6.

could set in motion a chain reaction that might result in open civil war in Iraq. If the United States were to take punitive military action against Iran, Iranian leaders might fear that Washington was trying to remove the Islamic regime, in which case Tehran would likely resist with all possible measures.

Ultimately, it is conceivable that Iranian agitation could become so severe, or Tehran's nuclear brandishing so threatening, that U.S. leaders and allies would contemplate imposing regime change on Tehran. However, they would not likely attempt such an action once they weigh the risks it would entail. Launching a military operation to remove the Tehran regime would invite dramatic escalation. Faced with the prospect of losing power and, potentially, their lives, Iranian leaders would have little to lose in crossing the nuclear threshold. As in the North Korean and Pakistani scenarios, they would be unlikely to unleash a wholesale attack, expending their nuclear arsenals and inviting undeterred retribution. But if they have multiple weapons, using one or more while holding the others in reserve to threaten other regional targets would be a reasonable strategy.

Finally, Iran's potential for domestic instability is not as great as that of North Korea or Pakistan; consequently, a serious effort to take control of Iran's nuclear arsenal by force is less likely to cause state authority to disintegrate than might instability within or a military operation against either of the other two countries. Indeed, a forceful violation of Iranian sovereignty would likely rally domestic support around the Tehran regime. However, the danger that a conventional military intervention might devolve into a struggle against nuclear-armed substate actors still exists, as Tehran could deliberately dissolve its main ground units and resort to irregular warfare if confronted with an overwhelming coalition force and if it believed regime change were inevitable.[61] Such a scenario would create multiple paths for escalation, some of them catastrophic, and would increase risks that nuclear weapons would end up in the hands of other nonstate actors with interests inimical to those of the United States.

---

[61] Indeed, the Iran Revolutionary Guard Corps is organized for just such a contingency.

Conclusion

In many ways, the escalation dynamics evident in regions in which states have recently acquired or are seeking nuclear weapons resemble those that the United States and Soviet Union experienced during the early Cold War. Just as the United States relied on its atomic capability to offset Soviet conventional superiority in Europe, North Korea developed nuclear weapons (and Iran may resume seeking them) largely to underwrite their own security in the face of U.S. conventional superiority and a policy threatening regime change. Similarly, Pakistani leaders believe that their nuclear weapons ensure their survival against India's conventional superiority, and New Delhi joined the nuclear club with an eye on China. If self-preservation were the only element of the equation, the risks of escalation would be low. Unfortunately, there is more to it than that.

Too often, leaders of new nuclear states presume that the threat implied by their newly acquired weapons provides them an umbrella beneath which they can safely risk provocative actions against their rivals. Doing so is a dangerous game that can lead to direct confrontations and contests of brinkmanship, such as those in which Moscow and Washington engaged in Berlin and Cuba and those that New Delhi and Islamabad played in Kargil and along the Indo-Pakistani border. How Pyongyang and, potentially, Tehran will behave as new nuclear powers remains to be seen, but if the historical pattern holds true, they will be more aggressive in pursuing regional goals while trusting their nuclear capabilities to deter the United States from intervening to protect its interests.

In the meantime, escalation management will be a crucially important challenge for the United States and its regional allies. While resolving the Kashmir dispute is beyond anyone's sightline, U.S. leaders need to remain engaged with Islamabad and New Delhi, striving to be the honest broker, building trust, urging caution and restraint. Unfortunately, whether Washington can succeed in such a role will depend largely on events beyond U.S. control, as radical elements in India and Pakistan can act as spoilers in Indo-Pakistani relations. Much depends on whether moderate elements in both countries can continue steering their ships of state through the treacherous waters ahead.

Washington will have a more direct role in managing escalation if a future confrontation occurs with North Korea or Iran. A large part of escalation management is deterrence amidst conflict—that is, persuading the adversary that raising the intensity of a fight or broadening its scope will not work to his advantage. Deterrence generally involves threats of punishment—either communicated explicitly or done so implicitly by posturing forces—that unacceptable escalation on the adversary's part will provoke a reciprocal move inflicting costs on him that outweigh the probable benefits of his action. The United States is imminently capable of inflicting punishment on any potential adversary, whether using conventional or nuclear forces, but some adversaries may not fully appreciate the gravity of certain U.S. escalation thresholds or understand where they lie. Therefore, in the event of a conflict with North Korea or Iran, U.S. leaders should clearly advise the enemy what escalation thresholds are prohibited and the consequences of violating them.[62]

However, several factors tend to undermine the credibility of some U.S. threats, and regional adversaries may try to exploit those weaknesses. Pyongyang and Tehran may not find the threat of a nuclear counterstrike sufficiently credible to deter them from attacking a U.S. ally, particularly when they hold additional nuclear weapons in reserve. Similarly, U.S. threats to punish actions for which it lacks proportional responses, such as chemical or biological attacks or attacks on space assets, may suffer from doubts of credibility and fail to deter an adversary from escalating along those lines.

Consequently, the United States should bolster its ability to deter escalation in regional conflicts by developing means to defeat enemy efforts to escalate along prohibited paths. Developing effective ballistic and cruise missile defenses, as well as other means of defending U.S.

---

[62] That is not to suggest that U.S. leaders should attempt to create new thresholds in the heat of a crisis where none existed before. Thresholds can rarely be created by mere declaration, and attempting to do so may signal fear or vulnerability. However, clarifying which acts the United States truly considers to be unacceptably escalatory will reduce the risk that an adversary will commit those acts inadvertently.

forces and regional partners from asymmetric attack, should be top priorities. The United States also needs to enhance its ability to detect and interdict efforts to covertly deliver nuclear, chemical, and biological weapons, whether by air, land, or sea. Effective defenses enhance deterrence by reducing the chances that an enemy can succeed in the prohibited action, thereby denying it the benefits of escalation and rendering the action not worth the cost of U.S. retribution.[63]

We must remember, however, that escalation management is not solely about deterrence. Escalation is an interactive phenomenon, one in which both combatants are struggling to win a conflict, or at least not lose it, while keeping their costs within acceptable limits. Managing escalation involves not only deterring the adversary from violating dangerous thresholds, but also in recognizing and respecting its most salient thresholds as well. No state can hope to deter an adversary from using any means at its disposal to ensure its own survival. If regime change is the objective or if the adversary believes it is even when it is not, the conflict is no longer a limited war, and escalation management becomes inoperative.

During the Cold War, the United States and Soviet Union both came to realize that nuclear weapons made the costs of unlimited war intolerable. Consequently, the superpowers resigned themselves to the fact that limited gains and limited losses were the only affordable outcomes of conflicts between nuclear states. Escalation management is about keeping limited wars limited. As an increasing number of regional powers acquire nuclear weapons, they and the United States will need to remember the lessons of the Cold War or else relearn them at their peril.

---

[63] Strengthening defenses also has the advantage of reducing costs to U.S. forces and regional partners should deterrence fail. For a similar argument, see Michael Eisenstadt, "Deter and Contain: Dealing with a Nuclear Iran," in Henry Sokolski and Patrick Clawson, eds., *Getting Ready for a Nuclear-Ready Iran*, Carlisle, Pa.: Strategic Studies Institute, 2005, pp. 234–235.

CHAPTER FIVE
Escalation in Irregular Warfare

Among the most notable characteristics of the post–Cold War security environment are the collapse of state authority in several regions of the world and the rise of powerful nonstate actors with agendas that threaten U.S. interests and the safety of U.S. citizens. These characteristics, taken in conjunction with the increased willingness of U.S. policymakers to intervene in regional crises, raise the probability that U.S. military forces will be attacked by irregular combatants or will be called on to conduct operations best described as irregular warfare.[1]

During the Cold War, Western leaders thought about escalation in irregular warfare mainly in terms of the risks it generated for drawing the United States into direct confrontation with the Soviet Union or the People's Republic of China.[2] This chapter demonstrates that conflicts with nonstate actors present a far more diverse set of escalation risks than previously considered, and even seemingly low-threat activities such as peacekeeping, noncombatant evacuation operations, and humanitarian assistance can degenerate into conflict if the escalation risks are not anticipated and managed. Add the possibility that hostile nonstate actors could obtain access to nuclear, biological, or chemical

---

[1] In the context of this monograph, the term *irregular warfare* is used to describe violent conflict involving irregular combatants, individuals, or groups that are not members of regular military, police, or other internal security force.

[2] For a brief but insightful analysis of Cold War thought on deterring escalation in such asymmetric conflicts as Vietnam, see Lawrence Freedman, "Prevention, Not Preemption," *Washington Quarterly*, Vol. 26, No. 2, Spring 2003, p. 110.

weapons, and escalation management in irregular warfare becomes an issue of grave concern.

This chapter explores the dynamics of irregular warfare and offers insights for managing escalation in these kinds of conflict. It surveys the many ways in which escalation has occurred in operations against irregular combatants and identifies some common elements across cases. Next, the chapter examines two irregular-warfare cases more closely: Lebanon, 1982 to 1984, and Somalia, 1992 to 1994. These cases are particularly instructive for the current security environment, as they illustrate the complex escalation dynamics that emerge when multiple state and nonstate actors with divergent interests interact in ungoverned or undergoverned territories. Building on insights drawn from those experiences, this chapter then examines escalation in the context of global jihad, the campaign of terrorist violence that militant Islamists have waged against the United States for more than a decade, and explains how escalation management should factor into any strategy to counter that threat. The chapter closes with insights and implications from these observations.

Irregular Warfare's Many Paths of Escalation

Given the diverse geopolitical circumstances in which irregular warfare occurs and the wide range of threats encountered, no single pattern of escalation emerges across cases. Such diversity presents substantial challenges for escalation management. However, history does offer a list of potential paths of escalation, and recognizing such dangers is a precondition for managing them in the future.

First, it is important to understand that state behavior has often been the primary source of escalation in irregular conflicts. When confronted by irregular adversaries, states have frequently escalated conflicts, both deliberately and accidentally, in their efforts to defeat the insurgent or terrorist groups opposing them. This dynamic is often the result of desperation; unable to quell resistance with more measured strategies, states have deliberately escalated conflicts by applying ever-increasing levels of force or by broadening the areas of operations. Such acts have often been accompanied by accidental escalation, as frustrated soldiers resorted to unauthorized brutality in efforts to deter further resistance and coerce cooperation from local citizens.[3] Such responses are not surprising; there is almost always a dramatic power differential between a state and its nonstate opponents, providing the state an asymmetric strength that its leaders believe they can use to obtain victory—or, at least, security—through escalation dominance. But while irregular combatants usually lack the means to directly oppose a state's conventional military superiority, deliberate escalation does not guarantee that the state will achieve escalation dominance, and accidental escalation resulting from brutal treatment of noncombatants is almost universally counterproductive. As illustrated in France's experience in Algeria, the United States' experience in Vietnam, Israel's experience in Lebanon, and the Soviet Union's experience in Afghanistan, employing greater levels of conventional force may result in impressive tactical victories, but states have considerable difficulty applying their conventional asymmetric strengths in ways relevant to the long-term, strategic objectives in the conflict.

Moreover, even when states succeed in achieving escalation dominance, doing so may broaden the conflict in unanticipated ways. For instance, in 1970, the PLO, then based in the East Bank region of Jordan, challenged Amman's sovereignty when King Hussein tried to curtail PLO attacks into Israel, and fighting erupted between PLO forces and the Jordanian army. Charging that PLO leader Yasser Arafat was attempting to create "a state within a state," Hussein mobilized and employed his army en masse, driving out the PLO's main force in September, then destroyed its remaining guerilla bases in Jordan in early 1971.[4]

---

[3] For more on desperation as a motive for civilian victimization, see Downes, 2006. Downes limits the scope of his study to "the targeting of enemy noncombatants in interstate wars" (p. 158), but makes passing references to counterinsurgency and counterterrorism (pp. 154, 164 [fn42], 169).

[4] "The Palestine Resistance and Jordan," *Journal of Palestine Studies*, Vol. 1, No. 1, Autumn 1971; S. R. "Palestinian Report," Middle East Report No. 4, November 1971. See also Chaim Herzog, *The Arab-Israeli Wars: War and Peace in the Middle East from the War of Independence Through Lebanon*, New York: Random House, 1982, p. 222.

King Hussein's conventional offensive was successful in securing Jordan from a powerful nonstate adversary, but it inspired new waves of terrorism and set in motion a chain of events that resulted in the collapse of a neighboring state. Having lost its Jordanian sanctuary, the PLO moved its bases to southern Lebanon and resumed its attacks on Israel from there. In time, the PLO's growing presence in Lebanon altered that country's demographics, and the cross-border attacks provoked a Syrian intervention and an Israeli invasion of Lebanon, all of which upset the delicate balance of Lebanon's sectarian government, rendering it unable to quell a rising tide of factional violence. Ultimately, Beirut's descent into anarchy contributed to more than a decade of irregular warfare in the region. Moreover, Jordan's September 1970 offensive became a PLO symbol of martyrdom that inspired a generation of terrorists, including the group, Black September, that murdered 11 Israeli athletes and a German police officer at the 1972 Olympics in Munich.

While Lebanon's collapse is an extreme example of the costs of escalation in irregular warfare, the dynamics exemplified in that case are not unusual. When threatened by well-established irregular adversaries, states frequently respond by increasing their commitment in conventional ground forces and by employing those forces in combat operations in contested regions. Such acts may secure those regions in the short term, but they often antagonize local inhabitants, strengthening support for insurgents or terrorists and feeding further escalation over time.

This dynamic intensifies if authorities respond to irregular attacks with reprisals against local citizens. In Algeria, for instance, French use of a doctrine of collective responsibility to punish Algerian citizens for the terrorist acts of the separatist group Front de Libération Nationale (FLN) proved disastrous for Paris. In resorting to torture, large-scale internment, and occasionally even wholesale slaughter of Algerian civilians, French authorities played right into the FLN's long-term strategy. Although France eventually defeated the FLN, militarily, the harshness with which French authorities dealt with the Algerian people only deepened their commitment to achieve independence. At the same time, repeated accounts of French brutality horrified citizens in France, ultimately eviscerating Paris's political will to hold on to the colony.[5]

As the Israeli incursions have also demonstrated, deploying conventional forces near or across borders may raise security concerns in neighboring states, and those states may react by increasing their support to irregular combatants, or they may enter the conflict on the insurgents' side.

Irregular combatants have often been supported, overtly or covertly, by states or other entities sympathetic to their cause. As a result, states battling insurgents or trying to protect their citizens from terrorists have sometimes resorted to coercive bombing in efforts to compel rival actors to cease such support. These efforts have taken the form of punishment raids, such as Operation El Dorado Canyon, the U.S. bombing of Libya in 1986, or as sustained campaigns, such as Operation Rolling Thunder, carried out against North Vietnam from 1965 to 1968. Such operations may appear to yield short-term benefits—the incidence of Libyan-supported terrorism declined for a couple of years after El Dorado Canyon—but positive results are usually transitory, if they are achieved at all.[6] Often, punitive bombing inspires higher levels of commitment from those being bombed and, as China's involvement in the Vietnam War illustrates, may provoke other states to increase their support to the irregular combatants or the states being bombed or even to enter the conflict on their side.[7]

---

[5] For more on the French struggle in Algeria and the doctrine of collective responsibility, see Alistair Horne, *A Savage War of Peace: Algeria, 1954–1962*, New York: Penguin, 1977, especially pp. 113–115.

[6] While El Dorado Canyon appeared to intimidate Libyan leader Muammar Qaddafi and deter Libyan-supported terrorism for a time, on December 21, 1988, Pan Am Flight 103 exploded over Lockerbie, Scotland, killing all 259 people on board and 11 more on the ground. Investigators attributed the explosion to a bomb planted by Libyan terrorists in retribution for El Dorado Canyon. Two Libyan intelligence officers were charged for the crime. One was convicted in 2001, the other acquitted. See Donald G. McNeil, Jr., "The Lockerbie Verdict: The Overview; Libyan Convicted by Scottish Court in '88 Pan Am Blast," *New York Times*, February 1, 2001.

[7] There is a rich literature on the difficulties of achieving coercive effects from punitive bombing. See, for example, Pape, 1996; Byman, Waxman, and Larson, 1999; and Johnson, Mueller, and Taft, 2002.

Insurgency warfare is particularly prone to escalation in geographic scope. As many analysts have observed, insurgencies are hard pressed to survive without sanctuaries in locations where they can organize, train forces, and hoard or transit supplies. Insurgents often launch operations from sanctuaries then flee back to those locations when confronted by superior forces. Consequently, sanctuaries are usually located in areas adjacent to the territory being contested, in states that are nominally neutral in the conflict but either sympathetic to the rebel cause or unable to evict the insurgents from their own territory. Cross-border raids by guerillas and terrorists frustrate security forces and intimidate local citizens, who may come to question why their government cannot protect them. As a result, military leaders in threatened states often press their governments for authority to pursue insurgents across borders or to conduct operations against base camps in sanctuaries. When permitted, such operations tend to broaden the war, as the insurgents flee ever deeper into the neighboring state. There, the presence of well-armed foreign fighters whom local authorities cannot control or evict tends to weaken the state's credibility and empower local dissidents who ally themselves with the intruders. Once again, as the experience in Lebanon demonstrated, when irregular warfare spills into a neighboring state, it can destabilize that government, leading to its overthrow or collapse, as in Laos and Cambodia.[8]

During the Vietnam War, North Vietnamese regulars and the Viet Cong operated from base camps in Laos and Cambodia and established the infamous Ho Chi Minh Trail through portions of those countries to transit troops and supplies into South Vietnam. In both countries, Vietnamese communists established symbiotic relationships with communist dissidents there, fueling local insurgencies. U.S. bombing operations and South Vietnamese incursions into Laos, and later Cambodia, were largely ineffective in destroying communist forces or interdicting their lines of communication; rather, they drove the Vietnamese communists ever deeper into those states, impeding

---

[8] Iran's support for Hizballah in its recent conflict with Israel in Lebanon and its support for Shiite combatants in the ongoing struggle in Iraq demonstrate that the risks of horizontal escalation are just as relevant in irregular warfare today as they have been in past conflicts.

the ability of noncommunist authorities to govern in ever-wider regions and steadily eroding the states' credibility in the eyes of their citizens. Ultimately, both states fell to communist insurgencies in 1975, the same year that North Vietnamese forces conquered South Vietnam.[9]

But escalation in irregular warfare is not the sole prerogative of state actors; insurgents and even terrorists have frequently escalated conflicts with states unilaterally and for their own motives. Unlike weak conventional forces, whose recourse to deliberate escalation is generally limited by their capabilities, the elusiveness that irregular forces typically enjoy offers them opportunities to escalate against much stronger adversaries with less risk of destruction, and they do so when they believe escalation will work to their advantage.

Irregular combatants usually avoid direct engagement with conventional forces, but they can escalate a conflict in other ways. One common way is to broaden the categories of targets of their attacks. A group that may have attacked only military and police targets to date may turn to civilian targets if it believes that such attacks will elicit the response it desires. Similarly, insurgents and terrorists can increase the frequency of attacks or broaden the geographic scope of their operations, striking the enemy in regions not previously attacked. They can increase the destructiveness of individual attacks, perhaps by orders of magnitude, if they develop an innovative weapon or tactic.[10] And as Aum Shinrikyo's sarin nerve gas attack in the Tokyo subway demonstrated, terrorists can wreak considerable havoc if they manage to acquire nuclear, biological, or chemical weapons.[11] Thus, irregular

---

[9] For detailed analyses on how the Vietnam War contributed to the destabilization and overthrow of noncommunist governments in Laos and Cambodia, see Paul F. Langer and Joseph J. Zasloff, *North Vietnam and the Pathet Lao: Partners in the Struggle for Laos*, Cambridge, Mass.: Harvard University Press, 1970, and Gerald Cannon Hickey, *The War in Cambodia: Focus on Some of the Internal Forces Involved*, Santa Monica, Calif.: RAND Corporation, 1970.

[10] Prominent examples of such innovations include Hizballah's 1983 truck bomb attack on the barracks in Beirut, Lebanon, killing 241 U.S. military personnel, and the use of hijacked airliners as guided missiles on September 11, 2001.

[11] See Kyle B. Olson, "Aum Shinrikyo: Once and Future Threat?" *Emerging Infectious Diseases*, Vol. 5, No. 4, July–August 1999.

combatants can and frequently have escalated the scope and destructiveness of conflicts with eminently more powerful state actors.

But the kind of escalation that is often more difficult to anticipate is that which emerges in operations in which military forces are engaged in activities other than warfighting. The historical record suggests that peacekeeping and stability operations, noncombatant evacuation operations, humanitarian assistance, and various other forms of national assistance are prone to escalation. The nature of that escalation is often insidious in that the environment may appear relatively benign. Yet, as the following cases illustrate, escalation in these kinds of activities can be anything but benign. Although it may not entail a high number of U.S. casualties or a heavy drain on national economic resources compared to conflicts of greater intensity, it can be very costly in terms of international prestige and national confidence. These cases are particularly instructive, as both occurred in territories left in the wake of failed states, settings that have become all too common in the post–Cold War world.

Escalation in Stability Operations: Two Illustrative Cases

In 1982, the United States participated in a multinational force (MNF) that intervened in Beirut, Lebanon, to prevent an imminent clash between the Israel Defense Forces (IDF), the PLO, and Syrian troops that would likely have resulted in mass civilian casualties. Ten years later, the United States took part in a UN-led relief mission to Mogadishu, Somalia, to provide security for the distribution of food and medical supplies and to relieve a potentially catastrophic humanitarian crisis.[12]

In both these cases, local combatants permitted the insertion of MNFs, and the noncombatants at risk initially welcomed their presence. However, over time, intense rivalries between multiple actors polarized these environments, resulting in a steady escalation in violence

---

[12] The analysis that follows draws from more detailed case studies presented in Appendix B.

against MNFs. Consequently, what began as humanitarian missions in relatively benign, permissive environments evolved into combat operations. Unable to manage this escalation or adapt to the evolving threat, the United States paid a heavy price in both cases. In Beirut, a suicide truck bomber crashed into the U.S. Marine Corps Battalion Landing Team headquarters and barracks, killing 241 military personnel; in Mogadishu, a U.S. special operations task force became embroiled in an intense firefight with Somali militia forces and civilians, resulting in the deaths of 18 U.S. soldiers, several of whose bodies were then desecrated before an international television audience.

While Beirut and Mogadishu may be extreme examples of peace operations gone awry, the settings in which they took place are typical of those in which the United States and other countries have repeatedly found themselves since the end of the Cold War. During the past 15 years, irregular warfare has erupted in ungoverned or undergoverned regions of Africa; Latin America; the Balkans; the Middle East; and Central, South, and Southeast Asia, frequently drawing the United States and other Western countries into local conflicts. With the United States and its allies now engaged in a struggle against transnational Islamist extremism—a phenomenon that tends to fester in many undergoverned regions—U.S. involvement in this strain of irregular warfare will likely continue for the foreseeable future.

Beirut and Mogadishu vividly illustrate the factors that make managing escalation in irregular warfare, particularly that which takes place in ungoverned territories, so difficult. In typical failed- or failing-state scenarios, the interaction of multiple actors with divergent interests creates a complex strategic environment in which several conflicts may erupt and play themselves out simultaneously. ROE, an essential element of escalation management, cannot easily accommodate such complexity. More seriously, asymmetries of power, interest, and commitment among the actors often create a dynamic that eventually works against the efforts of state actors attempting to stabilize the situation. The following sections examine these factors explicitly.

Multiple Actors in a Complex Strategic Environment

It is almost axiomatic that conflicts in ungoverned territories are characterized by complex interactions between multiple actors. Typical crises involve several nonstate actors pursuing violent agendas and at least one state attempting to stabilize the situation and guide events to an outcome that serves its interests. Often, several states with divergent interests are involved. Moreover, it is not unusual for one or more intergovernmental organizations, such as the UN or NATO, to have stakes in how the crisis plays out, and nongovernmental organizations (NGOs) are frequently on the scene, attempting to provide relief to noncombatant victims of the war. Finally, we must not forget the important roles that noncombatants play in these conflicts, both as individuals and factions. They are the population whose loyalty is being courted and over which the conflict is being fought. Irregular combatants draw support from them and may use them as hostages, shields, or quasicombatants when it serves their purposes. In irregular warfare, civilians are always a pivotal element in the dynamics of escalation.

All of these factors can be seen in the two illustrative cases. The armed forces of seven states were involved in the Beirut crisis, along with several militia groups (each covertly backed by a state actor) and the PLO. The United Nations and the Arab League were peripheral players. In Mogadishu, conversely, the UN played a central role, acting through its various operational bodies: the UN Operation in Somalia (UNOSOM), UNOSOM II, and the UN-sanctioned Unified Task Force (UNITAF).

Additionally, key individuals representing the UN—Secretary-General Boutros Boutros-Ghali and Special Representative Admiral Jonathan Howe—were pivotal actors in the chain of escalatory events. The principal combatants in Mogadishu were initially rival subclans, led by Mohamed Farah Aidid and Ali Mohamed Mahdi. As the crisis evolved, various elements of UNOSOM and UNITAF became combatants when engaged by Somali militia forces, with a U.S. quick-reaction force (QRF) and Task Force (TF) Ranger eventually rounding out the list. Several states provided forces to the UN efforts, with Pakistan and the United States most entangled in the escalation dynamics. In both cases, noncombatants were sources of support and objects of leverage, victims of the violence and, in Somalia, targets of a brutal form of coercion: mass starvation.

Multiple Conflicts Exist Simultaneously
When multiple intergovernmental, state, and nonstate actors pursue their interests in ungoverned territories, it is not unusual for several conflicts to erupt over the course of an ongoing operation. Actors on all sides of a crisis tend to drag historical baggage to the scene, and new fights break out when the issues at hand bring the parties into confrontation over preexisting conflicts of interest. These parallel and crosscutting conflicts—some inextricably linked, others only marginally related—create a confusing environment in which issues become entangled and civilian loyalties vacillate between actors. Weaker combatants seek opportunities to manipulate the complex interactions to their advantage, currying favor from some actors while playing others against one another. The violence may seem random at times, as individuals and groups commit covert attacks to bring retribution to their adversaries, poison the attitudes of other combatant and noncombatant groups against rival actors, or otherwise alter tactical and strategic conditions to their advantage.

In Beirut, for instance, the Lebanese government and various militias engaged in a power struggle in the shadows of larger conflicts between Israel, the PLO, and Syria. The PLO, which first armed the Muslim and Druze dissidents, used the militias they helped create as proxies to fight the Israelis and their allies, the Christian militias. In September 1982, when hopes for stability emerged around the newly elected Lebanese President Bashir Gemayel—a kind of stability that Syria, the PLO, and Muslim militias may not have seen in their interests, as Gemayel, a Maronite Christian, was openly allied with Israel—he was anonymously assassinated, provoking Christian militia units to massacre hundreds of unarmed Palestinian men, women, and children in the Sabra and Shatila refugee camps, thereby triggering new waves of violence. Later, when the Lebanese government began trying to reassert sovereignty over its territory, the Lebanese Armed Forces (LAF) came into conflict with the Shiite militia in Beirut and the Syrian- and PLO-supported Druze militia in the Shouf Mountains east of the city, the latter of which broadened its fight to the U.S. component of the MNF when the Marines began training and patrolling with LAF personnel. Ironically, both the October 1983 bombing of the Marine headquarters and an earlier bombing of the U.S. Embassy were carried out by groups backed by Iran, a state in conflict with the United States over issues separate from those in Lebanon.

While the conflicts in Somalia were not as numerous as those in Lebanon, they were complicated enough to make escalation management a serious challenge. In this case, the initial combatants, Aidid and Mahdi, were confronted by UN-sanctioned forces arrayed in a succession of organizations (e.g., UNOSOM I, UNITAF, UNOSOM II, the U.S. QRF, TF Ranger), each with a separate mission, different ROE, and, at times, differing perceptions of the level of conflict in which they were engaged. Both clan leaders exploited these seams whenever possible, and Aidid, in particular, attempted to create additional fissures by targeting the Pakistani contingent and, later, the U.S. components in his most violent attacks.

Conflicts on the ground in Mogadishu were overshadowed by a long-standing enmity between Aidid and Boutros-Ghali, and Aidid may have believed that Boutros-Ghali was manipulating the UN Security Council to use U.S. forces as weapons against him personally. If so, this perception was no doubt heightened when Admiral Howe issued a warrant for Aidid's arrest, put a price on his head, and had TF Ranger deployed to capture him. Ultimately, Aidid, clothed in the aura of a Somali nationalist resisting neocolonial oppression and the victim of a vicious personal vendetta, was able to mobilize the citizens of Mogadishu to mob-attack U.S. and Pakistani forces whenever they ventured into the city.[13]

---

[13] After the disastrous October 1993 confrontation between TF Ranger and Aidid's Somali National Alliance (SNA), members of Aidid's Habr Gidr subclan stridently maintained that he was a nationalist who had rebelled against the tyranny of Siad Barre, Somalia's head of state, and was subsequently trying to unify Somalia. They claimed that Boutros-Ghali, during his earlier career as an Egyptian diplomat, had been a friend of Barre and had a personal vendetta against Aidid. See Mark Bowden, *Black Hawk Down: A Story of Modern War*, New York: Atlantic Monthly Press, 1999, pp. 69–70. For a Western assessment that supports the view of Aidid as a Somali nationalist, see Harold G. Marcus, "President Aidid's Somalia, September 1995," *H-Net*, undated.

ROE and the Challenge of Complexity

Realistic, carefully tuned ROE are an essential element of escalation management. But when multiple conflicts coexist in a dynamically shifting strategic environment, devising effective ROE and adjusting them to new threats as they emerge is nearly impossible. Multiple, simultaneous conflicts would suggest that a single set of ROE is inadequate; yet military personnel cannot be expected to learn and employ several sets of ROE, particularly in an irregular warfare setting in which combatants cannot easily be distinguished from noncombatants and members of one faction look like those of another. In the fog of multiple ongoing conflicts, it is difficult to recognize shifts in loyalty and enmity—groups that are friendly one day may be hostile the next—changes that military leaders may not discover before their forces are attacked and even then may not interpret correctly. In cases in which multiple ROE have been employed, the results have sometimes been disastrous. Beirut and Mogadishu are prime examples.

In Beirut, the U.S. MNF operated under peacetime ROE prohibiting the Marines from engaging in combat operations. Force was authorized in only self-defense, and commanders interpreted the constraints stringently:

> USMNF elements were enjoined to seek guidance from higher authority prior to using armed force for self-defense unless an emergency existed. . . . If non-LAF forces infiltrated or violated USMNF assigned areas or lines, they were to be informed they were in an unauthorized area and could not proceed. If they failed to depart, the USMNF Commander . . . was to be informed and would determine the action to be taken.[14]

After the March 1983 U.S. Embassy bombing, the ROE were made more realistic for marines detailed to guard the British Embassy and the Duraffourd Building, where embassy functions were reconstituted, but were kept the same for rest of the U.S. MNF, resulting in a

---

[14] *Report of the DoD Commission on Beirut International Airport Terrorist Act, October 23, 1983*, December 20, 1983, p. 45. Hereafter cited as the Long Commission Report.

"blue card/white card" system.[15] Individual marines were required to review their color-coded ROE cards and adjust their mindsets accordingly each time they were detailed to or from embassy security duty. The marines at the airport remained on peacetime ROE until the headquarters bombing, despite the fact that they were answering Druze mortar attacks with artillery fire, directing naval gunfire on Druze positions, and supporting the LAF in ways that made them combatants in the eyes of the militias opposing Lebanese government forces.

In Mogadishu, by the autumn of 1993, multiple UN-sanctioned forces were operating simultaneously, each with a different mission and different set of ROE. UNOSOM II operated under peacekeeping ROE (minimal force used only in self-defense) as it continued the relief effort begun by UNOSOM I and attempted to reestablish Somalia's civil institutions. The U.S. QRF was a separate force meant to be UNOSOM's mailed glove—its mission was to respond to attacks against UNOSOM II and NGO relief workers—and it carried out combat operations using combat ROE. Likewise, TF Ranger operated under combat ROE while conducting commando raids in the city, trying to capture Aidid and his subordinate SNA leaders. Perhaps most significantly, from June 1993 until shortly after the disastrous firefight in October, attack helicopters and AC-130 gunships flew combat sorties over Mogadishu, employing rockets and heavy gunfire in the city, striking weapon storage sites, vehicle depots, and Radio Mogadishu.

The use of multiple forces with contradictory ROE had deleterious effects on the attitudes of Somali citizens. While the conflict's irregular combatants may have known the differences among the various UN-sanctioned forces facing them, it was difficult for local residents to understand why Western forces that were feeding them were also killing their fellow citizens in rocket attacks and commando raids. Such seemingly capricious behavior not only fueled the spontaneous mob violence that resulted in the deaths of four Western journalists, it gave credence to Aidid's anti-Western propaganda, enabling him to mobilize mobs against UN forces when they attempted to remove militia roadblocks and against U.S. forces when they appeared in the city.

---

[15] Long Commission Report, 1983, pp. 8, 49–51, 135.

Dramatic Asymmetries of Power, Interest, and Commitment

Perhaps the most notable characteristic of irregular warfare in ungoverned territories is the existence of dramatic asymmetries of power, interest, and commitment among the actors. Typically, states that intervene in irregular conflicts can, if they choose, deploy overwhelming conventional military superiority in the field. Even when they send only lightly armed peacekeepers, they can usually call upon additional, more heavily armed forces if needed, tapping reservoirs of power unavailable to nonstate combatants. Given this asymmetric advantage in conventional force, there is a strong temptation for states to seek escalation dominance against nonstate combatants in an effort to impose stability and resolve the crisis. Such an approach may yield a degree of success in the initial stages, particularly if the intervening states' objectives are modest. Unfortunately, early success tends to inspire more ambitious objectives, provoking more concerted resistance from local combatants when those objectives impinge on their interests. Those actors may not be able to confront state forces directly, but the centrality of interests that local actors have in the issues at hand tends to arouse high levels of commitment and searches for asymmetric means of inflicting costs on the states threatening them. Conversely, states that participate in peacekeeping, stabilization, and nation-building efforts usually have only marginal interests in such regional issues. Thus, they lack comparable levels of commitment and are less willing to risk high numbers of casualties in the operation. This hamstrings them with an *asymmetric vulnerability* that irregular combatants have learned to exploit.

In both illustrative cases, U.S.-led MNFs achieved early success in averting crises, then embarked on more ambitious objectives. In Beirut, the mission grew from averting an urban battle between the IDF and the PLO to rebuilding the LAF and helping it reestablish Lebanese sovereignty. In Mogadishu, the mission evolved from providing security so that famine relief could proceed to supporting UNOSOM II's nation-building effort—an objective attempted with less force than was committed to the earlier, more modest mission—and finally, to apprehending Aidid and his key SNA subordinates.

In both cases, nonstate adversaries threatened by the new objectives escalated the levels of violence against U.S. forces until they imposed costs that exceeded what Washington was willing to pay. The Druze militia steadily increased the pressure on the U.S. MNF in Beirut, and Shiite terrorist groups inflicted catastrophic costs through the U.S. Embassy and Marine headquarters bombings, exceeding Washington's tolerance in the latter. In Mogadishu, Aidid escalated the violence against UN and U.S. forces, not only through SNA attacks, but also by mobilizing civilian mobs against them, culminating in the debacle of October 3, 1993. Ultimately, in both cases, *nonstate actors achieved escalation dominance over the most powerful state in the world.*

Irregular Warfare Undermines Traditional Escalation-Management Approaches

Complex asymmetric conflicts tend to undermine traditional approaches to escalation management. Typical escalation-management theories envisage symmetrical, two-party, interstate conflicts in which both participants are interested in limiting their costs by containing the scope and intensity of violence. In such a scenario, combatants can keep the conflict in check if each succeeds in deterring the other from escalating, respects the adversary's salient thresholds, and manages its forces in ways that avoid escalatory accidents. But states embroiled in irregular conflicts are confronted by a range of difficult-to-deter actors struggling in a dynamic strategic landscape in which escalation thresholds are fluid and difficult to ascertain. Deterrent threats suffer in credibility against irregular adversaries that cannot be found, whose followers mount suicidal assaults or attacks then melt away and blend with noncombatants. Deterrence is even less potent when the multiplicity of actors enables them to strike anonymously. Efforts to bolster the credibility of deterrent threats by punishing irregular actors with conventional raids and strikes rarely succeed for long. As Beirut and Mogadishu illustrate, as an irregular conflict progresses, conventional escalation tends to work against the state actors' objectives by antagonizing noncombatants, thereby driving them into the arms of irregular adversaries. In such cases, *conventional escalation ultimately serves the irregular adversary's cause.*

Escalation in the Global Jihad

Since the end of the Cold War, violent Islamic extremists have challenged the United States and its allies in what some analysts have described as *global jihad*.[16] This new and virulent strain of irregular warfare resembles earlier forms in some respects but differs from them in others. Jihadists have conducted guerilla warfare and rely heavily on terrorism, but unlike most Cold War–era irregular combatants, their violent acts are motivated less by secular political or nationalist ideologies than by a desire to eradicate what they see as the corrupting influences of Western culture from those parts of the world that they maintain once made up a vast Islamic caliphate, a region stretching from North Africa to Indonesia and particularly the Arabian Peninsula, home to the holy sites of Mecca and Medina.[17]

The jihadist phenomenon is the violent expression of an Islamist movement that hopes to replace existing states within the boundaries of this mythical caliphate, those governed along secular (and therefore Western) lines, with governments administered according to sharia, or Islamic law.[18] Jihadists have concluded that this objective cannot be obtained without first breaking the power of the West, and the most

---

[16] Analysts and academics debate whether the violence carried out by Islamist groups such as al Qaeda and its affiliates is better described as a form of insurgency warfare or simply as terrorism. While interesting, the debate is not central to the purpose of this study, so we describe Islamist violence using the neutral term, global jihad. For examples of arguments in the definitional debate, see "Bin Laden Expert Steps Forward," transcript of interview with Michael Sheuer, senior intelligence analyst, by Steve Kroft, *60 Minutes*, November 14, 2004; David J. Kilcullen, "Countering Global Insurgency," *Journal of Strategic Studies*, Vol. 28, No. 4, August 2005; and Bruce R. Pirnie, Alan J. Vick, Adam Grissom, Karl P. Mueller, and David T. Orletsky, *Beyond Close Air Support: Forging a New Air-Ground Partnership*, Santa Monica, Calif.: RAND Corporation, MG-301-AF, 2005.

[17] Walter Laqueur, *No End to War: Terrorism in the Twenty-First Century*, London: Continuum, 2003, p. 51. While large caliphates did exist at various times, none ever encompassed all the lands claimed in the Islamist interpretation of history.

[18] John C. Zimmerman, "Sayyid Qutb's Influence on the 11 September Attacks," *Terrorism and Political Violence*, Vol. 16, No. 2, Summer 2004, p. 223; Marc Sageman, *Understanding Terror Networks*, Philadelphia, Pa.: University of Pennsylvania Press, 2004, p. 1.

radical among them envision a future in which the entire earth is under the rule of Islam.[19]

The Roots of Global Jihad

The roots of modern Islamist extremism reach back to the 1928 founding of the Muslim Brotherhood in Egypt. Islamist ideology has since been cultivated in madrassas [religious schools] and other centers of Islamic thought, inspired by the writings of fundamentalists such as Egyptian Sayyid Qutb (1906–1966) and Pakistani Syed Abul Ala Maududi (1903–1979).[20] The current wave of jihadist violence was largely triggered by three coincident events in 1979: the dawn of a new Islamic century, the Islamic revolution in Iran, and the Soviet invasion of Afghanistan.[21]

Muslim tradition holds that the beginning of each new century brings with it the potential for dramatic change, and, indeed, 1979 was a watershed year in the Islamic world. The year began with the Iranian revolution, an event that infused Islamists with hope: For the first time in modern history, clergy-led Muslims had overthrown a corrupt, secular government and replaced it with an Islamic republic. Then, late in the year, the Soviet Union invaded Afghanistan, and the war that followed served as a rallying cry for Islamists, drawing volunteers from across the Muslim world to fight the "godless communists." The 10-year conflict provided a training ground for these "Afghan Arabs" to learn irregular warfare tactics and techniques that they later took back with them to their own countries.[22] Islamists saw the 1989 Soviet withdrawal from Afghanistan as a great victory for Islam, one that Walter Laqueur argues convinced many of them that "it might take only another decade to overthrow the present Arab and Muslim gov-

---

[19] Laqueur, 2003, pp. 54–56.

[20] Zimmerman, 2004, p. 222.

[21] David C. Rapoport, "The Fourth Wave: September 11 and the History of Terrorism," *Current History*, Vol. 100, No. 650, December 2001, p. 422.

[22] Analysts frequently refer to non-Afghan Muslims who volunteered to fight the Soviets as Afghan Arabs. The expression is a bit of a misnomer, as Muslims from non-Arab countries volunteered as well.

ernments and yet another few years to defeat America and the West."[23] One of the Islamists who reveled in that thought—and ultimately claimed a great deal of credit for the victory—was the son of a wealthy Saudi businessman, Osama Bin Laden.[24]

The Escalation Dynamics of Global Jihad

Bin Laden's role in the Soviet-Afghan war has been a subject of debate, as is the claim that he has been the main leader of a unified Islamist movement since the early 1990s. However, there are a number of details of which we are relatively certain regarding Bin Laden's activities and those of other jihadists, and a review of them provides an empirical foundation for understanding the escalation dynamics of global jihad.

Bin Laden founded al Qaeda ("the base") in the late 1980s to channel money and volunteers into the struggle against the Soviet Union. After the Soviet-Afghanistan war, he returned to private life in Saudi Arabia, but he and other Islamists were incensed when the Saudi government invited U.S. troops onto the Arabian Peninsula in response to the Iraqi invasion of Kuwait. For that desecration, Bin Laden spoke out against the monarchy with increasing venom and was put under house arrest before fleeing the country in April 1991. After a brief stay in Afghanistan, he moved al Qaeda headquarters from there to Sudan and reoriented the network to fund and coordinate violence against U.S. forces in Saudi Arabia, Yemen, and the Horn of Africa.[25]

---

[23] Laqueur, 2003, p. 49.

[24] Although Bin Laden and other Islamists boast that it was their efforts in the Soviet-Afghanistan war that drove out the Russians and ultimately resulted in the collapse of the Soviet Union, Western analysts argue that the number of foreign fighters in the struggle was relatively small compared to that of native Afghans and insignificant from a military perspective. Peter Bergen states,

> The war was won primarily with the blood of Afghans and secondarily with the treasure of the United States and Saudi Arabia, who between them provided approximately $6 billion in support. (Peter L. Bergen, *Holy War, Inc.: Inside the Secret World of Osama Bin Laden*, New York: Touchstone, 2002, p. 58).

[25] It is important to note that Sudan became the modern world's second regime to be governed, ostensibly, according to Islamic law following a 1989 coup and the institution in 1991 of a sharia-based legal code. Afghanistan under the Taliban, where Bin Laden went following his 1996 expulsion from Sudan, was also an Islamic regime.

According to most sources, al Qaeda's first attempt to attack U.S. forces probably occurred in December 1992, when two former Afghan Arabs blew up a hotel in Aden, Yemen, where U.S. soldiers had been quartered en route to Somalia.[26] Two months later, terrorists trained in al Qaeda camps and financially linked to Bin Laden set off a bomb in the garage under the World Trade Center, killing six people, but failed to bring the building down.[27]

Over the next several years, with training camps already operating in Afghanistan, Bin Laden established additional camps in northern Sudan, Yemen, Bosnia, and the Philippines, where Islamist rebels from countries throughout the Muslim world congregated to learn guerrilla warfare and terrorist techniques.[28] Bin Laden claims to have provided the training and advisors that enabled Aidid's militia to confront U.S. forces in Mogadishu, resulting in 18 dead Americans in October 1993, and is accused of doing so in a U.S. indictment against him, though the veracity of that claim is debated in intelligence circles.[29]

What is clear, however, is that Bin Laden used his time in Sudan to forge alliances with the other key Islamist groups in North Africa, the Middle East, and South Asia. In 1995, Bin Laden's benefactor in Sudan, Hassan al-Turabi, organized what he called the Islamic People's Congress, putting al Qaeda in contact with leaders of the Palestinian Islamic Jihad; Hamas; and terrorist groups from Pakistan, Algeria, and Tunisia. Bin Laden also formed alliances with Islamist groups from Egypt, Libya, Yemen, and Syria. Most significantly, al Qaeda established a relationship with Hizballah, the Shiite terrorist organization in southern Lebanon. Bin Laden met with Imad Mughniyeh, the

---

[26] U.S. troops had already left when the bomb exploded. It killed two Austrian tourists. Tim Weiner, "U.S. Fury on 2 Continents: The Protagonist; Man with Mission Takes On the U.S. at Far-Flung Sites," *New York Times*, August 20, 1998.

[27] Craig Pyes, Judith Miller, and Stephen Engleberg, "One Man and a Global Web of Violence," *New York Times*, January 14, 2001.

[28] Sageman, 2004, p. 44; Jeff Girth and Judith Miller, "Terror Money: A Special Report; Funds for Terrorists Traced to Persian Gulf Businessman," *New York Times*, August 14, 1996; Vernon Loeb, "A Global, Pan-Islamic Network; Terrorism Entrepreneur Unifies Groups Financially, Politically," *Washington Post*, August 23, 1998.

[29] Bergen, 2002, p. 22.

head of Hizballah's security service and mastermind of the 1983 suicide truck bombing of the Marine barracks in Beirut, and, in 1995, al Qaeda members went to Lebanon to study methods for bombing large buildings.[30]

That same year, Bin Laden began escalating his campaign against U.S. forces and friendly governments in the region. In May, Islamists linked to al Qaeda made a failed attempt to assassinate Egypt's President Hosni Mubarak while he was attending a conference in Addis Ababa, Ethiopia. In August, Bin Laden wrote an open letter to Saudi Arabia's King Fahd calling for guerilla attacks to drive U.S. forces out of the country. Three months later, on November 13, a car bomb damaged a U.S.-operated Saudi national guard training center in Riyadh, killing five Americans and two Indians. Bin Laden denied involvement but praised the attack. The bombers later admitted to having been inspired by his public statements.[31] One week later, jihadists in Pakistan devastated the Egyptian Embassy in Islamabad with a truck bomb, killing 15 people and injuring 80 others.[32]

Al Qaeda's escalation was not totally unilateral. One could argue that the Saudi government moved against Bin Laden before he began his violent attacks in the country. Riyadh stripped him of his Saudi citizenship and froze his financial assets in the country on April 9, 1994, and later that year, a team of gunmen opened fire on Bin Laden's house in Khartoum with AK-47 assault rifles—a bungled assassination attempt that biographer Peter Bergen believes was engineered by Saudi intelligence.[33] But the main response to al Qaeda's escalation during that period was limited to the judicial and diplomatic arenas. Already

---

[30] Al Qaeda's association with Hizballah is particularly significant, as fundamentalist Sunnis such as Bin Laden consider the Shiites to be an apostate sect of Islam. Their engagement in a cooperative relationship suggests that the Islamists and radical Shiites had decided to set aside their centuries-old animosities to fight a common enemy, the United States (Bergen, 2002, pp. 88–89).

[31] Sageman, 2004, p. 44.

[32] Kamran Khan, "Blast Laid to Muslim Radicals Kills 15 at Egyptian Embassy in Pakistan," *Washington Post*, November 20, 1995.

[33] Bergen, 2002, p. 92. For more on the attack, see Tina Susman, "Bin Laden's Plush Life in Sudan," *Newsday*, August 26, 1998; Tina Susman and Knut Royce, "Bin Laden Link: El

on the U.S. State Department's list of state sponsors of terrorism, Sudan yielded to mounting pressure from Cairo and Washington and expelled Bin Laden in May 1996. That did little if anything to impede his ability to inspire and coordinate Islamist violence. The al Qaeda leader simply returned to Afghanistan, where the Taliban welcomed him. A month later, a truck bomb destroyed Khobar Towers, U.S. military barracks in Dhahran, Saudi Arabia, killing 19 personnel. American investigators concluded that a radical Shiite group was responsible for the attack but believe that al Qaeda was somehow involved.[34]

On August 23, 1996, Bin Laden issued his "Declaration of War Against the Americans Occupying the Country of the Two Sacred Places." This lengthy formal statement, published in an Arab newspaper and picked up by various media outlets, called for Muslims to drive U.S. military forces off the Arabian Peninsula and overthrow the government of Saudi Arabia for its corruption, for its anti-Islamic policies, and for allowing infidel "American crusader forces" to enter and remain in the country.[35] In interviews with Western journalists in November 1996 and May 1997, Bin Laden reiterated his determination to wage Islamic holy war against the United States. In the May interview, he renewed his call for attacks on U.S. military personnel in Saudi Arabia and added that "he could not guarantee the safety of American civilians should they get in the way," suggesting that al Qaeda was not, at that point, targeting civilians directly.[36]

Shifa Factory Chief Lives in House He Used to Occupy," *Newsday*, August 27, 1998; and John Mintz, "U.S. Charges 2 as Bin Laden Aides," *Washington Post*, February 25, 2004.

[34] Loeb, 1998.

[35] See "Declaration of War Against the Americans Occupying the Land of the Two Holy Places," August 1996, English translation.

[36] Bergen, 2002, pp. 97–98. Some analysts argue that, between 1996 and 1998, leaders of the Islamist movement were engaged in an intense ideological debate over whether to target civilians directly and whether to prioritize their attacks against the "near enemy," targets in the Middle East, or the "far enemy," targets in other regions, including the United States and Europe. The general pattern of attacks suggests that the targeting strategy did indeed shift in 1998, though the 1993 World Trade Center bombing is a notable exception, being a pre-1998 civilian target of the "far enemy." See Christopher M. Blanchard, *Al Qaeda: Statements and Evolving Ideology*, Washington, D.C.: Congressional Research Service, RL32759, updated June 26, 2006, pp. 4–5; and Sageman, 2004, pp. 18–19.

But on February 23, 1998, Bin Laden signaled his intention to further escalate both the scope and the intensity of the jihad by issuing a joint declaration with four other extremist groups under the banner of the World Islamic Front.[37] In this fatwa [religious decree], the Islamists broadened the fight from attacking the Saudi government and U.S. military forces in Saudi Arabia to killing "Americans and their allies—military and civilian . . . in any country in which it is possible to do it."[38] Bin Laden underlined this decision to broaden the target set in an *ABC News* interview in May 1998, during which he said, "We do not have to differentiate between military and civilian. They are all targets."[39]

Meanwhile, a U.S. grand jury issued a sealed indictment on June 8, 1998, charging Bin Laden with "conspiracy to attack defense utilities of the United States," and the CIA allegedly began secret efforts to get the Afghan anti-Taliban opposition to help it capture or kill the al Qaeda leader in Afghanistan.[40] That month, Albanian authorities, with assistance from the CIA and FBI, conducted a series of raids that disrupted an Islamist effort to establish a terrorist network in and around the capital city of Tirana.[41]

On August 6, 1998, the al Qaeda–affiliated group Egyptian Jihad issued a statement warning the United States that it would soon deliver a message, "which we hope they read with care, because we will write it, with God's help, in a language they will understand."[42] The following day, truck bombs exploded simultaneously at the U.S. embassies in

---

[37] The other groups included the Jihad Group in Egypt, the Egyptian Islamic Group, the Jamiat-ul-Ulema-e-Pakistan, and the Jihad Movement in Bangladesh.

[38] See "Jihad Against Jews and Crusaders: World Islamic Front Statement," reprinted by the *Washington Post*, February 23, 1998.

[39] John Miller, "Interview: Osama Bin Laden," *ABC News*, transcript, May 1998.

[40] James Risen, "U.S. Pursued Secret Efforts to Catch or Kill Bin Laden," *New York Times*, September 30, 2001.

[41] R. Jeffrey Smith, "U.S. Probes Blasts' Possible Mideast Ties; Alleged Terrorists Investigated in Albania," *Washington Post*, August 12, 1998. For a detailed analysis of the Tirana raids, see Karl P. Mueller et al., pp. 212–222.

[42] Weiner, 1998.

Nairobi, Kenya, and Dar-as-Salaam, Tanzania, killing a total of 224 people, including 11 Americans, and injuring several thousand others. The United States launched an investigation and, over the next couple of weeks, assembled intelligence not only implicating al Qaeda in the attacks but also suggesting that Bin Laden was attempting to obtain chemical weapons for use against U.S. military installations. Consequently, on August 20, President William J. Clinton ordered cruise missile attacks against suspected al Qaeda training camps in Afghanistan and the al Shifa pharmaceutical plant in Khartoum, Sudan. Although approximately 80 missiles were fired at the two targets, the results were unsatisfying: Bin Laden escaped the attack in Afghanistan, and administration officials later admitted that they were wrong in their assessment that chemical weapons were being manufactured at al Shifa.[43]

Nor did the cruise missile strikes deter al Qaeda from further attacks. In December 1999, Jordan and the United States separately foiled related plots to bomb targets in the two countries. Around December 11, Jordanian security officials rounded up 13 suspects who had entered the country on fake passports with plans to blow up hotels, tour buses, and tourist sites where people were congregating for millennial religious celebrations.[44] Three days later, U.S. authorities arrested an Algerian citizen at the Canadian border when he tried to smuggle explosives into Washington state. Several other Algerians were soon apprehended in Washington and New York; the investigation that followed revealed that their intended target was Los Angeles International Airport.[45]

But U.S. authorities were not so lucky nine months later. On October 12, 2000, a pair of suicide bombers drove a motorboat laden

---

[43] "Dubious Decisions on the Sudan," *New York Times*, September 23, 1998; John Barry, Mark Dennis, and Alan Zarembo, "Tracking Terror," *Newsweek*, September 7, 1998.

[44] Barry Schweid, "State Department Issues New Worldwide Warning," Associated Press, December 21, 1999; "Urgent—US Confirms Arrests in Jordan Related to Potential US Attacks," Agence France Presse, December 15, 1999.

[45] "U.S. Investigations Link Osama Bin Laden to Suspected Algerian Terrorists," Agence France Presse, January 27, 2000.

with explosives up to the side of the destroyer, USS *Cole*, where it lay harbor in Aden, Yemen, and blew a large hole in the ship, killing 17 sailors and wounding 39 more. The subsequent investigation was hindered by strained cooperation between U.S. and Yemeni officials, prohibiting the United States from gathering enough information to target any specific Islamist group for reprisal, but the sophistication in planning and the materials used, as well as similarities to previous attacks, suggested that a group affiliated with al Qaeda was responsible.[46]

Islamists escalated their global jihad against the United States to its highest level of intensity on September 11, 2001, when teams of suicide bombers simultaneously highjacked four U.S. airliners and succeeded in flying two of them into the the World Trade Center towers and a third into the Pentagon, killing more than 3,000 people and bringing down the towers. The extensive planning, financing, training, and preparation for the attacks revealed the degree to which al Qaeda was then capable of inflicting coordinated violence against the U.S. homeland; the strike's audacity and brutality provoked a massive escalation by the United States and its allies, changing the face of the struggle between militant Islam and the West.

Escalation in Response to Global Jihad

On September 20, 2001, President George W. Bush declared a "global war on terrorism" and his determination to combat al Qaeda and any state harboring or supporting it.[47] The many U.S. and allied actions that followed entailed substantial escalation along multiple dimensions in the struggle against militant Islam. The first and most visible reac-

---

[46] David Johnson and Steven Lee Myers, "Investigation of Attack on U.S. Destroyer Moving Slowly," *New York Times*, October 29, 2000. In addition to the evidence gathered pointing to al Qaeda involvement, intelligence analysts have highlighted the fact that a few months prior to the attack, Bin Laden appeared in a video wearing a distinctive Yemeni dagger, something never seen in any previous picture of him. For details surrounding the Cole bombing and subsequent investigation, see Bergen, 2002, pp. 26, 27, 171–173, 188, 190–194, and 196–198.

[47] John F. Harris and Mike Allen, "President Details Global War on Terrorists and Supporters; Bush Tells Nations to Take Sides as N.Y. Toll Climbs Past 6,000," *Washington Post*, September 21, 2001.

tion to the September 11 attacks, however, was the forceful removal of the Taliban regime hosting Bin Laden, his key lieutenants, and some of al Qaeda's most important training camps.

Building on contacts that the CIA established in Afghanistan after the 1998 embassy bombings, U.S. intelligence operatives and special operations forces coordinated U.S. airpower support to Afghan forces opposing the Taliban regime. With U.S. help, those forces drove the Taliban out of Kabul in December 2001. The United States then began deploying regular military forces to the country and trying to capture Bin Laden and his associates as it replaced the ousted Islamist regime with one more moderate and accommodating to Western interests.

Meanwhile, Washington mounted a concerted effort to build international cooperation in areas of intelligence sharing, law enforcement, judicial extradition, and financial tracking in efforts to bring al Qaeda's global network to heel. Most states were quick to oblige; friends and allies were eager to cooperate with U.S. authorities, and, having witnessed Washington's willingness to remove regimes that openly harbored jihadists, even states that had been less than cooperative in the past declared their support for the struggle against Islamic extremism.[48]

These efforts yielded noteworthy results. By 2005, the United States and cooperating governments had killed or captured 15 of the top 37 al Qaeda operatives identified by U.S. agencies after September 11. Moreover, some "3,000 suspected al Qaeda members have been detained or arrested by about 90 countries," with 650 of the detainees under U.S. control.[49] The Bush administration also maintained that more than $142 million in terrorist assets had been frozen worldwide,

---

[48] The government of Yemen is a notable example. After seeing the United States' reaction to the September 11 attacks, Yemeni President Ali Abdullah Saleh, who previously courted the Islamic extremists in his country, pledged his support to the U.S.-led global war on terrorism and even allowed the CIA to assassinate a group of al Qaeda operatives in Yemen with a Hellfire missile fired from a Predator drone. For a detailed case study of the November 2002 Hellfire strike in Yemen, see K. Mueller et al., 2006, pp. 256–273.

[49] Kenneth Katzman, *Al Qaeda: Profile and Threat Assessment*, CRS Report to Congress, Washington, D.C.: Congressional Research Service, updated August 17, 2005, p. 6.

with around $77 million identified as related to al Qaeda.[50] Al Qaeda no longer had prominent sanctuaries where it could build infrastructure or operate training camps. And its ability to prepare, finance, and coordinate large-scale operations was undoubtedly hampered to some degree by the intense intelligence scrutiny to which global communication and financial linkages became subjected.

But it is difficult to determine the extent to which al Qaeda was really impaired. It is even harder to assess what impact the GWOT has had on the broader jihadist movement, and that is the more important question, given the widespread disagreement in Western government, intelligence, and academic circles about precisely what al Qaeda is. Bruce Hoffman lamented in 2003,

> It is remarkable that more than a decade after its founding, six years after it first came to international attention, and 18 months after the simultaneous attacks on the World Trade Center and Pentagon catapulted it to prominence, al Qaeda remains a poorly understood phenomenon. The ways in which it is variously described is a case in point. Is it a monolithic, international terrorist organization with an identifiable command and control apparatus or is it a broader, more amorphous movement tenuously held together by a loosely networked transnational constituency? Has it become a franchise operation with like-minded local representatives independently advancing the parent organization's goals or does it still function at the direction of some centralized command nucleus? Is al Qaeda a concept or a virus? An army or an ideology? A populist transnational movement or a vast international criminal enterprise? All of the above? None of the above? Or some of the above?[51]

Now, more than four years after Hoffman wrote those words, there is still disagreement over the degree to which al Qaeda, and more precisely, Bin Laden, exerts centralized control over the jihadist move-

---

[50] White House, "Three Years of Progress in the War on Terror," fact sheet, September 11, 2004.

[51] Bruce Hoffman, *Al Qaeda, Trends in Terrorism and Future Potentialities: An Assessment*, Santa Monica, Calif.: RAND Corporation, P-8078, 2003, p. 3.

ment. Some government officials maintain that killing or capturing Bin Laden and other key leaders, such as Egyptian Ayman al Zawahiri, would largely deflate the organization, making it much less threatening, but most officials and analysts argue that al Qaeda is now less central to the Islamist movement than it was on September 11, 2001.[52] Therefore, "it is no longer only al-Qa'eda itself but increasingly groups affiliated with al-Qa'eda, or independent ones adhering to al-Qa'eda's ideology, that present the greatest threat of terrorist attacks against U.S. and allied interests globally."[53] Whereas in the 1990s, Bin Laden operated al Qaeda along lines resembling a multinational business—with departments dedicated to specific functions and an array of local franchises sometimes acting on central direction and other times submitting proposals to a board of directors for approval and funding—the movement now more closely resembles an amorphous network of separate organizations.

Al Qaeda cells still exist, to be sure, but a substantial part of the jihadist movement now consists of local groups with objectives that are more nationalist in orientation. Some of these groups are openly affiliated with al Qaeda; others are not, or at least, are less explicit about their affiliation in the hopes of avoiding increased pressure from the United States or counterterrorism authorities in their own countries. Many members of these groups were trained in al Qaeda camps, and some are veterans of other jihads. The nature of these groups varies widely, and some of them amount to little more than criminal enterprises, but they all have at least two things in common: an affinity for Islamist ideology and a strong antipathy for the West. These traits make them susceptible to influence from Bin Laden and other transnational Islamist leaders who promise to help them achieve their regional goals while inspiring them to act in support of the broader, global jihad.[54]

---

[52] Katzman, 2005, pp. 6–7.

[53] U.S. Department of State, *Patterns of Global Terrorism 2004*, Washington, D.C: U.S. Government Printing Office, April 2005, p. 7, quoted in Katzman, 2005, p. 7.

[54] Jonathan Schanzer, *Al-Qaeda's Armies: Middle East Affiliate Groups and the Next Generation of Terror*, New York: Specialist Press International, 2005, pp. 22–24.

Given these changes in the character of the global jihad, it is not surprising that, between September 11, 2001, and the first quarter of 2007, Islamist violence deescalated in intensity while escalating in scope.[55] Allied military actions, increased international cooperation in law enforcement and intelligence operations, and, especially, the loss of sanctuary in Afghanistan, made it more difficult for al Qaeda and its affiliates to organize and execute large-scale terrorist attacks on the order of those of September 11. Yet jihadist violence did not abate. In fact, al Qaeda retained the ability to inspire, if less often fund and coordinate, a number of major events. Some of the most notable ones include[56]

- the October 2002 bombing of a nightclub in Bali, Indonesia, which killed 180
- the November 2002 bombing of an Israeli-owned hotel and the related shoulder-launched missile firings at an Israeli airliner in Mombassa, Kenya
- the May 2003 suicide car bomb attacks on three housing compounds in Riyadh, Saudi Arabia, which killed eight Americans and at least a dozen people of other nationalities
- the May 2003 suicide bomb attacks against five sites in Casablanca, Morocco, which killed 41 people
- the March 2004 commuter train bombing in Madrid, Spain, which killed approximately 300 people
- the August 2004 suicide bombings of a Russian airliner and a Moscow subway, which killed 57 people and wounded 50 others
- the September 2004 hostage standoff at a school in Beslan, Russia, that ended with 331 people dead and 727 others wounded
- the July 2005 suicide bomb attacks against three underground trains and a double-decker bus in London, which killed 56 people and wounded more than 700 others.

---

[55] As of this writing, composite data on worldwide terrorist incidents were available only through the first quarter of 2007.

[56] Drawn from Katzman, 2005, p. 6; Schanzer, 2005, p. 21; and the MIPT Terrorism Knowledge Base (current through July 18, 2005).

Moreover, the worldwide rate of terrorist attacks carried out by Muslim groups of all types (Islamist, nationalist, sectarian, and criminal) increased during the same period.[57] Much of this escalation is a direct result of the war in Iraq. In March 2003, the United States led a coalition that invaded that country to remove the Baathist regime of Saddam Hussein following its noncompliance with UN resolutions regarding disarmament and inspection. Some U.S. government officials also claimed that the Iraqi government had ties to al Qaeda, and analysts have since debated whether Operation Iraqi Freedom was a necessary step in the GWOT. Whether or not it was, Iraq subsequently became a focal point of Islamist terrorism, drawing foreign fighters from across the Muslim world, and a catalyst for escalating violence by local Islamist, sectarian, nationalist, and criminal groups there and elsewhere.

Figure 5.1 illustrates the extent to which terrorism escalated after September 11, 2001. It shows the quarterly rates of terrorist attacks committed by Muslim groups worldwide from the fourth quarter of 2001 through the first quarter of 2007.[58] The figure divides the data into two categories based on the location of the attacks (Iraq and all others), and the extent to which terrorism in Iraq escalated in intensity is

---

[57] Analysts frequently debate whether various violent Muslim groups are properly categorized as terrorist, insurgent, sectarian, or criminal, but such classifications are not mutually exclusive and few groups fall solely into any one of them. Terrorism is a tactic that all such groups use, and escalating violence by or against Muslim groups in one category tends to incite violence from Muslim groups in other categories, the result of affinities between them not shared with similarly classified groups outside the Muslim world.

[58] Figures 5.1 through 5.3 are based on data extracted from the MIPT Terrorism Knowledge Base, a comprehensive database of terrorist incidents worldwide. Only incidents clearly identifiable as terrorism—i.e., politically motivated violence by nonstate actors against nonmilitary targets—are included. Attacks against military patrols or bases, battles between insurgent groups or sectarian militias, criminally motivated violence (such as kidnapping for ransom), and incidents of random violence with no known political motivation are not included. For Figures 5.1 through 5.3, we filtered the MIPT data further, including only terrorist attacks for which Islamist groups accepted responsibility and for which no group accepted responsibility but that are reasonably attributable to local Islamist groups because of similarities in targets and methods.

Figure 5.1
Incidents of Terrorism in Iraq Compared to Terrorism by Muslim Groups Elsewhere in the World Since September 11, 2001

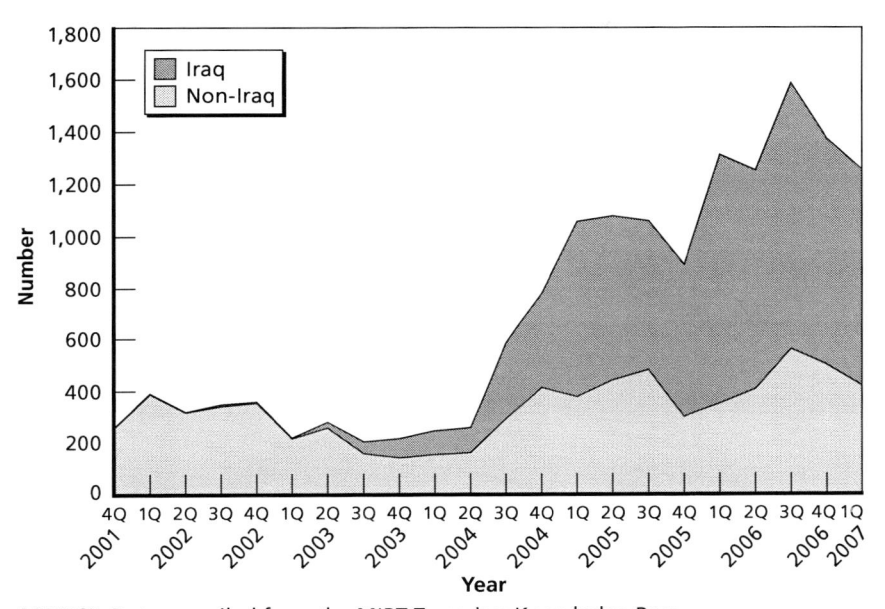

SOURCE: Data compiled from the MIPT Terrorism Knowledge Base.
RAND MG614-5.1

readily apparent.[59] Although the war in Iraq has become a focal point of terrorism and sectarian violence, the frequency of attacks by Muslim groups has escalated elsewhere as well.

---

[59] As of this writing, worldwide data on incidents of Muslim terrorism were not available beyond the first quarter of 2007; however, it must be noted that quarterly rates of terrorist incidents in Iraq and fatalities resulting from those attacks decreased significantly in the second half of that year. The decrease in violence in Iraq can be attributed to several coincident factors, including an increase in the number of U.S. forces in Baghdad, a change in U.S. and coalition strategy to one emphasizing the provision of security to Iraqi civilians, an increase in the competence and reliability of Iraqi military forces, the disaffection of Sunni insurgents and tribal leaders with al Qaeda in Iraq, and a truce between U.S. forces and Shiite militia and religious leaders. For a discussion on how these developments resulted in a deescalation of violence, see Bill Ardolino, "Why the Violence Has Declined in Iraq," *Long War Journal*, November 8, 2007.

148　Dangerous Thresholds: Managing Escalation in the 21st Century

Figure 5.2 provides the same information depicted in Figure 5.1 but with terrorist incidents in Iraq excluded and the remaining data sorted by location: Afghanistan, elsewhere in South Asia, Israel, Southeast Asia, and all other locations.[60] Filtering the data in this manner reveals that the rate of terrorism in Afghanistan escalated fairly steadily over the period. Otherwise, the frequency of attacks by Muslim groups worldwide declined by about half in 2003. This was largely the result of raised expectations in Israel, Gaza, and the West Bank following the 2002 Israeli-Palestinian agreement on a roadmap to a Palestinian state and a deliberate reduction in tensions in Kashmir following the 2002 Indo-Pakistani border crisis. However, in 2004, the frequency of terrorist attacks began escalating sharply as Israeli-Palestinian relations

Figure 5.2
Incidents of Terrorism by Muslim Groups Since September 11, 2001

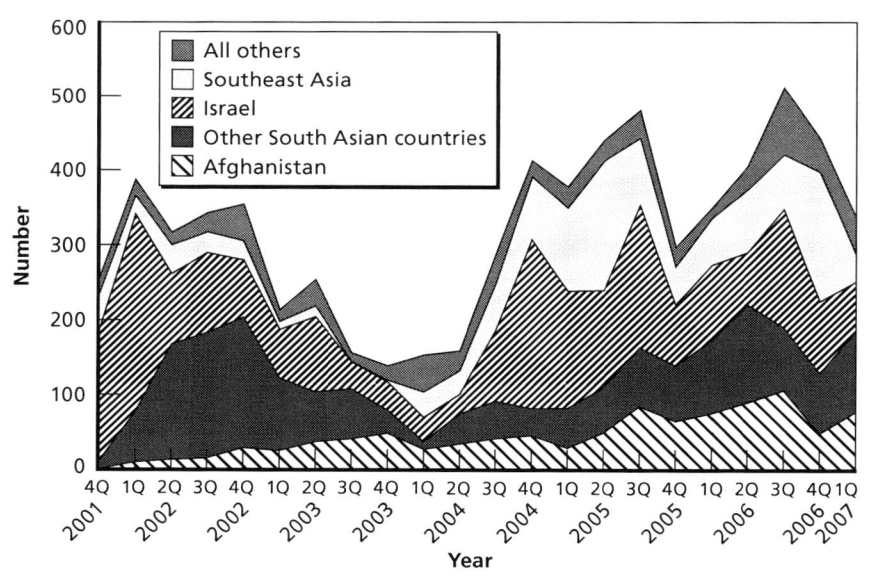

SOURCE: Data compiled from the MIPT Terrorism Knowledge Base.
NOTE: Excludes attacks in Iraq.
RAND MG614-5.2

---

[60] Terrorist incidents occurring in Gaza and the West Bank are grouped with those occurring in Israel.

faltered and terrorist incidents elsewhere increased coincident with the escalation seen in Iraq (compare with Figure 5.1). Yet numbers of incidents alone do not illustrate the full impact of terrorist attacks by al Qaeda and its affiliates.

Figure 5.3 depicts the total number of fatalities that resulted from Muslim terrorist attacks worldwide—excluding those in Iraq—from the fourth quarter of 2001 through the fourth quarter of 2007. Once again, the escalation in Afghanistan is evident. But what is more significant are the spikes appearing in the fourth quarter of 2002, the second quarter of 2003, the first and third quarters of 2004, and the third quarter of 2005. They represent, in part, death tolls from the Bali nightclub and Mombassa hotel bombings; the Riyadh and Casablanca suicide bombings; the Madrid train bombing; the airliner,

Figure 5.3
Fatalities Resulting from Terrorist Attacks by Muslim Groups Since September 11, 2001

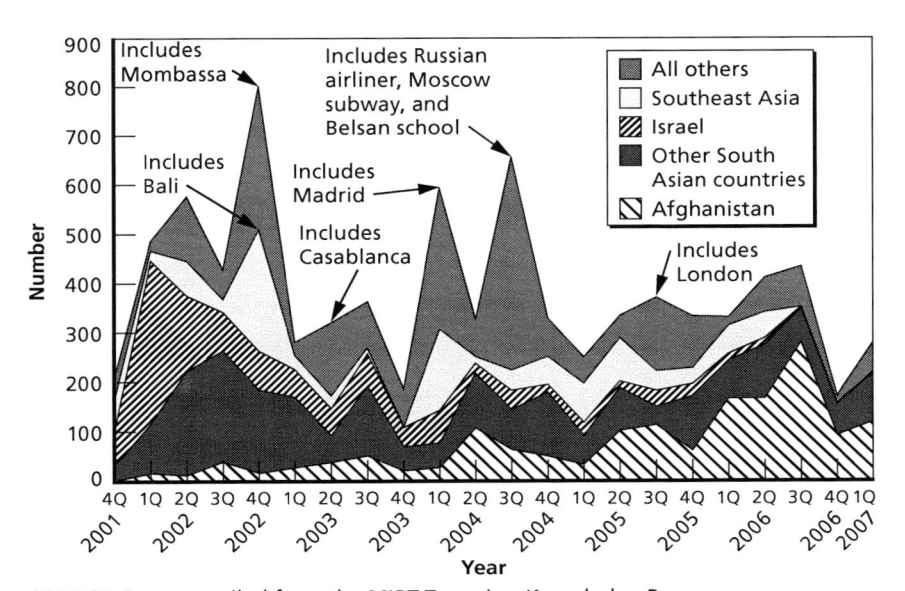

SOURCE: Data compiled from the MIPT Terrorism Knowledge Base.
NOTE: Excludes attacks in Iraq.
RAND MG614-5.3

subway, and school attacks in Russia; and the London transportation bombings, respectively. The magnitude of these spikes illustrates the high lethality of attacks carried out by groups affiliated with or inspired by al Qaeda. Although no terrorist attack since September 11, 2001, has managed to inflict a death toll comparable to that singular event, these data reveal that such groups were still capable of striking with enough lethality to dwarf the quarterly casualty rates suffered in the ongoing war in Afghanistan.[61]

Escalation Management in the Struggle Against Global Jihad

It is significant that no major terrorist attack has occurred in the United States since September 11. One might infer from that fact that the United States has, to some degree, successfully managed escalation in the global jihad. If that is the case, by what mechanism did it achieve such a feat? Managing an adversary's inclination to escalate generally implies deterring it from doing so, either by threats of punishment or by persuading it that such efforts will not meet with success. Have U.S. authorities deterred Bin Laden and his associates from attacking, either by punishing al Qaeda for September 11 or by making homeland defenses so strong as to discourage attempted attacks? Probably not.

If previous experience in irregular warfare is any indication, guerillas and terrorists are inherently difficult to deter. One should expect Islamic extremists, those infused with a fanatical religious ideology, to be all the more difficult to discourage. And, indeed, jihadist leaders appear unresponsive to threats of punishment. This is largely because such threats are difficult to make credible against elusive actors so radical that they reject the established order. Unlike nonstate groups, such as the Irish Republican Army (IRA), the PLO, and Hizballah—groups

---

[61] It is interesting to note that, although the rate of terrorist attacks in Israel, Gaza, and the West Bank began to rise again in 2004, fatality rates there did not. That is due to the frequent use of unguided rockets to attack Israeli targets during that period. Such tactics have a low level of lethality compared to the suicide bombings favored by al Qaeda and its imitators and the improvised explosive devices that Iraqi insurgents commonly employ.

invested in territory and that, in addition to their terrorist activities, pursue interests in the legitimate political arena—jihadists have little or no territory, visible infrastructure, or political capital to protect and, therefore, have little that an adversary can hold at risk.

Alternatively, deterrence via denial may have some limited effect: It may be possible to deter terrorists from attacking certain targets by defending those targets more aggressively, thereby discouraging them from escalating along certain lines. But such aspects of deterrence make, at best, only a limited contribution to escalation management, because jihadists can simply shift their attacks to lesser-defended targets.

Moreover, in addition to the many factors that undermine traditional escalation-management approaches in irregular warfare, efforts to manage escalation in any post–September 11 conflict between jihadists and the United States will inevitably encounter a fundamental contradiction: Escalation management involves tacit bargaining between adversaries, both of which have some interest in limiting the scope or intensity of a conflict, a condition that most observers would argue is no longer present in the United States' relationship with radical Islam, if indeed it ever was.[62]

In the latter half of the Cold War the United States and the Soviet Union had at least one common interest: Both wanted to keep confrontations from escalating to a nuclear exchange; that is, both wanted to survive. That common interest provided a purchase for tacit bargaining amidst enmity, motivating both states to avoid open confrontation wherever possible and enabling them to accept limited gains and losses when clashes did occur.[63] Today, the West appears to have no such common interest with global jihadists. Their declarations suggest they are determined to destroy the West—or at least hobble its power and drive it out of the Middle East—and those committed to defeating

---

[62] As the subsequent argument demonstrates, we generally share this opinion; however, we do not rule out the possibility that jihadists and the United States might indeed have some common interest in limiting the scope or intensity of a conflict that is yet to be realized. We recommend additional research on this question.

[63] Thomas C. Schelling was likely the first to recognize the importance of tacit bargaining as an element of mutual deterrence and escalation management during the Cold War. See Schelling, 1966, pp. 131–141.

radical Islamists are determined to destroy their networks and capture or kill their leaders. This leaves little if any space for negotiation. Al Qaeda strategist Abu 'Ubeid Al-Qurashi declared in 2002,

> Deterrence [is a principle] based on the assumption that there are two sides that seek to survive and defend their interests—but it is completely eliminated when dealing with people who don't care about living but thirst for martyrdom. While the principle of deterrence works well . . . between countries, it does not work at all for an organization with no permanent bases and with no capital in Western banks, that does not rely on aid from particular countries. As a result, it is completely independent in its decisions, and it seeks conflict from the outset. How can such people, who strive for death more than anything else, be deterred?[64]

Yet the case for this lack of negotiating space is far from certain. One RAND analyst has opined that the strong U.S. military response to the September 11 attack—driving the Taliban out of power in Afghanistan, thereby weakening al Qaeda and denying it sanctuary—may have suggested to jihadist leaders that further attacks of such magnitude might not be worth the cost of additional U.S. escalation.[65] Alternatively, Robert Pape argues that, as "suicide terrorism is a strategy for national liberation from foreign military occupation by a democratic state," the United States can reduce the jihadists' incentive to resort to that particular tactic and thereby deescalate the conflict with radical Islam by shifting U.S. strategy from one of occupation in the Muslim world to one of offshore balancing.[66] If either of these

---

[64] Abu 'Ubeid Al-Qurashi, "Fourth-Generation Wars," *Al-Ansar: For the Struggle Against the Crusader War* (biweekly Internet magazine published by al Qaeda), January 2002. Portions reprinted by the Middle East Media Research Institute, Special Dispatch Series, No. 344, February 10, 2002.

[65] Lowell Schwartz, RAND Corporation, interviews with Forrest E. Morgan, Pittsburgh, Pa., March 2006a; Lowell Schwartz, "Comments on Jed Peters Draft," email to Forrest E. Morgan, March 16, 2006b.

[66] Robert A. Pape, *Dying to Win: The Strategic Logic of Suicide Terrorism*, New York: Random House, 2005, pp. 45, 246–250.

viewpoints is accurate, there may be some common ground for the tacit negotiation necessary for escalation management.

But the record to date suggests that, if space for tacit negotiation does indeed exist in the global jihad, the United States has not yet found it. On October 6, 2005, the White House informed the U.S. public that U.S. authorities had foiled 10 terrorist plots since September 11 and disrupted five other attempted "casings and infiltrations."[67] Since that announcement, British authorities have disrupted a plot by at least 24 individuals to conduct multiple simultaneous suicide bombings of aircraft flying from London to the United States.[68] Thus, it does not appear that jihadists have been deterred from attacking U.S. targets, whether inside or entering U.S. borders; they have continued trying but simply have not succeeded since September 11. Consequently, while the United States seems to have achieved some level of homeland defense against the global jihad, Washington cannot claim to have managed escalation in any traditional sense of the word—nor should we optimistically expect it to do so in the future.

This does not suggest, however, that there is no role for escalation management in the struggle with militant Islam. But to understand that role, it is necessary to consider the strategies that global jihadists are attempting to employ in order to ascertain the most feasible means of defeating their efforts while minimizing the escalatory effects of both sides' actions.

Strategies in the Global Jihad

When considering the nature of jihadist attacks to date and comparing those attacks to the jihadist rhetoric, it becomes apparent that global jihadists are attempting to carry out a sophisticated strategy. In fact, jihadists tailor their attacks to send messages to multiple audiences. Dramatic attacks are designed to win followers on the Muslim

---

[67] Sara Kehaulani Goo, "List of Foiled Plots Puzzling to Some: White House Document Mixes Half-Baked Plans with Serious Terrorist Threats," *Washington Post*, October 23, 2005.

[68] "British Police Said to Foil Aircraft Plot," *Washington Post*, August 10, 2006; Dan Eggen and Spencer S. Hsu, "U.S. Responded to Plot with Speed, Secrecy," *Washington Post*, August 13, 2006.

street by demonstrating the viability of jihadists' extremist cause and ability to humble the West. The attacks transmit the same messages to the Muslim diaspora, to win international sympathy and economic support for their cause, along with additional followers. The attacks also speak directly to moderate Muslim regimes in an effort to coerce those governments to distance themselves from the West and accommodate Islamist policies.

But the global jihad has more instrumental goals vis-à-vis Western states. The immediate objectives of these attacks include provoking disproportionate, indiscriminate reprisals that alienate more moderate Muslims and push them into the extremist camp. When that happens, the Islamist movement gains momentum, escalating the struggle in the near term and planting the seeds for further conflict in decades to come. Both the jihadist attacks and the brutal reactions they are designed to provoke are also intended to cause divisions within the West, driving wedges into coalition seams and between those in the broader community of nations steadfast in their support of the struggle against militant Islam and those that waiver. Ultimately, the Islamist campaign of violence is part of a long-term war of attrition, a contest of will between radical elements in the Islamic world and the secular states that have interests there.

In recognizing the multifaceted nature of this strategy, one observes that the dynamics of militant Islam's long-term struggle with the West have a central element in common with other forms of irregular warfare: escalation—conventional escalation, in particular—usually works to the irregular adversary's advantage. Therefore, defeating the global jihad will depend, in part, on finding ways to disrupt and destroy Islamist networks without radicalizing ever-greater numbers of Muslims and thereby escalating the longer-term struggle. The United States and its allies must develop strategies for managing the escalatory effects of global jihad.

Managing the Escalatory Effects of Global Jihad

The popular assumption that terrorists cannot be deterred is one that deserves more critical analysis, but in the meantime, until a way can be found to credibly threaten something that jihadists hold dear, the United

States and its allies must accept their probable inability to deter such groups. In other words, given an opportunity, we should expect global jihadists to escalate to the maximum extent of their capabilities.

In such a circumstance, traditional two-player escalation management is largely disabled. Managing escalation then becomes a more complicated challenge: an effort to constrain and, preferably, eliminate the adversaries' ability to escalate the fight, but doing so in ways that minimize the escalatory effects that U.S. actions, and those of the jihadists, have on other actors in the environment. Said another way, the United States and its security partners must fashion and execute a strategy that maximizes their immediate security but does not, in doing so, jeopardize victory in the more important long-term political struggle with radical Islam.[69] Such a strategy would emphasize the following elements:

- *Vigilance, prevention, and defense.* Whether better defending key targets actually deters terrorists from attempting attacks or simply renders their efforts less effective is largely transparent from a strategic point of view. Either way, the only way to reliably constrain Islamists from escalating the global jihad is to deny them the ability to do so wherever possible. The United States and its partners in the struggle against terrorism should continue efforts to refine domestic and international security procedures, share intelligence, and develop new methods and technologies to detect, track, and seize terrorist suspects, weapons, and resources before they can be used against friendly targets.
- *Concentrating visible efforts in the diplomatic and judicial arenas.* Given that escalation generally serves the long-term objectives of global jihadists, the United States and its partners should avoid

---

[69] Defeating the global jihad will require a long-term strategy designed to cultivate and empower moderate elements in the Muslim world while simultaneously defending them and Western interests from radical Islamists. Developing the kind of comprehensive strategy needed—one that coordinates political, economic, and educational programs with military, intelligence, and law enforcement operations—is well beyond the scope of this study. We argue only that whatever strategy is devised must tailor the use of force against violent jihadists in ways that avoid escalating the conflict.

militarizing the conflict to the maximum extent possible. Operations against terrorists, particularly those visible to international audiences, should emphasize capture and trial rather than military strikes and invasions. Coercive diplomacy may be unavoidable when confronting states that support terrorism, but if conventional military force must be used, it should be used judiciously and with discretion.

- *Entrusting security operations in the Muslim world to local authorities.* Given the history of colonialism and the sense of Western victimization prevalent among many citizens in the Muslim world, Western powers should, to the greatest extent possible, leave military and law enforcement operations in those regions to local authorities. The West should keep its military footprints small to avoid projecting an air of occupation and neocolonialism.
- *Cooperation and foreign assistance.* Keeping the conventional footprint small does not mean noninvolvement. Entrusting security operations to local authorities requires helping states develop the capacity to perform those functions effectively and in ways that do not alienate their own citizens. The United States should cultivate cooperative relationships in the areas of intelligence, law enforcement, and military training and assistance. U.S. intelligence and military specialists need to work cooperatively with their regional counterparts to train and advise their forces and to develop intelligence resources to support U.S. security requirements. The initial phase of Operation Enduring Freedom and the CIA's cooperative efforts with Albanian authorities culminating in the 1998 Tirana raids stand as positive examples of effective operations in the struggle against militant Islam.
- *Restraint and discretion in force employment.* Despite the imperative to minimize conventional military operations, strategic considerations sometimes demand the deployment of conventional forces. When such forces are needed, they should be used, primarily, to provide security to citizens who would otherwise be exposed to extremist violence. Nevertheless, the use of conventional military force in more traditional combat roles may be desirable when opportunities to preempt terrorist attacks arise

and may be altogether unavoidable in cases of self-defense. Even then, however, managing escalation requires keeping the use of force to a minimum. This is particularly important in and around cities. Using conventional military force in populated areas, even when employing precision-guided munitions to minimize collateral damage, lends credibility to extremist propaganda and antagonizes noncombatants, strengthening the jihadist movement. When terrorist or insurgent targets of opportunity arise, every effort should be made to strike them away from cities.[70] The CIA's November 2002 employment of a Hellfire missile fired from a Predator drone, killing a high-ranking al Qaeda leader and several other operatives in rural Yemen, offers a positive example of the discrete use of force to achieve an important tactical objective.[71]

Conclusion

Given the wide range of operations that fall under the rubric of irregular warfare, there is no single approach to escalation management that will be effective in all scenarios. Efforts to manage escalation in these conflicts are subject to the fundamental paradox of irregular warfare: the need to employ deadly force in a struggle that is essentially political in nature. The tension that this apparent contradiction creates manifests in escalation management in various ways.

In humanitarian interventions and stability operations, *deploying* overwhelming conventional force at the onset of an intervention appears to deter escalation so long as objectives are modest; but *employing* force in pursuit of more ambitious objectives in these complex environments tends to trigger escalatory chain reactions with results that are difficult to predict. States can bring a preponderance of force to

---

[70] Daniel Byman, a Mideast expert at Georgetown University, has reached similar conclusions (see Lucy Stallworthy, "Analysis: Targeted Killings Often Work," United Press International, February 10, 2006).

[71] Unfortunately, the benefits of discretion in that case were sacrificed when word of it leaked to the press. See K. Mueller et al., 2006, pp. 256–273.

bear in such scenarios, but their relative lack of stakes limits their ability to tolerate casualties, hamstringing them with an asymmetric vulnerability that nonstate actors have learned to exploit.

These observations point to some obvious implications—states should intervene only when serious interests are at stake, then deploy ample force while keeping objectives modest—but such admonitions are not always practical, given the need to eliminate havens for terrorists, the political pressure generated when starving children are featured in news media, and the intractable nature of problems in failed and failing states.

Alternatively, September 11 generated a sufficient increase in threat perception to convince most Americans that U.S. stakes in the struggle against global jihad are very high. As a result, the U.S. population has been much more tolerant of casualties in operations they have associated with that effort, such as those in Afghanistan and Iraq. This heightened level of casualty tolerance has afforded U.S. political and military leaders a much freer hand to escalate those conflicts than any U.S. leaders have had in irregular conflicts since the Vietnam War, a freedom they have used not only in a struggle to defeat the irregular adversaries challenging Western interests there, but also in the pursuit of ambitious nation-building objectives. The long-term ramifications of such efforts remain to be seen.

CHAPTER SIX
Managing Escalation in a Complex World

This monograph has examined the risks of escalation in the 21st century and assessed implications for military confrontations with adversaries armed with nuclear weapons and asymmetric capabilities. The findings presented here offer insights for air- and spacepower strategy and should also inform national security policy and military operations more generally. To help the Air Force anticipate and manage escalation risks in today's complex environment, this analysis set out to answer three key questions:

1. What is the fundamental nature of escalation? That is, what are the motives and mechanisms that drive escalation in military conflict?
2. What escalation risks result when those motives and mechanisms engage during confrontations with adversaries in the three categories of threats that characterize the current security environment?
3. What can U.S. military and civilian leaders do to manage those risks?

This chapter integrates findings from the prior chapters to answer these questions and offers recommendations for the U.S. Air Force.

The First Step in Managing Escalation Is Understanding Its Nature

Escalation is a natural tendency in any form of limited human competition. When that competition turns to military confrontation or limited war, the pressure to escalate can become intense due to the weight of issues that bring actors into violent conflict and the potential costs of losing contests of deadly force. Escalation can be unilateral, but it is often reciprocal, as each combatant struggles ever harder to gain advantage over the enemy or counter disadvantages incurred due to enemy escalation. Left unchecked, escalatory chain reactions can occur, raising the costs of war to catastrophic levels for combatants and noncombatants alike.

Escalation management is about keeping military confrontations from erupting into war and keeping limited wars from spinning out of control. Most wars are fought for limited stakes; therefore, states have interests in limiting the costs of their involvement. In a world in which nuclear weapons are proliferating, the need to maintain limits on war is paramount. Even when facing conventionally armed opponents or irregular adversaries, the United States will usually want to keep wars limited to avoid the costs of extended conflict and, potentially, attacks by enemies using asymmetric weapons. Thus, escalation management should always be an important factor in U.S. policy and military planning.

Because escalation is an interactive phenomenon, one in which any party to a conflict can play a role, it can rarely be *controlled* in the normal sense of the word. However, by understanding the motives that drive escalation and the mechanisms through which it manifests, military and political leaders can manage the risks of escalation by manipulating the tacit negotiations with opponents that characterize confrontation and limited war.

Deterring Deliberate Escalation

The escalation mechanism and motive most easily recognized and understood is deliberate escalation done for instrumental reasons. In this mode, a combatant deliberately increases the intensity or scope of operations in ways that violate one or more of an adversary's thresholds to gain advantage or avoid defeat. Historical examples abound, as combatants in many wars have expanded target lists, introduced new weapons, or broadened those conflicts in the hopes of shifting military and political outcomes to their advantage.

Combatants also deliberately escalate conflicts, or indicate they are willing to do so, for suggestive purposes in efforts to send signals to the enemy. Deliberate, suggestive escalation has sometimes been done to punish enemies for earlier escalatory acts. In other cases, combatants have escalated in efforts to signal to enemies that they are at risk of even greater escalation if they do not comply with coercive demands, as was the case when the United States used gradual escalation in Operation Rolling Thunder in an attempt to compel North Vietnam to stop its aggressive campaign against the South. Either way, suggestively motivated escalation is a means of manipulating risk in the tacit negotiations between adversaries that characterize limited war. It is coercive communication through deed.

Threatening Punishment to Deter Deliberate Escalation. Because deliberate escalation, whether instrumental or suggestive, is an intentional act, the key to managing the enemy's propensity to resort to it lies in deterrence. The purpose is to deter the enemy from deliberately escalating a conflict along prohibited dimensions by convincing enemy leaders that the costs of such action will outweigh the any benefits they might expect to accrue from it. Deterrence is most often associated with threats of punishment, and, indeed, that is the most direct way of manipulating the enemy's cost-benefit calculations.

But deterrence via threat of punishment carries certain potential drawbacks. The most obvious is the burden of credibility. To make a threat of punishment credible, one must convince the adversary that one has both the capability and the will to carry it out. This can be more difficult than would appear, as enemy leaders may be confident in their ability to defend against the threatened punishment and may believe that the threatening party would incur prohibitive costs in carrying out the threat. In other words, they might conclude that the threat is a bluff. Establishing the credibility of a deterrent threat may require demonstrating one's capability and will to follow through—

perhaps punishing some smaller infraction in a measured way that holds the prospects of inflicting greater costs in reserve—but this risks triggering the very escalation one is hoping to avoid by suggesting to the adversary that greater escalation is on the way, escalation that may put it at a critical disadvantage if it does not escalate first.

More serious weaknesses emerge in punishment-based deterrence when there is a significant asymmetry of stakes between parties to the conflict. An adversary that perceives that its stakes in an issue are high will be willing to bear higher costs and therefore be less sensitive to threats of punishment. And if that enemy believes that the threatening party's stakes are low, it may also doubt that the threatener is willing to bear the reciprocal costs of escalation or pay the political costs of carrying out such threats. Unfortunately, the United States has often found itself in conflicts in which it held the low end of asymmetric stakes, and, as events in Lebanon, Somalia, and even Vietnam demonstrate, U.S. leaders have sometimes failed to appreciate how disproportionate interests might undermine the nation's will to continue before the costs of escalation exceed political tolerances.[1]

Denial-Based Deterrence Strategies. An approach to deterrence that is somewhat more resilient to these potential pitfalls is often called *denial*. Denial-based deterrence strategies entail discouraging an adversary from taking a prohibited action by convincing enemy leaders that such efforts can be countered sufficiently to deny their benefit. Denial strategies may encompass a wide range of activities, from deploying integrated air and missile defenses around friendly cities to tightening security measures at airports. An advantage of using denial to bolster escalation management is that doing so puts defensive capabilities in place that lessen the costs of escalation, should deterrence fail. In fact, critics sometimes argue that denial strategies are essentially indistinguishable from defensive or controlling strategies. Indeed, denial resembles those strategies in certain ways, yet it differs from them in

---

[1] For a seminal study of how disproportionate interests (asymmetry of stakes) hampered U.S. efforts to coerce Hanoi during the Vietnam War, see Alexander L. George, David K. Hall, and William E. Simons, *The Limits of Coercive Diplomacy: Laos, Cuba, Vietnam*, Boston: Little, Brown, 1971. See also George and Simons, 1994.

others. While denial, defensive, and controlling strategies all entail preparing to defend against or defeat an enemy, defensive strategies anticipate a fight, and controlling strategies seek dominance. Pure denial strategies, alternatively, while preparing for defense, focus on manipulating an enemy's decision calculus to deter it from escalating in the hopes of saving the costs of fighting at broader or more intense levels of conflict.

Moreover, there is another feature that distinguishes denial-based escalation-management strategies from those designed for defense or control, one that, if not properly understood during military planning, can result in a strategy that triggers inadvertent escalation. To manage escalation without provoking it, denial strategies should be truly defensive. Actions taken for denial should not violate an enemy's escalation thresholds or threaten an enemy that is not attempting to escalate, at least not in ways beyond the threats imposed by military operations at the current level of conflict. For instance, while defensive counter–air patrols over friendly territory and offensive counter–air strikes on enemy bases both work to deny the enemy the ability to bomb friendly cities, the first option would be consistent with a denial-based escalation-management strategy, but the second, while supporting defensive and controlling strategies, might be escalatory if bombing the enemy's homeland is a threshold not yet crossed.

Managing Inadvertent Escalation: A Matter of Clarifying Thresholds
While deliberate escalation is the form most easily recognized and understood, inadvertent escalation—that is, the mechanism that engages when a combatant deliberately takes actions that it does not perceive as escalatory but that the adversary does—has been a persistent problem in war. The cause of this phenomenon lies largely in the subjective nature of escalation thresholds. As discussed in Chapter Two, escalation thresholds are social constructs that exist in the minds of the actors rather than in objective reality. Although some thresholds are obvious to all combatants, certain ones may loom large for one side while remaining obscure or invisible to the other. Consequently, it may be difficult to divine what acts the enemy considers escalatory, beyond those most obvious, such as attacks on the homeland, deliberate attacks

on civilians or cherished sites, use of prohibited weapons, and so on. Therefore, the first step in managing this risk is to collect and analyze all available intelligence to determine where the enemy's salient escalation thresholds might lie. When likely thresholds are identified, U.S. leaders can respect those triggers to avoid inadvertent escalation or deliberately violate them if they conclude that escalation is affordable and will work to U.S. advantage. Either way, the choice to escalate or not becomes a conscious decision: It is managed. Similarly, U.S. leaders can reduce the risks that adversaries will inadvertently escalate a conflict by explicitly stating what actions the United States would consider to be seriously escalatory. As demonstrated during the first Gulf War, when Saddam Hussein was warned against using chemical weapons, such statements carry an implicit threat of retribution and therefore simultaneously serve both to clarify thresholds and deter escalation.

Unfortunately, clarifying escalation thresholds is not always so straightforward. Often, military and political leaders do not consider which enemy actions might be escalatory or how they might react to them until the enemy carries them out. Moreover, some escalation thresholds are fluid, changing over the course of a conflict as opponents' fortunes rise and fall. A change in targets or weapons that might not have been considered a serious provocation when a combatant was holding its own could be very escalatory when that party is losing and vulnerable. More seriously, when an actor clarifies a threshold, thereby revealing its proverbial bottom line, a skillful enemy may respond in ways that make the declared threshold ambiguous, posing a quandary to the threshold-declaring party that may be unanticipated. Finally, clarifying one's own escalation thresholds may even have negative value: Such declarations may imply that certain thresholds are not convincing enough to go without saying. Alternatively, it could encourage an adversary to deliberately escalate if it interprets the acknowledgment of a threshold as an admission of vulnerability. Political and military leaders must take all of these considerations into account when tailoring strategies to manage the risks of escalation. They should conduct a thorough and frank analysis of their own thresholds, as well as those of the enemy, and craft a strategy that clearly communicates well-defined thresholds in terms that make it difficult for the enemy to unhinge and that are backed by credible, though perhaps implicit, threats of reprisal.

Managing Forces to Avoid Accidental Escalation

The third fundamental mechanism of escalation is that which occurs by accident. While the strategy to defeat a particular adversary may include deliberately escalating along certain lines, no political or military leaders want escalatory accidents to occur, as they take the control of events out of their hands. Accidental escalation occurs when operators make mistakes, such a bombing the wrong targets or straying across geographical boundaries. While both sides may recognize that such acts violate escalation thresholds, the violator knows that its forces made a mistake, but the enemy typically believes that the act was deliberate and escalates in response. Accidental escalation can also occur when leaders fail to set appropriate ROE or fail to maintain adequate discipline over the forces under their command. Escalatory accidents are more prone to occur when forces must be configured to respond quickly, as was the case with U.S. and Soviet strategic forces during the Cold War.[2]

The risks of accidental escalation can never be completely eliminated, but the key to mitigating them lies in effective force management. Leaders must assess the potential costs of escalatory acts, establish appropriate ROE, and enforce those rules among subordinate forces. The risk of accidents is further reduced with diligent training and exercises before the engagement and effective command and control throughout the operation.

Dominance as a Means of Escalation Management

No nation today can rival U.S. power across the full range of nuclear and conventional military capabilities. Such sweeping superiority has led some military and civilian defense professionals to conclude that

---

[2] After the Cold War, U.S. and Soviet leaders reduced the chances that accidents might escalate into nuclear war by lowering the standing-alert levels of their nuclear forces and relaxing the command-and-control linkages between warning and weapon systems that previously raised concerns about launch on warning during crises.

the surest means of controlling escalation in a conflict is to impose escalation dominance—that is, to escalate the conflict in ways advantageous to the United States while denying the enemy the ability to reciprocate, either because it has no escalation options or because those available would not improve its situation. Once the enemy realizes that the United States has escalation dominance, they reason, not only should the enemy be deterred from trying to escalate, but it should also be malleable to U.S. demands for fear of further escalation.

Indeed, the United States commands a wide range of asymmetric strengths with which it might be able to achieve escalation dominance in some limited conflicts. However, cases examined in this monograph suggest that escalation dominance is difficult to achieve against a committed adversary, even in conflicts in which the combatant seeking it enjoys vastly disproportionate strengths. When significant issues are at stake, adversaries tend not to acknowledge their enemies' apparent dominance. Rather than concede, they seek ways to mitigate the strengths arrayed against them while striving for some asymmetric strength of their own—a way to impose greater costs on their enemies.

Thus, efforts to achieve escalation dominance risk triggering reciprocal escalation, even when asymmetric strengths are present. When escalation dominance does occur, it is more often the result of a combatant discovering, and effectively exploiting, some asymmetric vulnerability in its opponent, thereby imposing some cost that the opponent cannot avoid and is not willing to bear. For the United States, low stakes in some past conflicts have exposed such an asymmetric vulnerability in the form of casualty aversion, enabling adversaries to achieve escalation dominance over U.S. forces despite those forces' asymmetric strengths in conventional warfighting capabilities.

Ironically, escalation dominance is most achievable when escalation management is of least concern. The United States might well achieve escalation dominance when confronting a state that possesses limited conventional capabilities and is not armed with nuclear weapons. U.S. interventions in Grenada, Panama, Haiti, and even Kosovo offer examples of successful U.S. dominance. But in these cases, the need to manage the risks of escalation were significantly relaxed, so dominance became more a means to victory than a tool of escalation management. Moreover, even when facing an opponent with limited means of resistance, dominance in one form of war does not necessarily mean that the enemy will concede the long-term conflict, particularly if outside help is available. As events in Vietnam, Afghanistan, and Iraq have illustrated, enemies overmatched in conventional warfare may seek ways to alter the conflict to prolong the struggle and bring asymmetric strengths to bear.

If, on the other hand, the United States confronts a significant regional power—particularly one armed with nuclear weapons—escalation-management concerns rise to the fore and prospects of escalation dominance become more remote. Such an adversary would be less easily cowed by U.S. conventional superiority, and immense U.S. nuclear capabilities would largely be irrelevant in response to conventional aggression in a struggle for limited stakes. Were the United States to try to impose its dominance through conventional means, enemy leaders might conclude that their survival was at risk. Then, the conflict would no longer be a limited war from their prospective, making it more difficult to deter their escalation—and, potentially, their use of nuclear weapons—if they felt sufficiently threatened.

One might wonder how any rational enemy could resort to nuclear weapons in a conflict with a superpower, thereby risking its own annihilation. But a regional power's first step over the nuclear threshold would not likely entail a salvo that exhausts its arsenal, leaving it defenseless. Rather, a more reasoned strategy might involve a demonstration blast, a space detonation, a high-altitude electromagnetic pulse, or even an attack on some counterforce or minor countervalue target while keeping the rest of the arsenal in reserve to hold other, more significant regional countervalue targets at risk. Any of the foregoing developments would strain alliances and place the United States in a serious dilemma. U.S. leaders would be loath to leave an enemy regime in power after it had crossed the nuclear threshold. Yet the desire to remove such a regime would have to be considered in light of prospects for locating and destroying the enemy's remaining weapons and weighed against the potential cost of even a single nuclear strike on a major city of a regional friend or ally.

In sum, when even a few nuclear weapons are involved, attempting to impose dominance is a dangerous approach to escalation management.

The Role of Technology in Escalation and Escalation Management

The Air Force is a child of technology. Indeed, the very essence of air and space power lies in the orchestration of sophisticated technological capabilities, something the U.S. Air Force does better than any other institution in the world. Consequently, any effort to understand the nature of escalation in the current security environment would be remiss if it did not consider what role technology might play. It is almost axiomatic that *weapons do not escalate*; rather, *people escalate with weapons*. Yet we cannot leave this issue with so basic a finding. Closer examination reveals that certain technology-related issues bear on the dynamics of escalation and suggest important implications for escalation management.

First, it is important to keep in mind that any technology that enables a military force to fight with more speed, range, and lethality will enable that force to cross escalation thresholds faster. New capabilities may allow the United States to achieve escalation dominance where none was possible before, but technology cannot substitute for strategy, and ever-greater capability will enable U.S. warfighters to do all the wrong things to ever-greater, and potentially negative, effect.

Beyond that, deploying certain kinds of weapons or force structures may contribute to structural instabilities, making escalation more likely. Weapons or systems that appear very threatening to adversaries but are difficult for U.S. forces to defend present tempting targets for escalation if deployed within reach of an enemy's strike assets. The U.S. military's growing dependence on space may be an example of such a structural instability, as the U.S. orbital infrastructure enables its forces in enormous ways, yet that infrastructure is largely undefended, and portions of it may be within reach of more sophisticated adversaries.

On the other hand, lacking certain capabilities may also contribute to structural instabilities, prompting adversaries to escalate in ways for which the United States lacks proportionate responses. Leaving such options available to an adversary risks exposing U.S. leaders to an escalation dilemma, forcing them to choose between allowing painful enemy escalation go unanswered or responding with disproportionate escalation that may entail undesirable military or political cost.[3]

Managing Escalation Risks in Today's World

Confrontations with adversaries in any of the three categories of threat that characterize the current security environment would present significant risks of escalation.

Escalation Management in a Limited Conflict with China

China is an emerging great power, one with a nuclear arsenal and a growing ability to project conventional force in its region. While few analysts surmise that Beijing has expansionist ambitions per se, China is not constrained by any cultural predilection toward pacifism; Chinese leaders can be expected to use force to protect their interests when they calculate that the risks and potential benefits of doing so are favorable. Chinese leaders and security analysts seem aware of the need to control escalation, as are their U.S. counterparts, but operational military doctrines in both China and the United States emphasize surprise, speed, and deep strikes to seize the initiative and achieve dominance. Neither body of doctrine appears to consider how an adversary might react to such operations in a limited war—indeed, each seems to assume that it will suppress enemy escalation by dominating the conflict. Consequently, a Sino-American confrontation would entail significant risks of inadvertent escalation if military forces were permitted to operate in keeping with their doctrinal tenets without regard for escalation thresholds.

Managing escalation in a limited conflict with China will require U.S. leaders to take a firm hand, not only in controlling their own military forces, but also in clarifying thresholds and deterring the Chinese

---

[3] Examples might include enemy use of chemical, biological, or small tactical nuclear weapons. Would the United States respond to such escalatory acts with one or more strategic nuclear weapons? Would the enemy find the threat of such a response sufficiently credible to deter escalation? These are critical questions to consider.

from violating them. At the onset of a crisis, U.S. leaders will need to assess each side's interests and estimate how much cost the United States can bear in potential escalation. They will need to conduct an in-depth analysis of Chinese escalation thresholds and weigh the risks of violating them against operational necessity. At the same time, the United States should clearly state what forms of Chinese escalation are unacceptable and develop strategies for deterring Beijing from committing those acts. Because it may be difficult to make some threats of retribution credible in a limited conflict, such deterrent strategies should be fortified as much as possible by defensive capabilities to deny China success and benefits from attempted escalation.

Managing Escalation in Confrontations with Other Regional Nuclear Powers

Unlike China, whose nuclear doctrines are well developed and, to date, appear relatively benign, today's newly emerging regional nuclear powers present escalation risks, in part, by virtue of their lack of doctrine and experience in nuclear force management. New nuclear states typically develop their weapons first and only afterward work out the policies and doctrines for when and how they will use those weapons. Their operators lack training and experience, and it takes time to develop the necessary equipment and protocols for positive control and nuclear surety. Such states initially lack survivable second-strike capabilities, and that generates use-or-lose pressures when they feel threatened. New nuclear powers have often engaged in provocative behavior soon after achieving nuclear capability, suggesting that the leaders of such states tend to overestimate the ability of nuclear weapons to deter conventional conflict. All of this suggests that emergent nuclear states are more liable to make catastrophic errors than are longer-established nuclear powers; their leaders and forces may precipitate a crisis and act unpredictably.

Complicating matters, all of the new and soon-to-be nuclear powers have bitter animosities with their neighbors, and some are embroiled in ongoing conflicts. India and Pakistan have gone to the brink of open war twice since demonstrating their initial nuclear capabilities in 1998. North Korea, despite occasional diplomatic flirtation with the South, keeps its military forces deployed for war and continues raising anxieties in Northeast Asia. North Korea and Iran are hostile to the United States, and Washington has singled them out as rogues and members of an axis of evil, a club that once included Saddam Hussein's Iraq. Therefore, they may be anxious that the United States will attempt to impose regime change on them, raising risks of escalation should U.S. forces intervene in crises in their regions. Finally, some of these states have domestic problems that threaten their stability, and factions within them have known links to terrorist groups.

Strategies for managing risks of escalation in confrontations with new nuclear states will resemble those for conflicts with other nuclear powers, but they must hedge against a greater potential for miscalculation. As in the case of China, escalation management will require the clarification of thresholds and the development of deterrent strategies, but U.S. statements about thresholds and deterrent threats will need to be more explicit. Beyond this, the United States should focus on developing effective ballistic and cruise missile defenses as well as other means of defending U.S. forces and regional friends and allies from asymmetric attack. Such capabilities will enhance deterrence by reducing the chances that an enemy can succeed in the prohibited action, thereby denying it the benefits of escalation and rendering it not worth the cost of U.S. retribution.

Yet threats and defenses alone may not deter an adversary that believes its survival is at stake. Given the insecurities new nuclear states suffer due to the questionable survivability of their nuclear forces and the anxieties that North Korea and Iran, in particular, feel regarding potential U.S. designs for regime change, in any limited conflict with them, the United States may want to balance its threats with assurances. For deterrence to remain viable in limited war, enemies must be reasonably confident that if they respect critical escalation thresholds, U.S. forces will as well. At the same time, the United States will need to develop a damage-limitation strategy and put forces in place to execute it should deterrence fail.

All of this assumes, of course, that U.S. objectives in such a conflict would not include regime change—that is, that the conflict would indeed be limited. While escalation management is a function of limited war, regime change is an unlimited objective (although one may still set limits on what means may be used to impose it). When targeted for regime change, enemy leaders have little incentive to restrain the scope or intensity of their resistance. The United States may attempt to deter them from violating certain thresholds, such as the use of nuclear weapons, by balancing threats of postconflict war-crime prosecution with promises of benefits, such as life in exile and immunity from prosecution, but it is highly questionable whether enemy leaders will factor such postconflict trade-offs into their strategic calculations until the prospects of defeat and capture appear imminent. In the meantime, they are likely to see the weapons whose use the United States is trying to deter as available means for resisting the effort to destroy their regimes.

Moreover, there is another reason for the United States to limit its objectives in confrontations with emerging nuclear powers. All of these states have domestic problems to varying degrees, and some of them may be vulnerable to collapse in a serious military crisis. The disintegration of a nuclear state would raise critical questions regarding who has control of the weapons, what ideologies and loyalties motivate those groups, and what they intend to do. This would be particularly alarming if factions within the failed state have links to terrorist groups, as some of the factors that deter states from transferring nuclear weapons to extremists may not apply to substate elements.

Ultimately, whether efforts to impose regime change on a regional nuclear power are successful, the United States might find itself with the burden of having to stabilize and rebuild a failed state, an ungoverned territory ripe for terrorists and insurgents. As the next section explains, such scenarios present some of the greatest challenges for escalation management.

Escalation Management in Irregular Warfare

During the Cold War, concerns about escalation focused primarily on the risks that irregular conflicts, seen largely as proxy wars between the East and West, might draw the superpowers into direct confrontation. However, this monograph has found that risks of escalation even in that era were much broader and more diverse than was then appreciated. Cases such as the Vietnam War and Israel's incursions into Lebanon, among other scenarios, reveal that counterinsurgency warfare and counterterrorism operations are prone to horizontal escalation as state actors broaden the scope of conflict in efforts to eliminate enemy sanctuaries or punish third-party states supporting the irregular combatants. These conflicts also invite vertical escalation, with states employing ever-greater numbers of conventional forces in efforts to defeat nonstate adversaries. Even seemingly benign peace operations can escalate into dangerous crises, as the U.S. experience in Beirut, Lebanon, and the post–Cold War debacle in Mogadishu, Somalia, demonstrate.

In all the cases examined, state actors enjoyed dramatic asymmetric strengths in conventional force, and they often attempted to employ those strengths to gain escalation dominance against their irregular adversaries. In doing so, they frequently scored impressive tactical victories and achieved a range of operational objectives; however, rarely did they succeed in applying their asymmetric strengths in ways relevant to the strategic objectives in the conflict. In cases where conventional force was effective, it was used primarily to provide security for populations threatened by terrorists or insurgents. Alternatively, when offensive operations were emphasized, most often, conventional escalation ultimately served the irregular adversary's cause.

Escalation management is inherently difficult with nonstate actors for an assortment of reasons, not the least of which is that it depends largely on deterrence. For deterrence to hold force, parties to a conflict must be interested in limiting their costs, and each must be able to credibly threaten its adversaries with prospects of punishment should they attempt to escalate, a condition that is more the exception than the norm in conflicts between states and irregular adversaries. Global jihadists have been particularly unresponsive to threats of punishment to date, largely because such threats are difficult to make credible against elusive groups that reject the established order. Unlike other terrorist organizations, such as the IRA, the PLO, and even Hizballah—groups invested in territory and that, in addition to their terrorist activities, pursue interests in the legitimate political arena—jihadists have little or no territory, visible infrastructure, or political capital to protect and, therefore, have little that one can hold at risk. Alternatively, deterrence via denial has some effect: One can deter terrorists from attacking certain targets by defending those targets more aggressively, thereby denying adversaries the ability to escalate along certain lines, but such aspects of deterrence make only limited contributions to escalation management, because jihadists can simply shift their attacks to lesser-defended targets. Until a way can be found to credibly threaten something that the jihadists hold dear, we should expect them to escalate to the maximum extent of their capability.

Consequently, traditional two-player escalation management is disabled in the struggle with radical Islam, and limiting costs in this long-term conflict will present a more complicated challenge: U.S. forces must seek to constrain and, ideally, eliminate their adversaries' ability to escalate the fight, but they must do so in ways that minimize the escalatory effects that U.S. actions and those of the jihadists have on other actors in the environment. Put another way, the United States must fashion and execute a strategy that maximizes its immediate security, but that does not, in doing so, jeopardize its victory in the more important long-term political contest. Such a strategy should emphasize concentrating visible efforts in the diplomatic and judicial arenas. The United States and its partners should avoid militarizing the conflict to the maximum extent possible. Efforts should focus on cooperation and foreign assistance to help states build the capacity to provide for their own security. When military force is needed, the primary emphasis should be on providing security to populations threatened by terrorists or insurgents. Any employment of offensive force should be done with restraint and discretion to avoid antagonizing local citizens and thereby validating extremist propaganda and sowing the seeds of future escalation.

Recommendations for the U.S. Air Force

Escalation management is largely a matter of sound policy and good strategy, functions that lie mainly in the realm of political and joint military leadership. But there are several steps that the U.S. Air Force can take to organize, train, and equip its airmen to support these important tasks more effectively. This monograph offers the following recommendations:

- *Identify and resolve potential escalation dilemmas.* The Air Force should conduct a thorough assessment of its current and future force structure to determine if it provides the necessary flexibility to offer joint commanders proportionate responses to potential paths of enemy escalation. When gaps are identified, the Air Force should consider programming new capabilities to fill them. In cases in which fiscal or political costs might preclude developing certain weapons that potential adversaries possess (such as chemical or biological weapons), the Air Force should concentrate on developing defenses against them and working with combatant commands to develop strategies to deter their use.
- *Train air-component commanders and their staffs on the principles of escalation management.* While developing military strategy is the purview of combatant commanders under the direction of political leaders, air-component commanders and their staffs play essential roles in developing COAs, evaluating prospective COAs, and conducting operational planning. Therefore, they have a fiduciary responsibility to advise joint commanders and policymakers on the escalation risks that prospective COAs present and to offer recommendations for managing those risks. To prepare airmen for that responsibility, they need to be taught that escalation management entails more than just establishing and enforcing rules of engagement. Determining enemy escalation thresholds should be an intelligence priority before and during the campaign planning process and it should continue to be so as the fight progresses. Finally, commanders and planners should eschew plans that escalate in ways that offer tactical advantages at the risk of great strategic cost.
- *Codify the principles of escalation management in airpower doctrine.* The Air Force should revise relevant passages in its doctrine to better acknowledge the risks of escalation and the need to manage those risks. Doctrine should stress knowing the political limits

of conflict and understanding why those limits are important. It should explain the relationship of thresholds to escalation and emphasize understanding the enemy's critical thresholds and how they can change over the course of a conflict. Finally, while the ability to impose shock, paralysis, and rapid dominance may be a useful tool for the Air Force to bring to the fight, doctrine must acknowledge that such tools may not be appropriate to employ in some limited conflicts.

- *Teach escalation management in Air Force schools.* The Air Force should provide all airmen a firm grounding in the concept of limited war, the risks of escalation, and the principles of escalation management. These topics should be stressed in professional military education programs and at the School of Advanced Air and Space Studies. They should also be emphasized in war games and exercises.

APPENDIX A
China, Force, and Escalation: Continuities Between Historical Behavior and Contemporary Writings

Debate continues in the United States over whether a rising China will be increasingly militaristic and willing to use force. Until the 1990s, the dominant view of both Western and Chinese scholars was that, since imperial times, China has been a relatively peaceful country that has tried to both avoid wars and limit its actions when undertaking military conflict.[1] It was generally believed that the influence of Confucianism and Daoism or the Sun Zi teaching "to subdue the enemy without fighting" were the sources of China's relative pacifism.[2]

This scholarship has, in part, led to a widespread Chinese belief in what China scholar Andrew Scobell calls the "Cult of the Defense," a shared self-conception depicting the Chinese as a peace-loving people who are not aggressive or expansionist and who use force only in self-defense.[3] Shared beliefs such as these may become self-fulfilling expectations when they are held so strongly that they shape a kind of strategic

---

[1] For references to the many Western and Chinese scholarly works that depict China as nonaggressive and antimilitaristic, see Alastair Iain Johnston, *Cultural Realism: Strategic Culture and Grand Strategy in Chinese History*, Princeton, N.J.: Princeton University Press, 1995, p. 26; Alastair Iain Johnston, "China's Militarized Interstate Dispute Behaviour 1949–1992: A First Cut at the Data," *China Quarterly*, No. 153, March 1998, pp. 6–8; and Andrew Scobell, *China's Use of Military Force: Beyond the Great Wall and the Long March*, New York: Cambridge University Press, 2003, pp. 16–23.

[2] Johnston, 1998, p. 7.

[3] Scobell, 2003, p. 27.

culture that biases decisionmaking about the use of force.[4] However, as Scobell points out, working against these pacific elements in the Chinese self-conception are "a strong reverence for national unification and a heightened sense of threat perception," which may actually increase the likelihood of China going to war.[5]

In fact, the notion that China is more peace loving than are other countries has been called into question in recent years. In a 1998 *China Quarterly* article, China scholar Alastair Iain Johnston extracted data from the Militarized Interstate Dispute (MID) database to statistically analyze China's use of threats or military force against other states short of actually going to war between 1949 and 1992.[6] He found that during the period in question, China was the second-most dispute-prone state, with an average 2.74 MIDs per year, trumped only by the United States, with an average of 3.93 disputes per year.[7] Moreover, "while the first 15 years of [China's] existence were more dispute-prone than the subsequent 25, there has been a fairly constant level of hostility and violence across Chinese MIDs up to the end of the 1980s."[8]

---

[4] The concept of strategic culture has been vigorously debated in the security studies literature. Scholars disagree as to how to define strategic culture, whether strategic cultures really exist, and, if so, by what mechanisms they affect the behavior of states and other international actors. For a critique of this debate and a theoretical construction of how culture influences decisionmaking, see Forrest E. Morgan, *Compellence and the Strategic Culture of Imperial Japan: Implications for Coercive Diplomacy in the Twenty-First Century*, Westport, Conn.: Praeger, 2003, pp. 5–8, 15–36.

[5] Scobell, 2003, p. 28.

[6] The MID data are compiled by the Correlates of War research group at the University of Michigan, which defines MIDs as "united historical cases in which the threat, display or use of military force short of war by one member state is explicitly directed towards the government, official representatives, official forces, property, or territory of another state" (Daniel M. Jones, Stuart A. Bremer, and J. David Singer, "Militarized Interstate Disputes, 1816–1992: Rationale, Coding Rules, and Empirical Patterns," *Conflict Management and Peace Science*, Vol. 15, No. 2, 1996, p. 168). This definition is also quoted in Johnston, 1998, p. 5.

[7] Johnston, 1998, p. 9.

[8] Johnston, 1998, p. 17. When Johnston did this work, MID data were available only through 1992. They are now available through 2001. Calculating the frequency with which China threatened, displayed, or used force from 1993 through 2001 yields an average of 2.89

In addition, Johnston observed that once China was in a militarized dispute, it "tended to resort to a higher level of force than other major powers."[9]

Adding to Johnston's findings, some observers point to what they describe as diverging trends in certain aspects of Chinese behavior. Although Beijing's tendency to resort to force (as opposed to threats alone) has declined in recent decades, the PLA's concepts for military operations have, if anything, increased their emphasis on offensive action.[10] This seemingly paradoxical behavior can be understood by distinguishing between changes in Beijing's grand strategy as it evolves in the post-Mao and post–Cold war eras and the PLA's recent efforts to revise its operational doctrines to employ its increasingly modern military forces against technologically sophisticated adversaries. During the Maoist era, China's leaders viewed the world in extraordinarily competitive terms and exhibited a confrontational attitude in international relations. Yet the PLA's strategic thinking was highly defensive. It mostly lacked the capability to fight wars beyond China's borders and declined to develop those capabilities even to the extent possible, preferring instead to draw enemies into the country and defeat them there.

However, in the decade and a half after Mao's death, Beijing's outlook began to change, and as the post–Cold War order took shape in the years that followed, China developed a grand strategy aimed at achieving great power status through market-led economic growth.[11] Such a strategy required maintaining amicable relations with other powers and relying to a greater extent on cooperative participation

---

MIDs per year (Faten Ghosn and Scott Bennett, *Codebook for the Dyadic Militarized Interstate Incident Data*, Version 3.0, 2003; using data set MIDB 3.02.csv as of June 27, 2007).

[9] Johnston, 1998, p. 15.

[10] We would like to thank our RAND colleague Eric Heginbotham for clarifying this distinction.

[11] See Michael D. Swaine and Ashley J. Tellis, *Interpreting China's Grand Strategy: Past, Present, and Future*, Santa Monica, Calif.: RAND Corporation, MR-1121-AF, 2000, and Avery Goldstein, *Rising to the Challenge: China's Grand Strategy and International Security*, Stanford, Calif.: Stanford University Press, 2005.

in regional and global multilateral institutions for conflict resolution. At the same time, however, the PLA began developing capabilities to project force beyond China's borders, enabling it to replace the defensive concepts that characterized its thinking in the Cold War era with operational doctrines that emphasize seizing the initiative. Nevertheless, despite these changes, the following analysis will demonstrate that there have been notable threads of continuity in Chinese thinking about how to use force and escalation in military operations from 1949 to the present.

Changes in grand strategy and operational doctrine aside, China's greater propensity to use force during the Maoist era may have been driven by two other factors. The first is the frequency with which China was involved in territorial disputes, owing to its size and Beijing's sensitivity to threats to Chinese territory. During the Cold War, the PRC had land and ocean borders with 15 to 21 states. As Johnston asserts, new states are generally "more sensitive to territorial issues because the territorial integrity of the state will be central to establishing the legitimacy of the regime."[12] A second reason for China's use of military force during that period may be explained by inconsistency theory. According to this theory, when there is a perception of a large gap between the status desired by an actor and the status ascribed or bestowed by other actors, the frequency of conflicts should increase.[13] Data drawn from the MID database suggest that during periods when Chinese leaders were likely dissatisfied with what they perceived to be China's status in the eyes of other states, the propensity for entering into disputes did increase. Conversely, during periods when China was more satisfied with its perceived international status, it was less likely to enter into disputes. Whatever the reasons, the research suggests that, since 1949, China has not shied away from using force and, in fact, is a state that has frequently threatened and employed force to resolve disputes.

Andrew Scobell's work also challenges the notion that China is more prone to peaceful dispute resolution than are other countries. He argues that Chinese strategic culture is really a blend of realpolitik and

---

[12] Johnston, 1998, p. 17.

[13] Johnston, 1998, pp. 25–26.

a belief that China consistently prefers nonviolent solutions to interstate disputes.[14] This mixture of hard-nosed international behavior and pacific self-perception has led to a belief that China fights only "just wars" of self-defense. In fact, many military actions have been deemed self-defense counterattacks by the Chinese government.

Although the Chinese may widely believe that their country uses military force only as a last resort, China has engaged in many military conflicts since 1949, including several against Taiwan, the United States, India, the Soviet Union, and Vietnam. In each instance, Chinese leaders rationalized taking military action, and even striking first in some cases, on the basis of territorial sovereignty and national integrity. In fact, analyses of historical patterns in China's use of force suggest a preference for preemption and surprise to inflict shock on military adversaries and their political leaders, even during periods when the PLA's operational concepts were couched in defensive terms.[15] All of this suggests that the Chinese belief that their country only fights just wars and that these wars are purely defensive may lead China to resort to force more quickly in a dispute and Beijing may be more difficult to deter. The notion of China as inherently peaceful may also hinder the ability of Chinese leaders to recognize that actions they see as purely defensive may appear threatening to other countries.[16] This may especially be true in a conflict over Taiwan, which China regards as its territory.

However, once again, we should distinguish the views of political leaders from those of operational military planners. Efforts made in recent years to improve transparency with India and several central Asian neighbors and engage them in confidence-building measures suggest that senior Chinese leaders now recognize that those states might view some of China's defensive actions as threatening. Unfortunately, writings recently published in military journals and theoretical

---

[14] Scobell, 2003, p. 38.

[15] Mark Burles and Abram N. Shulsky, *Patterns in China's Use of Force: Evidence from History and Doctrinal Writings*, Santa Monica, Calif.: RAND Corporation, MR-1160-AF, 2000, pp. 5–21.

[16] Scobell, 2003, p. 198.

treatises suggest that Chinese military thinkers have not reached the same conclusion.

In fact, China's self-image as a just, nonaggressive power finds particular expression in how it plans to fight wars, especially in the strategic guiding concept of active defense. Active defense was first formulated by Mao Zedong in the 1930s with regard to operations against the Nationalist forces that had surrounded the Communists. According to Mao, defensive operations are divided into active defense and passive defense. Active defense is described as "offensive defense or defense through decisive engagements" and is "for the purpose of counter-attacking and taking the offensive." Mao then adds, "Only a complete fool or a madman would cherish passive defense."[17]

The strategic principle of active defense has been reformulated into a more offense-oriented concept in modern Chinese writings on the operational level of war. According to an internally distributed Chinese military book, *The Science of Campaigns*, "The core of the strategic principle of active defense is to actively seize the initiative and to annihilate the enemy and requires being based on conducting operations from one's own territory and gaining mastery after the enemy has struck."[18] Because the strategic guideline of active defense is couched in terms of protecting national sovereignty and territorial integrity, it reinforces the Chinese belief that the country fights only just wars. Campaigns fought using the strategic principle of active defense are conducted by seizing the initiative through offensive strikes. In the context of escalation management, it is particularly important to recognize that, in conducting active defense, China intends to "mobilize all forces that can be mobilized and utilize all operational methods in order to form a military force that can defeat the enemy."[19]

Yet any strategic concept that emphasizes gaining mastery only after the enemy has struck would seem to have an inherent weak-

---

[17] Mao Zedong, *Selected Military Writings of Mao Tse-Tung*, Beijing: Foreign Languages Press, 1967, p. 105.

[18] Wang Houqing and Zhang Xingye, eds., *Zhanyixue* [*The Science of Military Campaigns*], Beijing: National Defense University Press, 2000a, p. 90.

[19] Wang and Zhang, 2000a, p. 90.

ness, given the speed with which modern conventional warfare is conducted, a detail not lost on Chinese military analysts. PLA strategists have closely studied U.S. military performance since Operation Desert Storm in 1991 and have come to understand that modern war is rapid and highly destructive and may consist of only one campaign with overall victory depending on success in the opening clash.[20] As one *Liberation Army Daily* article argues, "In a high-tech local war, a belligerent which adopts a passive defensive strategy and launches no offensive against the enemy is bound to fold its hands and await destruction."[21] Chinese analysts fully recognize that the strategies used by Iraq in Operation Desert Storm and Operation Iraqi Freedom led to its defeat and that permitting the U.S. military to become fully prepared before launching an operation will enable it to gain the upper hand. In the words of PLA Major General Lu Linzhi,

> If [the PLA] just sits there and waits for the enemy to complete assembling its full array of troops, China's fighting potential will certainly be more severely jeopardized because the enemy will then be in a position to put its overall combat superiority to good use, making it more difficult for China to win the war.[22]

Lu then concludes that the military that firsts seizes the initiative will achieve victory, writing,

> In a limited high-tech war, where the pace of action is fast and the duration short, a campaign often takes on a make-or-break char-

---

[20] Nan Li, "The PLA's Evolving Campaign Doctrine and Strategies," in James C. Mulvenon and Richard H. Yang, eds., *The People's Liberation Army in the Information Age*, Santa Monica, Calif.: RAND Corporation, CF-145-CAPP/AF, 1999, pp. 149–150.

[21] Huang Jialun, "Attach Importance to Operation at Outer Strategic Line," *Liberation Army Daily*, November 30, 1999, in Foreign Broadcast Information Service as "Operation at the Outer Strategic Line Viewed," December 14, 1999.

[22] Lu Linzhi, "Preemptive Strikes Are Crucial in Limited High-Tech Wars," *Liberation Army Daily*, February 7, 1996, in Foreign Broadcast Information Service as "Preemptive Strikes Endorsed for Limited High-Tech War," February 14, 1996.

acter. Clearly the quick and decisive battle assumes much more importance in such a war.[23]

The PLA's problems with adhering to a strategy of active defense are compounded by its self-acknowledged weaknesses in countering a military as advanced as that of the United States. In *The Science of Campaigns*, a book on military theory published by China's National Defense University Press, one passage reads,

> The most salient objective reality that the PLA will face in future campaign operations is the fact that it will be using inferior weapons to deal with an enemy that has superior arms.[24]

The passage goes on to note that the PLA's guiding concepts for military planning need to be developed with "a clear recognition of this reality."[25] Chinese analysts also acknowledge that a consequence of this deficiency is that China will likely absorb a great deal of damage and must be willing to "pay a heavy price" in any conflict with a technologically superior adversary such as the United States.[26]

Considering the requirement to gain the upper hand early in a war and the prospect of fighting a technologically superior opponent, how does the PLA propose to fight and win a high-tech local war while adhering to the strategic principle of active defense? If the emphasis in Chinese writings is a reliable indication, it intends to do so by seizing the initiative through surprise or preemption. According to *The Science of Campaigns*,

> Taking the enemy by surprise would catch it unprepared, would cause confusion in and huge psychological pressure on the enemy,

---

[23] Lu, 1996.

[24] See Wang and Zhang, 2000a, especially Chapter 3, on the "Objective Conditions of the PLA."

[25] Wang and Zhang, 2000a, p. 467.

[26] See, for example, Jiang Lei, *Xiandai Yi Lie Sheng You Zhanlue* [*Modern Strategy for Using the Inferior to Defeat the Superior*], Beijing: National Defense University Press, 1997, pp. 111–112.

and would help one win relatively large victories at relatively small costs.[27]

The timing of a surprise attack is critical. According to some Chinese analysts, the best time to conduct a surprise attack is during the deployment phase of a U.S. operation.[28] Similarly, the authors of a Chinese book on U.S. military strategy view the deployment phase as a critical period of weakness for the United States:

> In the opening stage, it is impossible to rapidly transfer enormous forces to the battlefield. Thus, [the the United States] is unable to establish superiority of forces and firepower, and it is easy for the U.S. military to be forced into a passive position from the start; this could very possibly have an impact on the process and outcome of the conflict.[29]

Preemptive strikes are also discussed in Chinese writings. If seizing the initiative at the beginning of battle is critical to the success of an operation, preemptively striking an opponent may be the best means of winning a war. A quick strike prior to or quickly following a formal declaration of hostilities could disrupt U.S. deployment of forces to the region, place the United States in a passive position, and deliver a psychological blow to the United States and its allies. As Major General Lu Linzhi argues,

> This makes it imperative that China launches a preemptive strike by taking advantage of the window of opportunity present before the enemy acquires a high-tech edge or develops a full-fledged combat capability in the war zone. Through a preemptive strike, China can put good timing and geographical location and the

---

[27] Wang and Zhang, 2000a, pp. 108–110.

[28] See, for example, Lu, 1996, and Nan Li, "The PLA's Evolving Warfighting Doctrine, Strategy and Tactics, 1985–95: A Chinese Perspective," *China Quarterly*, No. 146, June 1996, p. 457.

[29] Pan Xiangting and Sun Zhanping, eds., *Gao Jishu Tiaojian Xia Meijun Jubu Zhanzheng* [*The U.S. Military in Local Wars Under High-Tech Conditions*], Beijing: Liberation Army Press, 1994, p. 238.

support of the people to good use by making a series of offensive moves to destroy the enemy's ability to deploy high-tech weapons and troops and limit its ability to acquire a high-tech edge in the war zone, thus weakening its capacity to mount a powerful offensive. This is the only way to steer the course of the war in a direction favorable to China.[30]

These aspects of China's active defense strategy appear to conflict with the tenet of attacking only after the enemy has struck. Yet preemptive strikes and surprise attacks are viewed as consistent with a strategy of active defense:

The so-called preemptive strike means taking a series of decisive offensive actions in a battle to attack key targets of the enemy's in-depth campaign formations, diminishing its high-tech edge, impairing its readiness to attack, and creating an advantageous combat situation, all within a strategic framework of gaining mastery by striking only after the enemy has struck.[31]

This paradox is explained by defining the enemy's first strike as any "military activities conducted by the enemy aimed at breaking up China territorially and violating its sovereignty." By this definition, any military support or deployment in response to a military crisis could be interpreted as a "military activity aimed at breaking up China" and thereby could be rendered the equivalent of a "strategic first shot" that could serve as sufficient pretext for the PLA to launch a military strike against U.S. forces.[32]

China's Use of Force, 1950–1996: Eight Cases

This section serves to illuminate the previous discussion with an examination of the escalatory nature of China's use of force between 1950

---

[30] Lu, 1996.
[31] Lu, 1996.
[32] Lu, 1996.

and 1996. The analysis involves eight case studies: the Korean War, the 1954 operations against offshore islands, the 1958 shelling of Jinmen, the 1962 Sino-Indian conflict, China's involvement in the Vietnam War, the 1969 Sino-Soviet conflict, the 1979 Sino-Vietnam war, and the 1995–1996 Taiwan Strait exercises.

Evidence from this analysis supports Alastair Iain Johnston's assertion that territorial disputes have played a significant role in China's decision to use force. Territorial disputes were at play in six of the eight case studies (the exceptions being the Korean War and China's involvement in the Vietnam War). In four of the case studies (the 1954 operations against the offshore islands, the 1958 shelling of Jinmen, the 1962 Sino-Indian conflict, and the 1995–1996 Taiwan Strait exercises), territorial disputes were the prime motivation for China to use force, though it must be stressed that the operations in 1954, 1958, and even those in 1995 and 1996 can be seen as extensions of China's civil war.

Other motives for China's use of force include the desire to eliminate a threat on China's periphery, to contain the power of a regional competitor, and to reinforce China's image as a regional power. In the Korean War and in China's involvement in the Vietnam War, Beijing intervened in regional conflicts to deny a powerful adversary—the United States—access to territories on its periphery. In the 1969 Sino-Soviet conflict, China provoked a series of clashes on disputed islands in the Ussuri River to assert its military power in an effort to deter what Beijing perceived to be the risk of a Soviet intervention to stem the chaos of the Cultural Revolution.[33] Similarly, when China invaded Vietnam in 1979, Deng Xiaoping, then the de facto leader of China following Mao's death, said the objective was to "teach Vietnam a lesson" for invading and defeating Beijing's client state, Cambodia. However, tensions over escalating clashes along disputed stretches of the Sino-Vietnamese border, alleged mistreatment of Chinese residents in Vietnam, and the growing sense of encirclement that arose when Hanoi and Moscow signed a treaty of friendship and cooperation were

---

[33] Allen S. Whiting, "China's Use of Force, 1950–96, and Taiwan," *International Security*, Vol. 26, No. 2, Fall 2001, p. 117.

other factors that probably contributed to Beijing's decision to assert China's power.[34]

An examination of these cases also suggests that China's approach to military operations will pose challenges for escalation management in the event of a limited Sino-U.S. conflict. In five of the eight cases, China's operations were consistent with its strategic guideline of active defense and its emphasis on seizing the initiative early in a conflict. With the exception of China's support to Vietnam in the 1960s, the Sino-Indian conflict, and the Taiwan Straight exercises, China used significant force against its adversaries before they attacked, and in some cases, this force was massive. If Beijing continues this pattern in future conflicts, adversaries may have difficulty regaining the initiative or compelling China to deescalate.

But, significantly, while China has projected force beyond its borders eight times during the period in question and has used overwhelming force on some occasions, in each case, Beijing has also contained its use of force, in terms of both objectives and operations. For example, in all of the border disputes, save those involving Taiwan, China has withdrawn to its original LOCs once the operations were over. In fact, in the Sino-Indian and Sino-Vietnamese conflicts, China withdrew after taking considerable amounts of enemy territory. Conversely, one operational limitation imposed in nearly every conflict was on airpower. During the Korean War, People's Liberation Army Air Force (PLAAF) aircraft were not permitted to strike targets south of the 38th parallel. During the 1958 assault against Jinmen, aircraft were not permitted to bomb the island if Nationalist aircraft did not bomb the mainland. In conflicts with India in 1962, the Soviets in 1969, and the Vietnamese in 1979, neither side used airpower to provide close air support or to provide air cover.[35] And during the Taiwan Strait exercises, although the PLAAF deployed as many as 300 aircraft to coastal bases and employed them in a series of joint military maneuvers designed to intimidate Taiwanese voters during legislative and presi-

---

[34] Whiting, 2001, pp. 119–120.

[35] During the Sino-Soviet conflict, Soviet aircraft did make numerous passes on Chinese positions but never actually attacked.

dential elections, the planes stayed well away from Taiwan and the two U.S. carrier TFs deployed to the area in response to the exercises.[36]

It is difficult to determine why China did not employ airpower in these cases. One explanation may be that the PLAAF simply lacked the ability to conduct the kind of air operations required or, perhaps, it faced other operational constraints. For instance, in the invasion of Vietnam, the rugged mountains in the area of operations would have made effective close air support difficult, and the presence of Vietnam's advanced air defense systems would have made it costly, as the PLAAF lacked the sophisticated equipment and skills needed to suppress them.[37]

However, it is also clear that, in some cases, China limited air operations to prevent expansion of the conflict and to avoid air strikes against its own territory. The restriction on bombing below the 38th parallel during the Korean War, the prohibition against bombing Jinmen, and the tight constraints on airpower during the 1995–1996 exercises are three examples. During the Vietnam War, China provided North Vietnam extensive logistical, engineering, and air defense support, but it did not provide airpower. In fact, North Vietnamese aircraft that traveled to China for maintenance could not go directly to or from combat operations for fear of giving the appearance that China was being used as a sanctuary.[38]

It is unclear why China refrained from using airpower in its conflicts with India and the Soviet Union. In the Indian case, it may have reflected Beijing's desire to limit the conflict, which would have been consistent with China's many overtures to resolve the issue peacefully and other constraints Beijing placed on military action. In the Soviet case, China's self-restraint may have stemmed once again from a desire to limit the conflict, or it may have reflected a conscious decision to avoid clashing with a more capable air force, a contest that would have

---

[36] Whiting, 2001, pp. 120–123.

[37] Harlan W. Jencks, "China's 'Punitive' War on Vietnam: A Military Assessment," *Asian Survey*, Vol. 19, No. 8, August 1979, p. 809.

[38] Allen S. Whiting, *The Chinese Calculus of Deterrence*, Ann Arbor, Mich.: University of Michigan Press, 1975, p. 180.

been all the more mismatched given the deleterious effects that the Cultural Revolution had on the PLAAF during that period. Such calculated self-restraint was also apparent when facing superior U.S. airpower during the Korean War, suggesting that Chinese leaders have cannily avoided escalating conflicts along dimensions that would place them at a tactical disadvantage.

In several cases following the Korean War, Chinese leaders were highly motivated to avoid another direct confrontation with the United States, and Beijing limited its use of airpower accordingly. During the 1954 operations against the offshore islands, the PLA was ordered to avoid contact with the U.S. military and to fire only in self-defense, and then only if it would not put Chinese forces at risk. Operations were temporarily suspended while the U.S. Navy conducted an exercise in the region, then resumed after the U.S. ships departed the area due to the typhoon season. During the 1958 Jinmen operation, Mao ruled out an invasion and only authorized shelling the island. Ultimately, he was willing to accept defeat to avoid widening the conflict. During the Vietnam War, China provided air defense troops, which, according to Chinese accounts, shot down numerous U.S. aircraft, but Beijing kept quiet about the presence of these troops in North Vietnam in an effort to minimize U.S. domestic reaction. China, however, did promise to provide an increasing level of support, depending on how the United States escalated the conflict, including the use of ground troops in the case of a U.S. invasion of North Vietnam.

China's efforts to reduce risks of confrontation and escalation with the United States during the 1995–1996 exercises are particularly noteworthy. Although the PLA fired numerous ballistic missiles into ocean areas in the vicinity of Taiwan on several occasions, the missiles were unarmed and the launch schedules were announced in advance. More importantly, in February 1996, Beijing explicitly informed Washington that no attack on Taiwan would take place during the exercises, and the two countries subsequently established a high-level dialog throughout the remainder of the episode to minimize risks of misunderstanding.[39]

---

[39] Whiting, 2001, p. 123.

China's objectives were also quite limited in most of the cases examined. In one prominent exception, the Korean War, China wanted to remove all foreign forces from the peninsula. In the Sino-Indian conflict, however, Beijing's only objective was to restore the original boundary; the Chinese did not intend to advance deep into Indian territory, and they withdrew to the status quo ante at the operation's conclusion. During the Vietnam War, China's main goal was to deter the United States from invading North Vietnam, though it was prepared to engage in a large-scale war if deterrence failed. In its 1979 war with Vietnam, China meant only to punish its smaller southern neighbor, and Beijing sought to forestall Soviet intervention by publicly announcing that it would not advance into the Red River delta. In the confusing conflict with the Soviet Union, Chinese intentions appear limited to demonstrating its strength to its powerful neighbor to the north. In the 1995–1996 exercises, China engaged in coercive diplomacy, demonstrating its ability to project force beyond its borders to intimidate Taiwanese voters and discourage them from supporting pro-independence candidates in the legislative and presidential elections.

The Jinmen operation provided an opportunity to examine the escalation dynamics present in a three-party conflict: one involving China, Taiwan, and the United States. During this conflict, there was a universal perception on the part of U.S. government officials that the Nationalists were both holding back in their defense of Jinmen and overstating the threat posed to Jinmen to involve the United States more deeply in Taiwan's defense. Such posturing might have put considerable pressure on Washington to escalate had U.S. leaders been taken in by it. In addition, when the Nationalists recommended courses of action, they tended to focus on attacking the mainland instead of operations directly related to the relief of the garrison on Jinmen. These recommendations were viewed as too escalatory by the United States and were denied.

Conclusions

Trying to predict future behavior based on historical case studies is fraught with difficulty. Changes in international status, society, leadership, and military capabilities may lead to altered perceptions, goals, and conduct. Moreover, threats faced in future conflicts, and the domestic and international contexts in which those threats manifest, may differ so greatly from those in earlier cases that states may behave in ways that depart significantly from historical patterns.[40]

In many ways, today's China is clearly not the China of yore. Once surrounded by unfriendly states and plagued by border disputes, China has largely come to terms with its neighbors and resolved its territorial issues with all of them, except in the border dispute with India; contested claims on several small, unoccupied islands; and, of course, Taiwan. Indeed, seven of the eight cases of Chinese force employment examined for this study occurred before 1980. Since then, China's economy has roughly quadrupled in size, and its revolutionary leaders are no longer in power. Having changed its grand strategy to one emphasizing market-led development, China is becoming more ensconced in international norms and is more respected in the international community. At the same time, its military is much more capable and possesses world-class technology in selected niches.

Some of these changes suggest that China will be more restrained in its future use of force, more cautious about engaging in armed conflict, and more sensitive to the risks of escalation once combat commences. In most of the cases examined, China was a relatively young state, insecure in its standing and dominated by an aggressive leader willing to take risks. Beijing's political decisionmaking dynamic is now much changed. Today, no leader has the charisma or power of Mao. Former President Jiang Zemin was referred to as the core of the third-generation leadership, while the current top leaders are blandly described as the Party Central Committee with Comrade Hu Jintao as general secretary. Much of the decisionmaking is now done through consensus building, which may make it more difficult to go to war,

---

[40] Whiting, 1975, p. 196.

particularly given that China is heavily invested in the global economic system.

Yet China's increasing military capability and the growing sophistication of its operational concepts may also change Beijing's decision calculus about using force to advance China's regional interests. China now has modern fighter aircraft, comparable in performance to fourth-generation U.S. and Taiwanese models, capable of conducting air strikes against Taiwan. China's conventional ballistic missile arsenal and its submarine fleet continue to expand in numbers and increase in quality. And China is quickly developing the technology and expertise to project force beyond its borders in support of what Beijing calls "local wars under high-tech conditions."[41] In short, China's increasing military capabilities may give it more confidence, allowing it to be less constrained in its use of force than it has been in the past.

The PLA's growing prowess may also encourage Beijing to be more assertive in a confrontation with the United States. Chinese military analysts assume that the PLA will face the U.S. military in a confrontation over Taiwan and are devising ways to defeat a technologically superior opponent. Chinese writings are increasingly focusing on asymmetric strategies and information warfare to defeat the United States. These new operational concepts, coupled with improving technology, may give the Chinese government increased confidence that it can successfully strike at the U.S. military and accept the costs that may result from the ensuing conflict.

While there are vast differences between today's China and the China of Mao's era, there are also continuities that will be important to understand for managing escalation in the event that Washington finds itself in a confrontation with Beijing. First, the recent scholarship refuting notions that cultural factors somehow restrain China's use of force is just as relevant for future conflicts as it is concerning historical cases. China is no more peaceful than any other country and cannot be expected to refrain from the use of force out of cultural predilection.

However, where culture does matter is in how China's self-conception enables Chinese leaders to rationalize their use of force in

---

[41] Burles and Shulsky, 2000, pp. 29–32.

terms of self-defense. The Chinese appear to have a tautological belief that China fights only just wars in defense of Chinese sovereignty and territorial integrity, and, thus, all future military actions, even those that China initiates, will be justified because they will somehow involve defending Chinese sovereignty and territorial integrity. Consequently, because Chinese leaders see China as fighting only just wars, deterring China from using force or escalating a conflict may be difficult. In fact, attempts to deter Chinese escalation or to persuade China to deescalate may require strong demonstrations of force. Yet attempting to manage escalation in such a manner risks further aggravating Chinese perceptions of threat and intensifying Beijing's belief in the righteousness of further resistance. This could lead to a contest for escalation dominance that would be costly—and potentially catastrophic—for both sides.

If China decides to conduct a military operation, it may attempt to seize the initiative through surprise or preemption. This has been a frequent element in the historical pattern, and contemporary writings suggest that it remains a common theme in Chinese strategic thought. When Beijing decides to enter a conflict, the initial action could involve a wide range of weaponry and operational methods, and it could be quite intense, presenting a significant challenge for escalation management.

Chinese military writings suggest that the PLA prefers to use overwhelming force when it engages in combat, but the evidence from historical cases reveals that Beijing has usually placed substantial constraints on the PLA's use of force. These constraints have been imposed on the PLA's objectives, geographic scope, targets, and operational methods and have, among other things, served to reduce the chances of conflict with the United States and to avoid attacks on the Chinese mainland. This suggests two things: First, Chinese leaders understand the importance of limiting escalation, and second, Beijing may consider attacks on the Chinese mainland a significant escalation threshold.

Finally, should the United States find itself in a conflict with China over Taiwan, Washington will need to appreciate how the behavior of U.S. allies may affect the escalation dynamics. Particularly important are the actions of Taiwan's government. In the Jinmen conflict, Taiwanese leaders tried to shift an inordinate share of the burden for defending the Nationalist regime to the United States by downplaying Taiwan's defensive capabilities and overstating the threat from the mainland. Taiwan's current resistance to increasing its defense spending and recent statements by Taiwanese leaders about U.S. promises to defend their country suggest a similar mindset today.[42] Such a position could tempt Chinese adventurism by leading Beijing to believe that Taipei is timid about its own defense. Conversely, in the event of a conflict, Taiwan's military enthusiasm for attacking the Chinese mainland could complicate U.S. efforts to manage escalation.

---

[42] See, for example, "Parris Chang Says the US, Japan Will Defend Taiwan," Central News Agency, August 14, 2005.

APPENDIX B
Case Studies of Escalation in Stability Operations

This appendix examines two cases that illustrate the escalation dynamics that emerge when states attempt to stabilize ungoverned territories: Beirut, 1982–1984, and Mogadishu, 1992–1994. These case studies are not definitive accounts of the operations examined; rather, they focus on the difficulties states face in managing escalation when they undertake such challenges.

Beirut, 1982–1984

On October 23, 1983, a suicide bomber drove a truck loaded with the equivalent of more than 12,000 lbs of TNT into the U.S. Marine Corps Battalion Landing Team headquarters at Beirut International Airport, killing 241 military personnel and wounding 100 others.[1] Almost simultaneously, a similar truck bomb exploded at the French military barracks approximately two miles away, killing 58 paratroopers and wounding 15 others. The U.S. Marines and French soldiers were part of an MNF comprised of military components from France, Italy, and the United States that had come to Beirut more than a year earlier and also included troops from the United Kingdom, which had joined the effort in February 1993. Initially seen as impartial peacekeepers, the MNF was welcomed by noncombatants and tolerated by the many armed factions contesting for control of Lebanon's anarchic

---

[1] U.S. fatalities in the October 23 attack included 220 marines and 21 other U.S. military personnel.

territory. However, during the ensuing months, violent confrontations between the MNF and local combatants escalated in frequency and intensity, culminating in the catastrophic attacks of October 1983. To understand the dynamics driving this escalation, we must briefly examine the circumstances leading to the MNF's initial deployment in August 1982 and then review the chain of events that occurred after the forces arrived.

By the time the MNF landed in Beirut, Lebanon had already suffered several waves of anarchy and foreign intervention since civil war erupted in 1975. Earlier, the country's parliamentary "confessional" government, based on a 1926 constitution and a 1943 national pact, had established a delicate balance of power between the roughly half of Lebanon's citizens who were Christian and the Sunni and Shiite Muslims and Druze, who, collectively, constituted the other half.[2] The Lebanese were able to maintain this balance for more than two decades following the nation's 1946 independence from France, with clan and sectarian leaders brokering compromises on domestic issues as they arose. But sectarian relations grew strained as the Christians, who led the armed forces and held the presidency, became increasingly affluent while the Muslim and Druze segments of the population remained poor but grew proportionately larger as Palestinian refugees flowed into the country, fleeing the 1948 and 1967 Arab-Israeli Wars.[3] The tenuous balance was finally upset when the PLO arrived in late 1970, having been expelled from Jordan. Allying itself with dissident Muslims, the PLO militarized those factions, and the Christians formed their own private militias in response. When civil war broke out in 1975, the government of Lebanon found itself unable to employ the LAF to quell the insurrection for fear that it would fracture along sec-

---

[2] Lebanese Christians include Catholic and Orthodox groups and the politically dominant Maronites, a sect that existed in relative isolation from mainstream Christianity in the region of Mount Lebanon from the early Christian era until modern times. The Druze, a sect with a secret doctrine believed to be a blend of mystic Islamic and Christian tenets, also developed in relative isolation in the Shouf mountain range east of Beirut.

[3] By the time the civil war broke out in 1975, the Christian percentage of the population had shrunk to around 39 percent, and the Muslim and Druze proportion had grown to 59 percent.

tarian lines. Thereafter, the government functioned only sporadically, as multiple armed factions contested for power. Figure B.1 shows the geographical distribution of religious groups in 1983, just before the following events took place.

The next seven years saw successive waves of anarchy and foreign intervention interspersed with periods of relative calm. In 1976, hoping to preclude an Israeli invasion, Syria intervened on behalf of Lebanon's Christian president and imposed a temporary peace. Token forces from other Arab League countries joined Syria's 27,000 troops later that year, and the newly legitimized Arab Deterrent Force remained in the country, ostensibly to assure stability.[4] Nevertheless, the IDF invaded southern Lebanon in March 1978 to quell the tide of cross-border PLO attacks in Israel. The IDF withdrew later that year but turned the territory bordering Israel over to a Christian militia ally, the South Lebanese Army. In an effort to stabilize the situation, the United Nations established the UN Interim Force in Lebanon (UNFIL) to monitor the Israeli-Lebanese border, but PLO attacks resumed and intensified over the next several years.

On June 6, 1982, the IDF invaded Lebanon again, determined to eliminate the festering security threat on Israel's northern border. The IDF's operational objectives were to create a deeper security zone in southern Lebanon, neutralize the PLO's military and political power, and push Syrian troops out of the country. Beyond that, the Israelis hoped to break the political stalemate in Beirut and enable the establishment of a stable Christian government that would be friendly to Tel Aviv.[5] Within three days, the IDF reached the capital and linked

---

[4] The Arab Deterrent Force was a 30,000-strong military contingent constituted and funded by the Arab League in October 1976. It was, ostensibly, a pan-Arab peacekeeping force under command of the Lebanese president, but it was composed mainly of Syrian troops who reported to Damascus. See Richard W. Nelson, "Multinational Peacekeeping in the Middle East and the United Nations Model," in Anthony McDermott and Kjell Skjelsbaek, eds., *The Multinational Force in Beirut, 1982–1984*, Miami, Fla.: Florida International University Press, 1991, p. 11.

[5] Long Commission Report, 1983, p. 27. See also Nelson, 1991, pp. 8–9, and U.S. Department of State, Bureau of Near Eastern Affairs, "Background Note: Lebanon," February 2007.

200 Dangerous Thresholds: Managing Escalation in the 21st Century

Figure B.1
Geographical Distribution of Religious Groups in Lebanon as of 1983

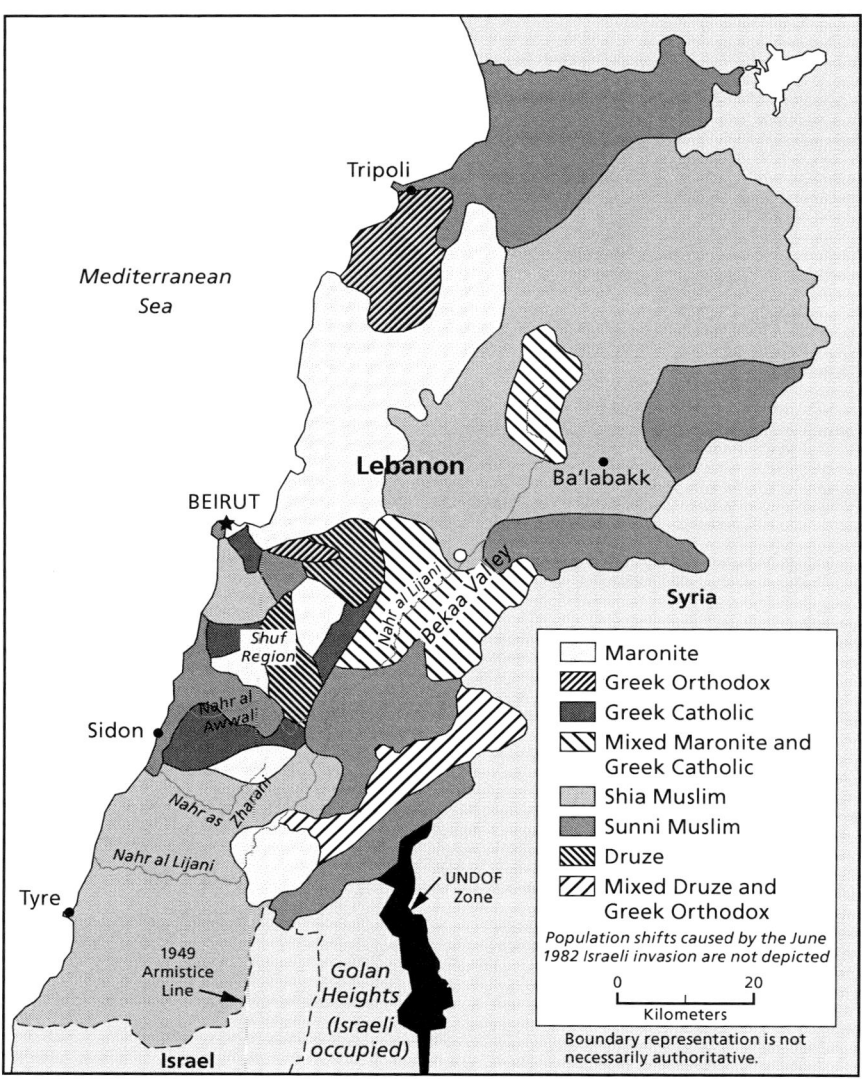

SOURCE: Central Intelligence Agency, Perry Castaneda Map Collection, University of Texas at Austin, 1983. Courtesy of the University of Texas Libraries, University of Texas at Austin.

RAND MG614-B.1

up with the Christian Lebanese Forces (LF) militia in East Beirut. Bolstered by the presence of the IDF, the LF began its own offensive against the Druze militia on June 28, engaging the Druze in their Shouf mountains stronghold east of Beirut. By July 2, the Israelis had blockaded Arab West Beirut, laying siege to more than 10,000 PLO fighters, along with 3,613 Syrian soldiers of the Arab Deterrent Force and several hundred foreign noncombatants, also mainly Syrian. The stage was set for a major urban battle that would have been costly for combatants and noncombatants alike.[6]

Over the next month and a half, diplomats from several countries frantically attempted to mediate a peaceful resolution to the siege while the IDF periodically bombarded West Beirut from the air and shelled the Muslim sector with artillery, tanks, and gunboats. Finally, the United States, at the request of the Lebanese government, persuaded the combatants to permit the insertion of an MNF to peacefully evacuate the Arab fighters.[7]

On August 25, 1982, a contingent of 850 U.S. marines landed in Beirut as part of the MNF that also included military components from France and Italy. Noncombatants of all factions welcomed the MNF, and the combatants accepted the intervention. President Ronald Reagan, in a speech to the American people, explained that the mission was purely humanitarian, as the United States had no strategic interest in Lebanon. U.S. troops would be out of Beirut within 30 days. Indeed, the MNF succeeded in evacuating the Arab fighters and then withdrew in early September.[8]

The immediate crisis was averted, but on September 14, Lebanese President-elect Bashir Gemayel, a Christian with Israeli backing, was assassinated in a covert bombing of his political headquarters. In response, the IDF occupied West Beirut, then stood by as Christian militia units massacred hundreds of unarmed Palestinian men, women, and children in the Sabra and Shatila refugee camps on Sep-

---

[6] Long Commission Report, 1983, p. 29; Nelson, 1991, p. 11.

[7] Nelson, 1991, pp. 9–10.

[8] Long Commission Report, 1983, p. 29; Nelson, 1991, p. 11.

tember 16–18.[9] This turn of events shocked the world, and the UN Security Council discussed sending UN observers to Beirut or moving UNFIL there from the Israeli-Lebanese border to stabilize the situation. But Lebanese officials doubted that unarmed observers could have any positive effect, and Israel indicated that the IDF would not permit UNFIL redeployment.

Consequently, at request of the government of Lebanon, the United States, France, and Italy reconstituted the MNF as MNF II. On September 26, the French and Italian contingents reentered Beirut, and on September 29, a 1,200-strong contingent of U.S. marines landed and took up positions in the vicinity of Beirut International Airport. The mission of MNF II, as agreed to in diplomatic notes exchanged between the governments of the United States and Lebanon, was broad and vague: "provide the multinational presence requested by the Lebanese government . . . to establish an environment which will permit the Lebanese Armed Forces to carry out their responsibilities in the Beirut area." Orders to the Marine contingent from the U.S. commander-in-chief, Europe, relayed this guidance and further specified that the marines were to "occupy and secure positions along a designated section of the line from south of the Beirut International Airport to a position in the vicinity of the Presidential Palace."[10] Their job was to "assist the LAF to deter the passage of hostile armed elements" into East Beirut, which, according to a November 2 change in orders, included conducting patrols in that part of the city. However, the orders made it clear that the Marines would not engage in combat and would not be responsible for the security of any given area and that peacetime ROE would be in force—that is, the use of force would be authorized only in self-defense or in the defense of any LAF unit colocated and operating with the Marines.[11]

---

[9] See Geoffrey Kemp, "The American Peacekeeping Role in Lebanon," in Anthony McDermott and Kjell Skjelsbaek, eds., *The Multinational Force in Beirut, 1982–1984*, Miami, Fla.: Florida International University Press, 1991, p. 131.

[10] Long Commission Report, 1983, p. 35.

[11] Long Commission Report, 1983, pp. 35–37.

As in the first MNF deployment, "the Marines were warmly welcomed and seemed genuinely to be appreciated by the majority of Lebanese."[12] However, the permissive environment that MNF II first enjoyed soon began to deteriorate. Interpreting their mission to assist the LAF broadly, marines undertook the task of rebuilding the Lebanese army. They began training Lebanese soldiers in small unit tactics starting in November 1982 and began helping them establish a rapid-reaction force in December.[13] This visible assistance to the Christian-led LAF began to taint the peacekeepers' impartiality in the eyes of Lebanon's non-Christian factions, and on March 16, 1983, five marines were wounded in a hand-grenade attack while on patrol.[14] More seriously, on April 18, a truck bomb destroyed the U.S. Embassy in Beirut, killing 17 U.S. citizens and 40 Lebanese.[15] The latter event triggered another enlargement of the Marines' mission—they were ordered to provide external security at the British Embassy and the Duraffourd Building, where U.S. Embassy functions were reconstituted.[16]

Meanwhile, it seemed apparent in Washington that the withdrawal of Israeli and Syrian forces was a prerequisite to establishing any national consensus in Lebanon, so U.S. diplomats increasingly urged Beirut and Israel to work toward that objective. On May 17, following a round of shuttle diplomacy by U.S. Secretary of State George Shultz, Tel Aviv signed an agreement with the government of Lebanon stipulating that a "state of war" between them no longer existed, and Israel

---

[12] Long Commission Report, 1983, p. 39.

[13] According to Eric Hammel,

> The decision to honor the Lebanese Ministry of Defense's request to help train and upgrade the sadly deficient and largely impotent Lebanese Armed Forces was casual, an attempt by a MAU commander concerned over the effects of garrison life on his highly motivated troops, an effort to allow Marines largely trapped within the BIA to kill time by doing one of the things Marines do best: training. (Eric Hammel, *The Root: The Marines in Beirut, August 1982–February 1984*, New York: Harcourt Brace Jovanovich, 1985, p. 57)

[14] The Italian contingent was also attacked that day, sustaining casualties but no fatalities.

[15] The pro-Iranian Islamic Jihad Organization claimed responsibility for the bombing (Nelson, 1991, p. 14).

[16] Kemp, 1991, p. 136; Long Commission Report, 1983, p. 37.

would withdraw the IDF if Syria would pull its forces out concurrently. Unfortunately, Syria was not party to the agreement. Damascus and Lebanon's Muslim factions were angered that it granted Israel supervisory authority over a security region in southern Lebanon. Consequently, the Syrians refused to withdraw, and the IDF remained in place as well.[17]

As these events transpired, factional conflicts escalated, and MNF II progressively lost its status as an impartial peacekeeper. Fighting intensified in the Shouf region between the Christian LF militia and the Druze, and in May, each combatant began periodically shelling its adversary's neighborhood in Beirut. The Marines began conducting combined patrols with the LAF on June 25, shortly before the LAF was pulled into the Shouf conflict on July 14, when the Druze militia ambushed a Lebanese army patrol. The following day, the LAF also engaged the Iranian-backed Amal militia in Beirut after an attempt to evict Shiite squatters from a schoolhouse erupted in violence. That month, Lebanese President Amin Gemayel (Bashir Gemayel's brother) visited Washington and secured a U.S. promise to expedite the delivery of arms to the LAF. And on July 23, Druze leader Walid Jamblatt announced the formation of the Syrian-backed National Salvation Front, dedicated to removing the Gemayel government and repudiating the May 17 agreement.[18]

As July drew into August, fighting in the Shouf region became more frequent and intense, with the IDF presence there serving as the last remaining barrier to unrestricted warfare between the Druze militia and the LAF and its Christian partner, the LF militia.[19] Meanwhile, the U.S. Marines, still operating under peacetime ROE, were increasingly seen as LAF allies and, therefore, co-combatants in the conflicts in which the Lebanese army was becoming embroiled. On July 22, the Druze shelled Marine positions at Beirut International Airport for the first time, wounding three marines and forcing a temporary closure of the airport. Druze artillery and mortar fire grew in intensity

---

[17] Nelson, 1991, p. 14.

[18] Long Commission Report, 1983, pp. 30–31.

[19] Kemp, 1991, pp. 136–137.

in August, closing the airport again from August 10 to 16 as the Druze made explicit their objection to LAF deployments in the Shouf. On August 28, the Marines returned fire for the first time, and the following day, they silenced a Druze battery after two marines were killed in a mortar attack. Two days later, the LAF swept through a Shiite neighborhood in Beirut, temporarily routing the Amal militia.[20]

On September 4, 1983, with domestic pressure against the Lebanon imbroglio building in Israel, the IDF abruptly withdrew from its positions in Alayh and the Shouf without forewarning the Lebanese government or coordinating with the LAF.[21] The next day, the Druze, reinforced by PLO and Syrian elements, routed the LF militia in the village of Bhamdun, inflicting heavy casualties and eliminating the LF as a viable combatant. This forced the LAF to occupy the village of Suq-al-Gharb, positioned on a ridgeline in the Shouf foothills, to avoid ceding all of the high ground overlooking the airport to the Druze. As these events unfolded, the Marines came under near-constant indirect fire from Druze mortar and artillery positions. On September 5, the Marines began using counterbattery radar to return the fire, and two days later, the U.S. Navy began flying airborne reconnaissance missions over the Shouf. On September 8, the Marines received naval gunfire support from U.S. destroyers off the Lebanese coast.[22]

As the situation grew dire, U.S. authorities determined that the defense of Suq-al-Gharb was vital to the Marines' safety at the airport, and they granted U.S. ground commanders broad authority to call in air strikes and naval artillery fire to defend themselves, other MNF II units, and the LAF.[23] On September 14, the United States began an emergency ammunition resupply to the LAF. Five days later, U.S. Navy destroyers shelled Druze positions in the Shouf in support of the LAF defenders at Suq-al-Gharb, even though, in that instance, the marines at the airport had not been threatened.

---

[20] Long Commission Report, 1983, p. 31.

[21] Kemp, 1991, p. 137.

[22] Long Commission Report, 1983, pp. 31–32.

[23] Nelson, 1991, pp. 15–16.

On September 25, the battleship USS *New Jersey* arrived in Lebanese waters, and that day, the warring factions reached an uneasy cease-fire. On October 1, Walid Jamblatt declared a separate government for the Shouf and called for Druze members of the Christian-led LAF to defect. For the time being, the army held together, and although sporadic clashes and sniper fire occurred, the cease-fire held in name for several weeks. The United States used the relative calm to resupply the LAF, rushing in armored personnel carriers, tanks, and howitzers, and the Marines resumed training the Lebanese army. On October 14, factional leaders agreed to meet in Geneva, Switzerland, to discuss national reconciliation, but the tenuous truce was clearly fraying. Factional clashes were increasing and sniper attacks on MNF II contingents were becoming commonplace. On October 19, four marines were wounded when a bomb in a parked car detonated beside an MNF II convoy.[24]

At 6:22 a.m. on Sunday, October 23, a yellow Mercedes-Benz stake-bed truck sped across a public parking lot at Beirut International Airport, crashed through a barbed wire and concertina fence, and plunged into the lobby of the Marine headquarters and barracks, where it exploded, bringing the building down on more than 300 marines while they slept. Between the fence and the building, the truck passed between two guard posts and flattened the sergeant-of-the-guard's hut, but the Marines, still operating under peacetime rules of engagement, did not open fire.[25]

As Geoffrey Kemp has said, "[F]rom the U.S. perspective, the bombing of the Marines meant that it was not a question of whether we would leave, but when."[26] In the weeks following the disaster, Israel withdrew its forces to the southern security zone along the Israeli border, and the LAF increasingly lost ground to Druze and Muslim militias. The Marines came under persistent sniper, mortar, artillery, and rocket attack. In December 1983, the U.S. Navy began shelling militia strongholds and Syrian positions using the *New Jersey*'s 16-inch

---

[24] Long Commission Report, 1983, p. 32.

[25] Long Commission Report, 1983, pp. 32–33.

[26] Kemp, 1991, p. 139.

guns, much to the consternation of French officials, who feared that such escalation would provoke retribution on MNF II.[27]

The bombardment was but a prelude to withdrawal. Although President Reagan insisted that the United States was committed to remaining in MNF II and achieving stability in Lebanon, domestic support for the operation had declined steeply and the U.S. Department of Defense had long wanted to pull the Marines offshore, keeping them available but safe at sea. On February 7, 1984, the White House announced that the U.S. contingent of MNF II would redeploy to the ships. Enthusiasm for MNF II also waned in Europe. Britain withdrew its troops on February 8, and the last Italian soldiers departed on February 20. France redeployed its MNF II troops to UNFIL on the Israeli-Lebanese border on March 31, one day after President Reagan notified Congress that U.S. involvement in MNF II was over.[28]

As the IDF and MNF II withdrew, Druze and Muslim militia units took up the positions they vacated and the LAF virtually disintegrated along sectarian lines. On March 5, 1984, under pressure from Damascus and Lebanon's non-Christian factions, the Gemayel government cancelled the May 17 agreement with Israel.

Mogadishu, 1992–1994

On October 3, 1993, elements of TF Ranger, a joint special operations TF assembled the previous August to apprehend Somali warlord Mohamed Farah Aidid, launched a raid to capture some of Aidid's key lieutenants meeting in the market district of Mogadishu. Over the course of the raid, an intense firefight erupted between U.S. Army Rangers and Aidid's followers, resulting in the deaths of hundreds of Somalis, the loss of two U.S. Army helicopters, and 18 American soldiers killed in action, several of whose bodies Somali mobs later des-

---

[27] Nelson, 1991, p. 18.

[28] Kemp, 1991, pp. 140–141; Nelson, 1991, p. 20.

ecrated in the streets of Mogadishu as an international television audience watched in horror.[29]

The October 3 raid was the culmination of almost a year and a half of U.S. involvement in efforts to relieve a humanitarian disaster and provide stability in the failed state of Somalia. Over the course of that involvement, the U.S. role progressed from airlifting and sealifting relief workers, food, and medical supplies to leading an international coalition protecting relief efforts on the ground to helping UN forces in efforts to disarm Somalia's warring factions so that nation building could commence and, finally, to attempting to bring a major clan leader to justice for violence against UN peacekeepers. Early efforts looked promising: Security provided by the U.S.-led coalition stabilized the situation, enabling aid distribution to proceed and easing the immediate humanitarian crisis. Somali citizens warmly welcomed the intervention. But as UN and U.S. objectives grew evermore ambitious, violence escalated against UN and coalition forces, and many Somalis who first embraced the international effort ultimately sided with the factions that forcefully opposed it. To understand how a humanitarian relief effort can escalate so violently, we must briefly examine the circumstances leading to the initial UN intervention, then review the escalation dynamics that came into play after UN and coalition forces arrived.

In January 1991, the regime of strongman Mohamed Siad Barre collapsed and Somalia descended into chaos as heavily armed militias, organized along clan and subclan lines, battled for control of the country (see Figure B.2). This collapse followed more than a decade of brutal civil war that brought agriculture to a halt and destroyed the Somali economy, plunging the nation into abject poverty and starvation. As civil authority disintegrated, a severe drought added to the humanitarian crisis, and international relief organizations were hamstrung in their efforts to provide assistance. They set up refugee camps, paid protection money to warlords, and attempted to distribute food

---

[29] See Keith B. Richburg, "Battle Killed 12 Americans, Wounded 78," *Washington Post*, October 5, 1993. The early count of 12 dead and 78 wounded as reported by Richburg changed as more facts became available.

Case Studies of Escalation in Stability Operations   209

Figure B.2
Geographical Distribution of Somalia's Clans and Subclans in 1992

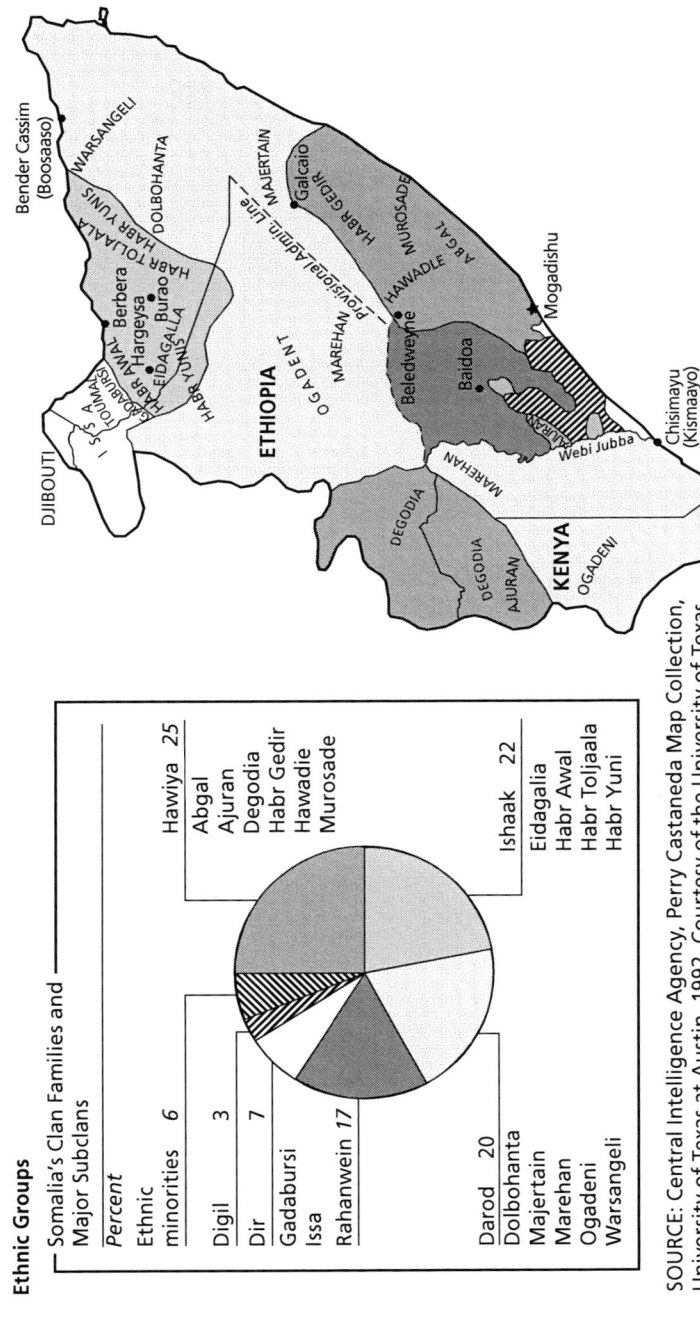

Ethnic Groups

Somalia's Clan Families and Major Subclans

Percent

Ethnic minorities 6

Digil 3

Dir 7

Gadabursi
Issa

Rahanwein 17

Darod 20
Dolbohanta
Majertain
Marehan
Ogadeni
Warsangeli

Hawiya 25
Abgal
Ajuran
Degodia
Habr Gedir
Hawadie
Murosade

Ishaak 22
Eidagalia
Habr Awal
Habr Toljaala
Habr Yuni

SOURCE: Central Intelligence Agency, Perry Castaneda Map Collection, University of Texas at Austin, 1992. Courtesy of the University of Texas Libraries, University of Texas at Austin.

RAND MG614-B.2

to the Somali people, but little aid reached those who needed it. The militias fought over food supplies, raiding storehouses and distribution points, and used access to food as a weapon to secure clan loyalty.[30]

By the end of 1991, fighting in the capital of Mogadishu had coalesced around factions of the Hawiya clan supporting General Mohamed Farah Aidid, the former army chief of staff under Barre and leader of the Habr Gidr subclan, and those allied with Ali Mohamed Mahdi, an Abgal subclan leader. An estimated 300,000 people died of starvation in Somalia that year—many of them children—and some 2 million citizens fled their homes. "By 1992, almost 4.5 million people, more than half the total number in the country, were threatened with starvation, severe malnutrition and related diseases."[31]

With the impending catastrophe attracting media attention, the UN Security Council imposed a general arms embargo on Somalia in January 1992, and Secretary-General Boutros Boutros-Ghali urged the warring factions to cease hostilities so that relief operations could proceed. On March 3, Aidid and Mahdi signed a cease-fire agreement and, after more than two additional months of consultation, finally consented to the deployment of UN observers. Meanwhile, on April 24, the Security Council urged the secretary-general to immediately send 50 unarmed observers to Somalia and further authorized the deployment of a security force there, establishing UNOSOM I.[32]

The mission of UNOSOM I, in addition to monitoring the cease-fire, was to protect relief personnel, equipment, and supplies at the seaports and airports in Mogadishu; escort deliveries of humanitarian supplies from there to distribution centers in and around the city; and, starting in August 1992, protect humanitarian convoys and distribution centers throughout Somalia.[33] Over the next several months, UN member nations raised $20 million in food aid for the relief effort, and

---

[30] Richard W. Stewart, *The United States Army in Somalia, 1992–1994*, Washington, D.C.: Center for Military History, U.S. Department of the Army, 2002, p. 6.

[31] United Nations Department of Public Information, "Somalia—UNOSOM I: Mission Backgrounder," March 21, 1997a.

[32] See United Nations Security Council, Resolution 751 (Somalia), April 24, 1992.

[33] United Nations Department of Public Information, 1997a.

Pakistan provided UNOSOM's initial 550-strong security force.[34] To support the operation, the United States stood up joint TF Operation Provide Relief in August 1993, supplying airlift and sealift, but did not provide troops to the ground contingent.

These efforts proved inadequate in the face of continued resistance from the heavily armed militias. Despite pledges from Aidid and Mahdi to allow relief operations to proceed, control of food was a major source of power in Somalia, and none of the factions was willing to surrender that lever to the perceived advantage of its rivals. Pakistani peacekeepers attempted to protect the distribution system but were unable to do so. Although the contingent was reinforced twice in the summer and autumn of 1992, bringing its strength to 3,500 and then 4,219 troops, it lacked heavy weapons and was regularly outgunned by militia "technicals." Efforts to accomplish their mission brought the Pakistanis into frequent confrontations with militia gangs, and, on October 28, Aidid declared that the UNOSOM Pakistani battalion would no longer be tolerated in Mogadishu. Soon afterward, Aidid's forces began shelling and sniping at UNOSOM troops controlling the airport. Mahdi, alternatively, angered that Aidid's followers were seizing food shipments as soon as they were offloaded from ships, wanted UNOSOM to take full control of Mogadishu's port. When it could not, his forces began shelling ships as they attempted to enter the harbor, turning one back in November.[35]

Meanwhile, Somalis continued dying of starvation, and poignant news reports of their plight raised public distress in the United States and elsewhere. On December 3, 1992, the UN Security Council unanimously accepted a U.S. offer to raise and lead an international coalition, UNITAF, and authorized it to use all necessary means under Chapter VII of the UN Charter "to establish as soon as possible a

---

[34] See Versalle F. Washington, "Setting the Stage," in Robert F. Baumann and Lawrence A. Yates with Versalle F. Washington, *"My Clan Against the World": US and Coalition Forces in Somalia, 1992–1994*, Ft. Leavenworth, Kan.: Combat Studies Institute Press, 2004, pp. 9–22 (p. 18).

[35] Kenneth Allard, *Somalia Operations: Lessons Learned*, Ft. McNair, Washington D.C.: National Defense University Press, 1995, pp. 15–16; Washington, 2004, pp. 18–19; United Nations Department of Public Information, 1997a.

secure environment for humanitarian relief operations in Somalia."[36] Thus, UNITAF began assembling on December 8, 1992, under the U.S. code name Operation Restore Hope.[37]

At its peak, UNITAF was composed of approximately 28,900 U.S. troops and 10,000 soldiers from 23 other countries.[38] Troops from the 1st Marine Division and the Army's 10th Mountain Division composed the bulk of the U.S. ground force, and Headquarters, 1st Marine Expeditionary Force, provided the command element. The other services also supplied essential capabilities, as did U.S. Special Operations Command. The first elements of Operation Restore Hope came ashore in Somalia unopposed in the predawn hours of December 9, and, before the day was out, the Marines had secured the U.S. Embassy compound and the airport outside Mogadishu. The rest of UNITAF's forces flowed in quickly, seizing port facilities and creating a security zone in the capital, then deploying to nearby towns and securing the lines of communication linking the major relief centers in south and central Somalia.

Overwhelmed by the sudden deployment of nearly 39,000 troops supported by armor, artillery, and attack helicopters, the clan militias in UNITAF's area of operations largely stopped interfering with relief efforts and entered into an uneasy truce. Consequently, by the end of December 1992, UNOSOM I and UNITAF had made considerable progress in alleviating the human suffering in Mogadishu and the surrounding areas. More than 40,000 tons of grain had been off-loaded

---

[36] United Nations Security Council, Resolution 794 (Somalia), December 3, 1992, p. 3.

[37] Stewart, 2002, p. 9.

[38] Lawrence A. Yates, "Operation Restore Hope Phases I and II, December 1992," in Robert F. Baumann and Lawrence A. Yates with Versalle F. Washington, *"My Clan Against the World": US and Coalition Forces in Somalia, 1992–1994*, Ft. Leavenworth, Kan.: Combat Studies Institute Press, 2004, p. 30; Stewart, 2002, p. 10; United Nations Department of Public Information, 1997a. The other participating nations were Australia, Belgium, Botswana, Canada, Egypt, France, Germany, Greece, India, Italy, Kuwait, Morocco, New Zealand, Nigeria, Norway, Pakistan, Saudi Arabia, Sweden, Tunisia, Turkey, United Arab Emirates, United Kingdom, and Zimbabwe.

and were being shipped in convoys and delivered from distribution centers secured by UNITAF troops.[39]

Encouraged by this success, Secretary-General Boutros-Ghali began efforts to bring about a national reconciliation between the warring factions. In January 1993, he convened a meeting with Somalia's leading political organizations and persuaded them to hold a conference on national reconciliation, which met in Addis Ababa, Ethiopia, on March 15–27, 1993. There, leaders of 15 political movements agreed on a basic framework for disarmament and security, rehabilitation and reconstruction, restoration of property, and settlement of disputes in Somalia during the period of national reconciliation.[40]

Yet despite having made considerable progress in defusing the humanitarian crisis, Somalia was still far from secure. Clashes between clan militias continued to occur, and the threat to UN personnel and international relief workers remained high in some parts of Mogadishu and the surrounding countryside. Moreover, there was no UNITAF presence in the northeast or northwest regions of Somalia or along the Ethiopian-Somali border. Nor would there be, as the White House was eager to withdraw the majority of U.S. ground forces and turn over those forces' responsibilities to the UN. Consequently, on March 3, the secretary-general recommended that the UN Security Council transfer most of UNITAF's security responsibilities to an expanded and reconstituted UNOSOM (UNOSOM II), which would be tasked with restoring peace and stability throughout Somalia and rebuilding the political, economic, and social institutions essential to creating a democratic state.[41]

The UN Security Council accepted that recommendation on March 26 and authorized the creation of UNOSOM II. The new force, envisaged to include 28,000 peacekeepers from 21 nations, was given wide-ranging Chapter VII authority to disarm militias and enforce peace. It was also tasked with clearing mines, repatriating refugees, and

---

[39] Stewart, 2002, p. 10.

[40] United Nations Department of Public Information, "Somalia—UNOSOM II: Mission Backgrounder," March 21, 1997b.

[41] United Nations Department of Public Information, 1997b.

rebuilding Somalia's civil institutions, in addition to providing security for relief efforts throughout the country.[42] Boutros-Ghali appointed Turkish Lieutenant General Cevik Bir to command the operation and urged him to work closely with the secretary-general's newly assigned special representative to Somalia, retired U.S. Admiral Jonathan Howe. The deputy commander of UNOSOM II would be U.S. Army Major General Thomas Montgomery. Montgomery would also serve as commander of U.S. Forces in Somalia (USFORSOM), which, after UNITAF drew down, would consist of 2,600 logistical personnel, a special operations element, and a 1,100-strong QRF drawn from the 10th Mountain Division.[43]

On May 4, having reached approximately 30 percent of its projected strength, UNOSOM II relieved UNITAF of responsibility for UN security operations in Somalia. The peacekeepers then, as their mandate required, began trying to disarm the militias in Mogadishu, and it quickly became apparent that General Aidid had little respect for the new organization. Over the next couple of weeks, confrontations between Aidid's followers and UNOSOM II personnel grew frequent and tense, and Radio Mogadishu, operated by Aidid's United Somali Congress and SNA, began vilifying the disarmament effort as neocolonialism. Then, on June 5, Aidid's forces ambushed a group of Pakistani peacekeepers attempting to conduct a short-notice inspection of a weapon storage site, killing 24 and wounding 44 others. The UN Security Council condemned the violence the following day, authorized UNOSOM II to take more aggressive measures against Aidid, and urged member states to accelerate delivery of the additional personnel and equipment promised to the effort.[44]

---

[42] United Nations Security Council, Resolution 814 (Somalia), March 26, 1993, pp. 4–5. Participating nations were Australia, Bangladesh, Belgium, Botswana, Canada, Egypt, France, Germany, Greece, India, Indonesia, Ireland, Italy, Kuwait, Malaysia, Morocco, Nepal, New Zealand, Nigeria, Norway, Pakistan, Republic of Korea, Romania, Saudi Arabia, Sweden, Tunisia, Turkey, United Arab Emirates, United States, and Zimbabwe.

[43] Allard, 1995, pp. 18–19; Stewart, 2002, pp. 15–16.

[44] United Nations Security Council, Resolution 837 (Somalia), June 6, 1993, pp. 2–3.

The peacekeepers and Admiral Howe moved aggressively to regain control of the situation. Pakistani and Italian forces immediately began conducting armored patrols in the sector in which the ambush occurred and at other critical traffic nodes in the city. U.S. Central Command requested that the Pentagon make four AC-130 gunships available to USFORSOM; they arrived on June 7, and USFORSOM began flying combat sorties over the streets of Mogadishu on June 11, striking Aidid's weapon storage facilities, vehicle depots, and Radio Mogadishu over the next several days. On June 17, Admiral Howe issued a warrant for Aidid's arrest and offered a $25,000 reward for information leading to the clan leader's apprehension. Thereafter, clashes between Aidid's forces and the peacekeepers became more frequent and intense, and on July 12, the USFORSOM QRF raided Aidid's command compound with attack helicopters and airmobile troops.[45]

Yet none of these actions brought UNOSOM II any closer to catching Aidid, and the violence continued escalating. After the raid on the clan leader's compound, a crowd of Somalis pulling dead and wounded from the rubble attacked a group of Western journalists that had come to cover the story, killing four of them.[46] At Admiral Howe's urging, UNOSOM II focused its intelligence assets on locating Aidid and other SNA leaders responsible for the June and July violence, and the QRF organized teams to "attack, snatch, and secure" the clan leader once he was found. But Aidid proved both elusive and able to fight back. Intelligence sources reported that the SNA had put a bounty on the heads of UN and U.S. personnel.[47] On August 8, SNA fighters set

---

[45] Robert F. Baumann, "UNOSOM II: Part II, The Battle of Mogadishu," in Robert F. Baumann and Lawrence A. Yates with Versalle F. Washington, *"My Clan Against the World": US and Coalition Forces in Somalia, 1992–1994*, Ft. Leavenworth, Kan.: Combat Studies Institute Press, 2004, pp. 110–118; Stewart, 2002, p. 16.

[46] See Andrew Hill and Richard Dowden, "Air Raid Puts Aid at Risk: UN Secretary-General Rejects Call to Suspend 'Peace By Force' After Attack Kills at Least 16 and Avenging Crowds Beat Journalists to Death," *The Independent*, July 13, 1993.

[47] Baumann, 2004, p. 118.

off an explosive device beneath a passing military police vehicle, killing four U.S. soldiers.[48]

With efforts to capture Aidid failing, Admiral Howe requested help from Washington. In response, Secretary of Defense Les Aspin ordered the deployment of a joint special operations TF, and TF Ranger was in Somalia by August 28, 1993. Comprised largely of elements of the 75th Ranger Regiment and 1st Special Forces Operational Detachment–Delta (Delta Force), TF Ranger was put under the command of Major General William Garrison and given the singular task of apprehending General Aidid or, at least, crippling his command structure by capturing his top lieutenants.[49] Between its arrival and the end of September 1993, the TF carried out six missions, including one in which it captured Osman Otto, Aidid's financial aide and close adviser.[50]

Even as TF Ranger seemed to be making headway, the conflict between UNOSOM II and Aidid's SNA continued to escalate. On September 8, Somali militias attacked a group of U.S. and Pakistani soldiers with 106-mm recoilless rifles, rocket-propelled grenades (RPGs), and small arms as the peacekeepers were clearing roadblocks. The Somali assault was so determined that it took intensive ground fire and rotary-wing air support to drive the attackers away. Militia fighters, along with a mob of around 1,000 Somali civilians, attacked the same UNOSOM II element again later that day, injuring six peacekeepers. Several U.S. soldiers were wounded on September 13 when a QRF raid on an SNA compound drew militia fighters from surrounding neighborhoods, resulting in an extended firefight. Roadblock-clearing teams were attacked again on September 16 and 21; in the latter incident, Pakistan lost an armored personnel carrier in which two soldiers were killed and nine were wounded. And on September 25, militia fighters shot down an MH-60 Black Hawk helicopter with RPGs, killing three U.S. soldiers. By the end of September, the militia fighters were exhibiting an ever-greater ability to quickly coordinate and mass their people

---

[48] Stewart, 2002, p. 17.

[49] Baumann, 2004, p. 140.

[50] Stewart, 2002, p. 18.

against specified objectives. Whenever UN or U.S. forces attempted to deploy anywhere in the SNA-controlled regions of the city, they came under intense pressure from civilian mobs and militia fighters within 20 to 30 minutes.[51]

On October 3, 1993, General Garrison believed that he had an opportunity to employ TF Ranger with considerable effect. Real-time intelligence indicated that a group of Aidid's top lieutenants would be meeting that afternoon in a building near the Olympic Hotel, located in Mogadishu's Black Sea slum district, an SNA stronghold. General Garrison and the TF quickly assembled a plan to capture the SNA leaders in a daring daylight raid involving 160 troops, 19 aircraft, and 12 vehicles. According to the plan, Delta Force commandos and rangers would fly to the objective in helicopters. The commandos would drop down on the building as Ranger teams fast-roped to the ground in four "chalks" to secure the approaches along adjoining streets. With the Ranger blocking force thus isolating the objective, Delta Force would raid the building and capture the targets. Then a truck convoy would rush in and evacuate TF Ranger and its detainees.[52]

The task force launched from its airport compound at around 3:30 p.m.; then, a series of mishaps, combined with an unexpectedly ferocious SNA response, led to an intense firefight that lasted the rest of the day and through the night. The teams were on the ground at the objective by 3:45 p.m. One helicopter mistakenly put its Rangers down one block away from their assigned station and, coincidentally, a soldier in that team was seriously injured in the fast-rope attempt, but within 30 minutes, despite increasingly heavy militia fire, the commandos had succeeded in securing the objective and had 24 detainees ready for pickup.

Then disaster struck. One of the Black Hawk helicopters providing cover for the operation was hit by an RPG and crashed approximately three blocks away. Immediately, an MH-6 Little Bird helicopter rushed to the crash site and, landing amid a firefight between survivors and militia forces, evacuated two wounded soldiers. Soon afterward, a

---

[51] Baumann, 2004, pp. 123–133; Stewart, 2002, p. 19.

[52] Baumann, 2004, pp. 142–143.

six-strong Ranger team arrived from its blocking station and joined the defenders at the crash site as a second Black Hawk reached the scene and began deploying a combat search-and-rescue team. That helicopter, too, was hit but managed to finish deploying the team and limp back to the airport.[53]

The situation quickly grew worse as hundreds of SNA fighters and clan supporters converged on the area. Two more Black Hawks were hit—one managed to get back to the airport, but the other went down in the city, around a mile south of the first crash site. There, Somali mobs overran the survivors' desperate defenses and killed everyone on board except for the injured pilot, whom they took prisoner. As these events transpired, the truck convoy with the detainees set out in an effort to reach the first crash site, as did the remaining assault and blocking forces still on foot. The foot soldiers drew heavy fire and took casualties along the way, but they reached the site and joined their comrades in defensive positions from which they fought through the night. The truck convoy, alternatively, was unable to find the site. After making two passes through the neighborhood under intense fire, it headed back to the airport, joining a rescue convoy on the way. A company from the QRF attempted to reach the second crash site, but heavy SNA fire drove it back.[54]

As besieged soldiers at the first crash site fought into the night, USFORSOM coordinated with Pakistani and Malaysian elements of UNOSOM II to assemble a relief column with the requisite armor to penetrate the city's many roadblocks and weather the RPG fire. Finally, a 60-vehicle convoy, spearheaded by Pakistani tanks and supported by AH-1 Cobra and AH-6 Little Bird attack helicopters, set out from the New Port area of the city and reached the crash site at around 1:55 a.m. on October 4. There, they loaded the wounded into armored personnel carriers and worked for several hours under heavy fire to free the helicopter pilot's body from the wreckage. Meanwhile, an infantry company proceeded to the second crash site but found none of the crew or soldiers there. At dawn, the column moved out, with the armored

---

[53] Stewart, 2002, pp. 19–20.

[54] Baumann, 2004, p. 147.

vehicles providing cover for the soldiers on foot, and the combined force fought its way to the Pakistani stadium compound in the northeast sector of the city, arriving at around 6:30 a.m.[55]

Thus ended what the U.S. Army described as "one of the bloodiest and fiercest urban firefights since the Vietnam War."[56] U.S. losses on October 3–4 included 18 killed and 77 wounded. The Malaysians suffered two dead and seven wounded, and two Pakistanis were also wounded that night. Somali casualty estimates have ranged from 500 to 1,500.[57]

This costly battle, punctuated by the shocking spectacle of dead U.S. soldiers being dragged through the streets of Mogadishu, had a deleterious effect on U.S. will to continue supporting the UN effort.[58] The U.S. contingent in Mogadishu grew sharply immediately following the incident; Washington deployed a new joint TF to Somalia that included armor and infantry battalions, a mechanized infantry company, more special operators, and additional AC-130 gunships. But the mission of this TF was limited to protecting UN and U.S. forces during the U.S. withdrawal. On October 6, the White House directed TF Ranger and USFORSOM to stop all actions against Aidid except those required in self-defense. The following day, President Clinton announced that U.S. forces would be out of Somalia by March 31, 1994.[59]

---

[55] Baumann, 2004, pp. 150–154; Stewart, 2002, pp. 22–23.

[56] Stewart, 2002, p. 23.

[57] Stewart, 2002, p. 23.

[58] See, for example, Tamara Jones, "Grim Skepticism Grows on the Home Front," *Washington Post*, October 5, 1993; Michael Ross and Art Pine, "Angry Lawmakers Threaten to Push for Somalia Pullout," *Los Angeles Times*, October 6, 1993; and Thomas Friedman, "Clinton Reviews Policy in Somalia as Unease Grows," *New York Times*, October 6, 1993.

[59] Ann Devroy and John Lancaster, "Clinton to Add 1,500 Troops in Somalia, Considers a March 31 Withdrawal Date," *Washington Post*, October 7, 1993. See also Lawrence A. Yates, "Buildup and Withdrawal, October 1993–March 1994," in Robert F. Baumann and Lawrence A. Yates with Versalle F. Washington, *"My Clan Against the World": US and Coalition Forces in Somalia, 1992–1994*, Ft. Leavenworth, Kan.: Combat Studies Institute Press, 2004, pp. 167–168.

Without U.S. support on the ground, UN involvement did not last much longer. UNOSOM II returned to a noncoercive approach in its efforts to mediate an end to clan warfare in Somalia, and the principal combatants entered into another uneasy truce in 1994. However, as negotiations bogged down time and again, it became clear that none of the factions was willing to relinquish power to a central governing authority. By the end of the year, the international community had lost patience with the lack of progress in Somalia. The UN Security Council voted to end UNOSOM II not later than March 31, 1995, and the withdrawal was completed by March 28.[60]

---

[60] United Nations Department of Public Information, 1997b.

APPENDIX C
Modified Method for Delphi Analyses

As part of the research effort for this study, we conducted two exercises using a modified version of the Delphi method of analysis. The first exercise was conducted on June 1, 2005, to examine the escalation dynamics that could emerge in a Sino-U.S. military confrontation over Taiwan. The second exercise was conducted on July 20, 2005, to explore the risks of escalation among new nuclear powers and among states and nonstate actors in the event of a collapse of government authority in Pakistan. Both exercises were conducted in the RAND Corporation's Washington office and involved the participation of RAND researchers and selected military and civilian staff members from Headquarters, U.S. Air Force.

The Delphi method is a forecasting technique involving iterative, structured examinations of specific issues by teams of experts in fields relevant to those issues. Developed at RAND in the late 1940s, early Delphi analyses used questionnaires to solicit the opinions of experts who were geographically separated to preserve their anonymity, thereby preventing the opinions of more prominent individuals from exerting undue influence on the others.[1]

For this project, an approach was developed for employing the Delphi method in a format resembling a war-game seminar. It thereby

---

[1] See Norman C. Dalkey, *Project Delphi*, Santa Monica, Calif.: RAND Corporation, D-1005, August 21, 1951. For an exhaustive examination and critique of the many variations of the Delphi method that had evolved by 2002, see Harold A. Linstone and Murray Turoff, eds., *The Delphi Method: Techniques and Applications*, Newark, N.J.: New Jersey Institute of Technology, 2002.

replaced expert anonymity with direct player interaction in a way designed to reveal the range of escalation dynamics that might emerge in particular military confrontations. This format involved specifying an initial crisis situation, then querying the seminar participants about how each of the principal actors (countries or nonstate actors) involved in the crisis might respond to the initial situation and the actions of the other actors. Seminar participants included area specialists, security policy analysts, military strategists, and nuclear effects experts.

The structural flow of the seminar resembled, in many respects, an informal war game, with some participants representing specific actors (or groups of actors) and with plays carried out in sequential turns. Participants received background and intelligence workups on the notional crisis that each scenario entailed and were supplied with realistic catalogs of each actor's military order of battle or, in the case of nonstate actors, the irregular combatants at their disposal. Unlike a more traditional war game, however, instead of choosing a single COA in each turn, the participants were asked to describe a range of plausible COAs each actor might take. Once all reasonably plausible COAs were identified, participants were asked to describe a range of plausible responses to each of these COAs.

In each full turn, play proceeded from one actor to the next until all had listed their prospective COAs. At that point, the line of inquiry returned to the first actor, and the entire process was repeated until all plausible escalation paths had been explored as thoroughly as possible within the time constraint of the seminar, one working day. The process of examining all combinations of actions and responses resulted in the exploration of an entire decision tree, as illustrated in Figure C.1, rather than a single path through that tree, as would have been the case using the standard approach of a traditional war game.

During these exercises, only participants who were expert on the political culture, military doctrine, or operational style of a given country or nonstate actor were allowed to speak for that actor. This was because COAs that might have seemed viable to U.S. experts on military operations, viewing the situation solely from the perspective of military operational utility, may not have been plausible within the

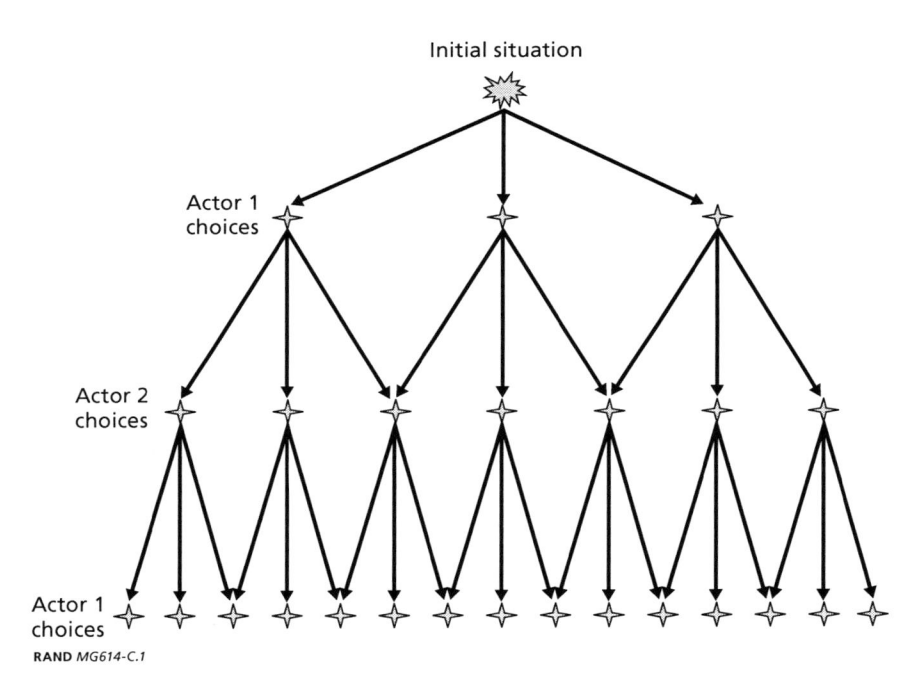

Figure C.1
Example of a Delphi Analysis Decision Tree

political and cultural context of that country or nonstate actor. Although the beliefs of U.S. specialists on a country or nonstate actor about how that actor would behave in a particular scenario are not guaranteed to be correct, the views of regional specialists may be presumed to be more accurate than the views of nonexperts. Alternatively, during the course of the analyses, participants who did not have specialized expertise on a country or nonstate actor were allowed to suggest possible courses of action by that actor to the relevant regional specialists, who were then free to accept or reject those suggestions. If the regional specialists chose to reject suggested COAs, they were required to explain why they believed them to be implausible.

Over the course of the two seminars, several potential paths of escalation were identified, evaluated, and cataloged. Alternatively, other potential paths of escalation about which some participants worried before the exercises were analyzed and found to be of much lower risk than previously assumed. These findings were used to inform the analyses presented in Chapters Three through Five of this monograph.

Bibliography

"A General of the People's Liberation Army and Arms Control Experts Discuss Chinas' Nuclear Policy in the New Period," *Liaowang Dongfang Zhoukan*, No. 32, August 11, 2005, pp. 38–39, 41, in Foreign Broadcast Information Service as "PRC Arms Control Experts Discuss China's Nuclear Policy."

Ahmad, Munir, "Musharraf Fans Flames with Threat to Unleash a 'Storm,'" *The Advertiser* (South Australia), May 31, 2002, p. 26.

Albertini, Luigi, *The Origins of the War of 1914*, three vols., Isabelle M. Massey, ed. and trans., Oxford, UK: Oxford University Press, 1952–1957.

Allard, Kenneth, *Somalia Operations: Lessons Learned*, Ft. McNair, Washington, D.C.: National Defense University Press, 1995. As of August 10, 2007: http://www.ndu.edu/inss/books/books%20-%201990%20to%201995/Somalia%20Lessons%20Learned%20Jan%2095/SOLL.pdf

Allison, Graham T., *Essence of Decision: Explaining the Cuban Missile Crisis*, Boston: Little, Brown, 1971.

Al-Qurashi, Abu 'Ubeid, "Fourth-Generation Wars," *Al-Ansar: For the Struggle Against the Crusader War* (biweekly Internet magazine published by al Qaeda), January 2002. Portions reprinted by the Middle East Media Research Institute, Special Dispatch Series, No. 344, February 10, 2002. As of February 22, 2007: http://memri.org/bin/articles.cgi?Page=archives&Area=sd&ID=SP34402

Ardolino, Bill, "Why the Violence Has Declined in Iraq," *Long War Journal*, November 8, 2007. As of December 21, 2007: http://www.longwarjournal.org/archives/2007/11/why_the_violence_has.php

Armstrong, Anne, *Unconditional Surrender: The Impact of the Casablanca Policy upon World War II*, New Brunswick, N.J.: Rutgers University Press, 1961.

Baldwin, David A., "The Power of Positive Sanctions," *World Politics*, Vol. 24, No. 1, October 1971, pp. 19–38.

Barry, John, Mark Dennis, and Alan Zarembo, "Tracking Terror," *Newsweek*, September 7, 1998, p. 20.

Baumann, Robert F., and Lawrence A. Yates with Versalle F. Washington, *"My Clan Against the World": US and Coalition Forces in Somalia, 1992–1994*, Ft. Leavenworth, Kan.: Combat Studies Institute Press, 2004. As of August 30, 2007:
http://handle.dtic.mil/100.2/ADA465677

Baumann, Robert F., "UNOSOM II: Part II—The Battle of Mogadishu," in Robert F. Baumann and Lawrence A. Yates with Versalle F. Washington, *"My Clan Against the World": US and Coalition Forces in Somalia, 1992–1994*, Ft. Leavenworth, Kan.: Combat Studies Institute Press, 2003, pp. 139–164. As of August 30, 2007:
http://handle.dtic.mil/100.2/ADA465677

Bell, General B. B., Commander, UN Command; Commander, Republic of Korea–U.S. Combined Forces Command; and Commander, U.S. Forces, Korea, statement before the Senate Armed Services Committee, March 7, 2006. As of July 13, 2006:
http://armed-services.senate.gov/statemnt/2006/March/Bell%2003-07-06.pdf

Bergen, Peter L., *Holy War, Inc.: Inside the Secret World of Osama Bin Laden*, New York: Touchstone, 2002.

Betts, Richard K., *Nuclear Blackmail and Nuclear Balance*, Washington, D.C.: Brookings Institution Press, 1987.

"Bin Laden Expert Steps Forward," transcript of interview with Michael Sheuer, senior intelligence analyst, by Steve Kroft, *60 Minutes*, November 14, 2004. As of January 10, 2005:
http://www.cbsnews.com/stories/2004/11/12/60minutes/main655407.shtml?CMP=ILC-SearchStories

Bin, Yu, "What China Learned from Its 'Forgotten War' in Korea," in Mark A. Ryan, David M. Finkelstein, and Michael A. McDevitt, eds., *Chinese Warfighting: The PLA Experience Since 1949*, New York: M. E. Sharpe, 2003, pp. 123–142.

Blainey, Geoffrey, *The Causes of War*, 3rd ed., New York: Free Press, 1988.

Blanchard, Christopher M., *Al Qaeda: Statements and Evolving Ideology*, Washington, D.C.: Congressional Research Service, RL32759, updated June 26, 2006. As of August 10, 2007:
http://handle.dtic.mil/100.2/ADA444823

Bowden, Mark, *Black Hawk Down: A Story of Modern War*, New York: Atlantic Monthly Press, 1999.

"British Police Said to Foil Aircraft Plot," *Washington Post*, August 10, 2006, p. A20.

Brodie, Bernard, *Escalation and the Nuclear Option*, Princeton, N.J.: Princeton University Press, 1966.

Burkitt, Laurie, Andrew Scobell, and Larry M. Wortzel, eds., *The Lessons of History: The Chinese People's Liberation Army at 75*, Carlisle, Pa.: Strategic Studies Institute, 2003. As of August 10, 2007:
http://www.strategicstudiesinstitute.army.mil/pubs/display.cfm?pubID=52

Burles, Mark, and Abram N. Shulsky, *Patterns in China's Use of Force: Evidence from History and Doctrinal Writings*, Santa Monica, Calif.: RAND Corporation, MR-1160-AF, 2000. As of August 10, 2007:
http://www.rand.org/pubs/monograph_reports/MR1160/

Bush, George W., *The National Security Strategy of the United States of America*, Washington, D.C.: White House, September 2002. As of August 10, 2007:
http://www.whitehouse.gov/nsc/nss.pdf

Byman, Daniel, and Matthew Waxman, *The Dynamics of Coercion: American Foreign Policy and the Limits of Military Might*, Cambridge, UK: Cambridge University Press, 2002.

Byman, Daniel L., Matthew C. Waxman, and Eric Larson, *Air Power as a Coercive Instrument*, Santa Monica, Calif.: RAND Corporation, MR-1061-AF, 1999. As of August 10, 2007:
http://www.rand.org/pubs/monograph_reports/MR1061/

Carus, W. Seth, *Defining "Weapons of Mass Destruction,"* Center for the Study of Weapons of Mass Destruction Occasional Paper 4, Washington, D.C.: National Defense University Press, February 2006. As of August 10, 2007:
http://handle.dtic.mil/100.2/ADA446692

Castillo, Jasen J., "Nuclear Terrorism: Why Deterrence Still Matters," *Current History*, Vol. 102, No. 668, December 2003, pp. 426–431.

Center for Nonproliferation Studies, "Country Profiles: What Are the Threats from Weapons of Mass Destruction?" Nuclear Threat Initiative, Web page, updated continuously. As of August 10, 2007:
http://www.nti.org/e_research/profiles/

Central Intelligence Agency, map of distribution of religious groups in Lebanon, Perry Castaneda Library Map Collection, University of Texas at Austin, 1983. As of August 10, 2007:
http://www.lib.utexas.edu/maps/middle_east_and_asia/lebanon_religions_83.jpg

———, map of ethnic groups in Somalia, Perry Castaneda Library Map Collection, University of Texas at Austin, 1992. As of August 10, 2007:
http://www.lib.utexas.edu/maps/africa/somalia_ethnic92.jpg

Chandrasekaran, Rajiv, "Pakistan, India Mass Troops: Tensions Escalate as New Delhi Considers Strike," *Washington Post*, December 24, 2001, p. A1.

Chang Xianqi, "Space Strength and New Revolution in Military Affairs," *Zhongguo Junshi Kexue* [*China Military Science*], March 2003, p. 59.

Chen, Jian, *China's Road to the Korean War: The Making of the Sino-American Confrontation*, New York: Columbia University Press, 1994.

———, "China's Involvement in the Vietnam War, 1964–1969," *China Quarterly*, No. 142, June 1995, pp. 356–387.

"China Plans to Launch 100 Satellites Before 2020 to Form an Observation Network," Xinhua, November 16, 2004.

Christensen, Thomas J., "Threats, Assurances, and the Last Chance for Peace: The Lessons of Mao's Korean War Telegrams," *International Security*, Vol. 17, No. 1, Summer 1992, pp. 122–154.

Clausewitz, Carl von, *On War*, Michael Howard and Peter Paret, eds. and trans., Princeton, N.J.: Princeton University Press, 1976.

Clodfelter, Mark, *The Limits of Air Power: The American Bombing of North Vietnam*, New York: Free Press, 1989.

Coll, Steve, "The Standoff: How Jihadi Groups Helped Provoke the Twenty-First Century's First Nuclear Crisis," *New Yorker*, February 13–20, 2006, pp. 126–139. As of August 10, 2007:
http://www.newyorker.com/archive/2006/02/13/060213fa_fact_coll

Cordesman, Anthony H., *The Asian Military Balance: An Analytic Overview*, Washington, D.C.: Center for Strategic and International Studies, May 1, 2003. As of August 10, 2007:
http://www.csis.org/index.php?option=com_csis_pubs&task=view&id=1502

Dalkey, Norman C., *Project Delphi*, Santa Monica, Calif.: RAND Corporation, D-1005, August 21, 1951.

Dasgupta, Sunil, review of Kanti P. Bajpai, P. R. Chari, Pervaiz Iqbal Cheema, Stephen P. Cohen, and Sumit Ganguly, *Brasstacks and Beyond: Perception and Management of Crisis in South Asia*, New Delhi: Manohar, 1995, *Bulletin of the Atomic Scientists*, Vol. 52, No. 1, January–February 1996, pp. 57–58.

"Declaration of War Against the Americans Occupying the Land of the Two Holy Places," August 1996, English translation. As of August 10, 2007:
http://www.pbs.org/newshour/terrorism/international/fatwa_1996.html

Devroy, Ann, and John Lancaster, "Clinton to Add 1,500 Troops in Somalia, Considers a March 31 Withdrawal Date," *Washington Post*, October 7, 1993, p. A1.

"Dier Paobing Junshi Xueshu" ["Second Artillery Military Studies"], in *Junshixue Yanjiu Huigu yu Zhanwang* [*Military Academic Research Review and Prospects*], Beijing: Academy of Military Sciences Press, 1995, pp. 358–371.

Downes, Alexander B., "Desperate Times, Desperate Measures: The Causes of Civilian Victimization in War," *International Security*, Vol. 30, No. 4, Spring 2006, pp. 152–195.

"Dubious Decisions on the Sudan," *New York Times*, September 23, 1998, p. A28.

Eberstadt, Nicholas, "The Persistence of North Korea," *Policy Review*, No. 127, October–November 2004. As of August 10, 2007:
http://www.hoover.org/publications/policyreview/3436436.html

Eggen, Dan, and Spencer S. Hsu, "U.S. Responded to Plot with Speed, Secrecy," *Washington Post*, August 13, 2006, p. A1.

Eisenstadt, Michael, "Deter and Contain: Dealing with a Nuclear Iran," in Henry Sokolski and Patrick Clawson, eds., *Getting Ready for a Nuclear-Ready Iran*, Carlisle, Pa.: Strategic Studies Institute, 2005, pp. 225–256. As of August 10, 2007:
http://www.strategicstudiesinstitute.army.mil/pdffiles/pub629.pdf

Epstein, Joshua M., "Horizontal Escalation: Sour Notes on a Recurrent Theme," *International Security*, Vol. 8, No. 3, Winter 1983–1984, pp. 19–31.

"Ershiyi Shiji Chu Erpao Junshi Lilun Fazhan yu Chuangxin" ["The Development and Innovation of 2nd Artillery Military Theory in the 21st Century"], in National Military Philosophy and Social Science Planning Office, ed., *Ershiyi Shiji Chu Junshi Xue Xueke Jianshe yu Chuangxin* [*Development and Innovation of Military Science in the 21st Century*], Beijing: Junshi Kexue Chubanshe, 2004, pp. 342–348.

Evans, Michael, and Phillip Webster, "Britain Fears Nuclear War Over Kashmir: Plans Being Drawn Up to Get Britons Out of India, Pakistan," *Ottawa Citizen*, May 24, 2002, p. A8.

"Exploring India's Options," *Indian Express*, May 16, 2002.

Finkelstein, David, "Thinking About the PLA's 'Revolution in Doctrinal Affairs,'" in James Mulvenon and David Finkelstein, *The Revolution in Chinese Military Doctrinal Affairs*, Santa Monica, Calif.: RAND Corporation, forthcoming.

Foot, Rosemary J., "Nuclear Coercion and the Ending of the Korean Conflict," *International Security*, Vol. 13, No. 3, Winter 1988–1989, pp. 92–112.

Freedman, Lawrence, "Prevention, Not Preemption," *Washington Quarterly*, Vol. 26, No. 2, Spring 2003, pp. 105–114. As of August 10, 2007:
http://www.twq.com/03spring/docs/03spring_freedman.pdf

Friedman, Thomas, "Clinton Reviews Policy in Somalia as Unease Grows," *New York Times*, October 6, 1993, p. A1.

Gao Rui, ed., *Zhanluexue* [*The Science of Military Strategy*], Beijing: Junshi Kexue Chubanshe, 1987.

George, Alexander L., David K. Hall, and William E. Simons, *The Limits of Coercive Diplomacy: Laos, Cuba, Vietnam*, Boston: Little, Brown, 1971.

George, Alexander L., and William E. Simons, eds., *The Limits of Coercive Diplomacy*, 2nd ed., Boulder, Colo.: Westview Press, 1994.

Ghosn, Faten, and Scott Bennett, *Codebook for the Dyadic Militarized Interstate Incident Data*, Version 3.0, 2003. Dataset MIDB 3.02.csv, as of June 27, 2007.

Girth, Jeff, and Judith Miller, "Terror Money: A Special Report; Funds for Terrorists Traced to Persian Gulf Businessman," *New York Times*, August 14, 1996, p. A1.

Glaser, Charles L., *Analyzing Strategic Nuclear Policy*, Princeton, N.J.: Princeton University Press, 1990.

———, "Political Consequences of Military Strategy: Expanding and Refining the Spiral and Deterrence Models," *World Politics*, Vol. 44, No. 4, July 1992, pp. 497–538.

GlobalSecurity.org, "U.S. Forces, Japan," updated April 26, 2005. As of August 30, 2007:
http://www.globalsecurity.org/military/agency/dod/usfj.htm

———, "Active Duty Uniformed Troop Strength," updated January 25, 2006a. As of August 10, 2007:
http://www.globalsecurity.org/military/world/active-force.htm

———, "U.S. Forces, Korea/Combined Forces Command Combined Ground Component Command (GCC)," updated May 8, 2006b. As of August 30, 2007:
http://www.globalsecurity.org/military/agency/dod/usfk.htm

Goemans, H. E., *War and Punishment: The Causes of War Termination and the First World War*, Princeton, N.J.: Princeton University Press, 2000.

Goldstein, Avery, *Rising to the Challenge: China's Grand Strategy and International Relations*, Stanford, Calif.: Stanford University Press, 2005.

Goldstein, Lyle J., "Return to Zhenbao Island: Who Started Shooting and Why It Matters," *China Quarterly*, No. 168, December 2001, pp. 985–997.

Goo, Sara Kehaulani, "List of Foiled Plots Puzzling to Some: White House Document Mixes Half-Baked Plans with Serious Terrorist Threats," *Washington Post*, October 23, 2005, p. A6.

"Government Opens Defence Umbrella in Pak Face," *Indian Express*, May 20, 2002.

Gu Dexin and Niu Yongjun, *Heyouling De Zhengdong: Ershishiji Hewenti Huihu Yu Sikao* [*Rumblings of the Nuclear Specter: Looking Back at and Considering the Nuclear Problem in the 20th Century*], Beijing: Guofang Daxue Chubanshe, 1999.

Halperin, Morton H., *The 1958 Taiwan Straits Crisis: A Documented History*, Santa Monica, Calif.: RAND Corporation, RM-4900-ISA, 1966. As of August 30, 2007:
http://www.rand.org/pubs/research_memoranda/RM4900/

Hammel, Eric, *The Root: The Marines in Beirut, August 1982–February 1984*, New York: Harcourt Brace Jovanovich, 1985.

Haqqani, Hussein, "Pakistan's Terrorist Dilemma," in Satu P. Limaye, Mohan Malik, and Robert G. Wirsing, eds., *Religious Radicalism and Security in South Asia*, Honolulu: Asia-Pacific Center for Security Studies, 2004, pp. 351–361. As of August 10, 2007:
http://www.apcss.org/Publications/Edited%20Volumes/ReligiousRadicalism/ReligiousRadicalism.htm

Harris, John F., and Mike Allen, "President Details Global War on Terrorists and Supporters; Bush Tells Nations to Take Sides as N.Y. Toll Climbs Past 6,000," *Washington Post*, September 21, 2001, p. A1.

He Diqing, ed., *Zhanyixue Jiaocheng* [*A Course on the Science of Campaigns*], Beijing: Military Sciences Press, 2001.

Headquarters, U.S. Air Force Doctrine Center, *Strategic Attack*, Air Force Doctrine Document 2-1.2, September 30, 2003. As of August 10, 2007:
http://www.dtic.mil/doctrine/jel/service_pubs/afdd2_1_2.pdf

Henley, Lonnie D., "War Control: Chinese Concepts of Escalation Management," in Andrew Scobell and Larry M. Wortzel, eds., *Shaping China's Security Environment: The Role of the People's Liberation Army*, Carlisle, Pa.: U.S. Army War College, October 2006, pp. 81–104. As of August 10, 2007:
http://www.strategicstudiesinstitute.army.mil/pubs/display.cfm?pubID=709

Herzog, Chaim, *The Arab-Israeli Wars: War and Peace in the Middle East from the War of Independence Through Lebanon*, New York: Random House, 1982.

Hickey, Gerald Cannon, *The War in Cambodia: Focus on Some of the Internal Forces Involved*, Santa Monica, Calif.: RAND Corporation, 1970.

Hill, Andrew, and Richard Dowden, "Air Raid Puts Aid at Risk: UN Secretary-General Rejects Call to Suspend 'Peace By Force' After Attack Kills at Least 16 and Avenging Crowds Beat Journalists to Death," *The Independent*, July 13, 1993, p. 1.

Hoehn, Andrew R., Adam Grissom, David Ochmanek, David A. Shlapak, and Alan J. Vick, *A New Division of Labor: Meeting America's Security Challenges Beyond Iraq*, Santa Monica, Calif.: RAND Corporation, MG-499-AF, 2007. As of August 10, 2007:
http://www.rand.org/pubs/monographs/MG499/

Hoffman, Bruce, *Al Qaeda, Trends in Terrorism and Future Potentialities: An Assessment*, Santa Monica, Calif.: RAND Corporation, P-8078, 2003. As of August 10, 2007:
http://www.rand.org/pubs/papers/P8078/

Hong Bing and Liang Xiaoqiu, "Guanyu Kongjian Zhanlue Lilun de Jige Jiben Wenti" ["The Basics of Space Strategic Theory"] *Zhongguo Junshi Kexue* [*China Military Science*], Vol. 1, 2002, pp. 23–31.

Horne, Alistair, *A Savage War of Peace: Algeria, 1954–1962*, New York: Penguin, 1977.

Huang Jialun, "Attach Importance to Operation at Outer Strategic Line," *Liberation Army Daily*, November 30, 1999, p. 6, in Foreign Broadcast Information Service as "Operation at the Outer Strategic Line Viewed," December 14, 1999.

Hu Guangzheng, *Zhongwai Junshi Zuzhi Tizhi Bijiao Jiaocheng* [*Teaching Materials on a Comparison of Chinese and Foreign Military Organizational Systems*], Beijing: Junshi Kexue Chubanshe, 1999.

Irfani, Suroosh, "Pakistan's Sectarian Violence: Between the 'Arabist Shift' and the Indo-Persian Culture," in Satu P. Limaye, Mohan Malik, and Robert G. Wirsing, eds., *Religious Radicalism and Security in South Asia*, Honolulu: Asia-Pacific Center for Security Studies, 2004, pp. 147–169. As of August 10, 2007:
http://www.apcss.org/Publications/Edited%20Volumes/ReligiousRadicalism/ReligiousRadicalism.htm

Jahn, George, "Experts Describe Tight-Knit Nuclear Black Market: Millions in Sales Motivated by 'Personal Greed and Ambition,'" *Washington Times*, February 3, 2004, p. 11.

Jencks, Harlan W., "China's 'Punitive' War on Vietnam: A Military Assessment," *Asian Survey*, Vol. 19, No. 8, August 1979, pp. 801–815.

Jervis, Robert, *Perception and Misperception in International Politics*, Princeton, N.J.: Princeton University Press, 1976.

———, "Cooperation Under the Security Dilemma," *World Politics*, Vol. 30, No. 2, January 1978, pp. 167–214.

———, *The Illogic of American Nuclear Strategy*, Ithaca, N.Y.: Cornell University Press, 1984.

Jiang Lei, *Xiandai Yi Lie Sheng You Zhanlue* [*Modern Strategy for Using the Inferior to Defeat the Superior*], Beijing: National Defense University Press, 1997.

"Jihad Against Jews and Crusaders: World Islamic Front Statement," reprinted by the *Washington Post*, February 23, 1998. As of January 31, 2006:
http://www.washingtonpost.com/ac2/wp-dyn?pagename=article&node=&contentId=A4993-2001Sep21

Johnson, David E., Karl P. Mueller, and William H. Taft V, *Conventional Coercion Across the Spectrum of Operations: The Utility of U.S. Military Forces in the Emerging Security Environment*, Santa Monica, Calif.: RAND Corporation, MR-1494-A, 2002. As of August 10, 2007:
http://www.rand.org/pubs/monograph_reports/MR1494/

Johnson, David, and Steven Lee Myers, "Investigation of Attack on U.S. Destroyer Moving Slowly," *New York Times*, October 29, 2000, p. A10.

Johnston, Alastair Iain, *Cultural Realism: Strategic Culture and Grand Strategy in Chinese History*, Princeton, N.J.: Princeton University Press, 1995.

———, "China's Militarized Interstate Dispute Behaviour 1949–1992: A First Cut at the Data," *China Quarterly*, No. 153, March 1998, pp. 1–30.

———, "Toward Conceptualizing the Concept of a *Shashoujian* (Assassin's Mace)," unpublished manuscript, August 2002. As of August 10, 2007: http://www.people.fas.harvard.edu/%7Ejohnston/shashoujian.pdf

Joll, James, *The Origins of the First World War*, New York: Longman, 2nd ed., 1992.

Jones, Daniel M., Stuart A. Bremer, and J. David Singer, "Militarized Interstate Disputes, 1816–1992: Rationale, Coding Rules, and Empirical Patterns," *Conflict Management and Peace Science*, Vol. 15, No. 2, 1996, pp. 163–212.

Jones, Rodney W., "America's War on Terrorism: Religious Radicalism and Nuclear Confrontation in South Asia," in Satu P. Limaye, Mohan Malik, and Robert G. Wirsing, eds., *Religious Radicalism and Security in South Asia*, Honolulu: Asia-Pacific Center for Security Studies, 2004a, pp. 273–319. As of August 10, 2007: http://www.apcss.org/Publications/Edited%20Volumes/ReligiousRadicalism/ReligiousRadicalism.htm

———, "Nuclear Stability and Escalation Control in South Asia: Structural Factors," in Michael Krepon, Rodney W. Jones, and Ziad Haider, eds., *Escalation Control and the Nuclear Option in South Asia*, Washington, D.C.: Henry L. Stimson Center, November 2004b, pp. 25–55. As of August 10, 2007: http://www.stimson.org/pub.cfm?id=191

Jones, Tamara, "Grim Skepticism Grows on the Home Front," *Washington Post*, October 5, 1993, p. A12.

Kahn, Herman, *On Escalation: Metaphors and Scenarios*, Baltimore, Md.: Penguin, 1965.

Kapila, Subhash, "India's New 'Cold Start' War Doctrine Strategically Reviewed," South Asia Analysis Group, No. 991, May 4, 2004.

Kapur, S. Paul, "India and Pakistan's Unstable Peace: Why Nuclear South Asia Is Not Like Cold War Europe," *International Security*, Vol. 2, No. 5, Fall 2005, pp. 127–152.

Katzman, Kenneth, *Al Qaeda: Profile and Threat Assessment*, Washington, D.C.: Congressional Research Service, RL33038, updated August 17, 2005. As of August 10, 2007: http://handle.dtic.mil/100.2/ADA444819

———, *Iran's Influence in Iraq*, Washington, D.C.: Congressional Research Service, RS22323, updated February 7, 2007. As of August 10, 2007: http://fpc.state.gov/documents/organization/80209.pdf

Kaufmann, Chaim, "Possible and Impossible Solutions to Ethnic Civil Wars," *International Security*, Vol. 20, No. 4, Spring 1996, pp. 136–175.

Keegan, John, *The First World War*, New York: Vintage, 2000.

Kemp, Geoffrey, "The American Peacekeeping Role in Lebanon," in Anthony McDermott and Kjell Skjelsbaek, eds., *The Multinational Force in Beirut, 1982–1984*, Miami, Fla.: Florida International University Press, 1991, pp. 131–142.

Kenny, Henry J., "Vietnamese Perceptions of the 1979 War with China," in Mark A. Ryan, David M. Finkelstein, and Michael A. McDevitt, eds., *Chinese Warfighting: The PLA Experience Since 1949*, New York: M. E. Sharpe, 2003, pp. 218–227.

Khan, Kamran, "Blast Laid to Muslim Radicals Kills 15 at Egyptian Embassy in Pakistan," *Washington Post*, November 20, 1995, p. A14.

Khan, Muhammad Azam, "Indian Army Doctrine and Pakistan," *The Nation* (Pakistan), September 5, 2005.

Kilcullen, David J., "Countering Global Insurgency," *Journal of Strategic Studies*, Vol. 28, No. 4, August 2005, pp. 597–617.

Krepon, Michael, "The Stability-Instability Paradox, Misperception, and Escalation Control in South Asia," in Michael Krepon, Rodney W. Jones, and Ziad Haider, eds., *Escalation Control and the Nuclear Option in South Asia*, Washington, D.C.: Henry L. Stimson Center, November 2004, pp. 1–24. As of August 10, 2007:
http://www.stimson.org/pub.cfm?id=191

Krepon, Michael, Rodney W. Jones, and Ziad Haider, eds., *Escalation Control and the Nuclear Option in South Asia*, Washington, D.C.: Henry L. Stimson Center, November 2004. As of August 10, 2007:
http://www.stimson.org/pub.cfm?id=191

Labs, Eric J., "Beyond Victory: Offensive Realism and the Expansion of War Aims," *Security Studies*, Vol. 6, No. 4, Summer 1997, pp. 1–49.

Lakshmi, Rama, "Indians Blame Attacks on Pakistan-Based Group," *Washington Post*, December 15, 2001, p. A23.

Lambeth, Benjamin S., *NATO's Air War for Kosovo: A Strategic and Operational Assessment*, Santa Monica, Calif.: RAND Corporation, MR-1365-AF, 2001. As of August 10, 2007:
http://www.rand.org/pubs/monograph_reports/MR1365/

Langer, Paul F., and Joseph J. Zasloff, *North Vietnam and the Pathet Lao: Partners in the Struggle for Laos*, Cambridge, Mass.: Harvard University Press, 1970.

Laqueur, Walter, *No End to War: Terrorism in the Twenty-First Century*, London: Continuum, 2003.

Larson, Eric V., *Casualties and Consensus: The Historical Role of Casualties in Domestic Support for U.S. Military Operations*, Santa Monica, Calif.: RAND Corporation, MR-726-RC, 1996. As of August 10, 2007:
http://www.rand.org/pubs/monograph_reports/MR726/

Lavoy, Peter, "The Strategic Consequences of Nuclear Proliferation," *Security Studies*, Vol. 4, No. 4, Summer 1995, pp. 739–740.

Lebow, Richard Ned, "Windows of Opportunity: Do States Jump Through Them?" *International Security*, Vol. 9, No. 1, Summer 1984, pp. 147–186.

Legro, Jeffrey W., *Cooperation Under Fire: Anglo-German Restraint During World War II*, Ithaca, N.Y.: Cornell University Press, 1995.

Li Daguang, *Hangtian Zhan [Space Warfare]*, Beijing: Military Science Press, 2001.

Li Daguang and Wan Shuixian, "Zhengduo Zhi Tian Quande Jiben Tezheng" ["The Fundamental Features of the Struggle for Space Dominance"], *Zhuangbei Zhihui Jishu Xueyuan Xuebao [Journal of the Academy of Equipment Command and Technology]*, December 2003, pp. 37–42.

Li, Nan, "The PLA's Evolving Warfighting Doctrine, Strategy and Tactics, 1985–95: A Chinese Perspective," *China Quarterly*, No. 146, June, 1996, pp. 443–463.

———, "The PLA's Evolving Campaign Doctrine and Strategies," in James C. Mulvenon and Richard H. Yang, eds., *The People's Liberation Army in the Information Age*, Santa Monica, Calif.: RAND Corporation, CF-145-CAPP/AF, 1999, pp. 146–174. As of August 10, 2007:
http://www.rand.org/pubs/conf_proceedings/CF145/

Li Tilin, "Dui Dier Paobing Xinxihua Jianshe de Sikao" ["Thoughts on the Development of Second Artillery Informatization"], *Junshi Ushu [Military Science]*, December 2004.

Li, Xiaobing, "PLA Attacks and Operations During the Taiwan Strait Crises," in Mark A. Ryan, David M. Finkelstein, and Michael A. McDevitt, eds., *Chinese Warfighting: The PLA Experience Since 1949*, New York: M. E. Sharpe, 2003, pp. 143–172.

Limaye, Satu P., Mohan Malik, and Robert G. Wirsing, eds., *Religious Radicalism and Security in South Asia*, Honolulu: Asia-Pacific Center for Security Studies, 2004. As of August 10, 2007:
http://www.apcss.org/Publications/Edited%20Volumes/ReligiousRadicalism/ReligiousRadicalism.htm

Linstone, Harold A., and Murray Turoff, eds., *The Delphi Method: Techniques and Applications*, Newark, N.J.: New Jersey Institute of Technology, 2002. As of February 15, 2007:
http://is.njit.edu/pubs/delphibook/

Loeb, Vernon, "A Global, Pan-Islamic Network; Terrorism Entrepreneur Unifies Groups Financially, Politically," *Washington Post*, August 23, 1998, p. A1.

Long Commission Report—see *Report of the DoD Commission on Beirut International Airport*.

Lu Linzhi, "Preemptive Strikes Are Crucial in Limited High-Tech Wars," *Liberation Army Daily*, February 7, 1996, in Foreign Broadcast Information Service as "Preemptive Strikes Endorsed for Limited High-Tech War," February 14, 1996.

Malik, Mohan, "The Stability of Nuclear Deterrence in South Asia: The Clash Between State and Anti-State Actors," in Satu P. Limaye, Mohan Malik, and Robert G. Wirsing, eds., *Religious Radicalism and Security in South Asia*, Honolulu: Asia-Pacific Center for Security Studies, 2004, pp. 321–350. As of August 10, 2007:
http://www.apcss.org/Publications/Edited%20Volumes/ReligiousRadicalism/ReligiousRadicalism.htm

Mao Zedong, *Selected Military Writings of Mao Tse-Tung*, Beijing: Foreign Languages Press, 1967.

Marcus, Harold G., "President Aidid's Somalia, September 1995," *H-Net*, undated. As of November 2, 2005:
http://www.h-net.org/~africa/confrpt/marcus.html

McDermott, Anthony, and Kjell Skjelsbaek, eds., *The Multinational Force in Beirut, 1982–1984*, Miami, Fla.: Florida International University Press, 1991.

McNeil, Donald G., Jr., "The Lockerbie Verdict: The Overview; Libyan Convicted by Scottish Court in '88 Pan Am Blast," *New York Times*, February 1, 2001, p. A1.

Medeiros, Evan S., "Undressing the Dragon: Researching the PLA Through Open Source Exploitation," in James C. Mulvenon and Andrew N. D. Yang, eds., *A Poverty of Riches: New Challenges and Opportunities in PLA Research*, Santa Monica, Calif.: RAND Corporation, CF-189-NSRD, 2003, pp. 119–168. As of August 10, 2007:
http://www.rand.org/pubs/conf_proceedings/CF189/

———, "Minding the Gap: Assessing the Trajectory of the PLA's Strategic Missile Forces," paper presented at Exploring the "Right Size" for China's Military: PLA Missions, Functions, and Organization, U.S. Army War College, Carlisle, Pa., October 6–8, 2006.

Meilinger, Phillip S., ed., *The Paths of Heaven: The Evolution of Airpower Theory*, Maxwell AFB, Ala.: Air University Press, 1997.

Mercer, Jonathan, *Reputation and International Politics*, Ithaca, N.Y.: Cornell University Press, 1996.

Milburn, Thomas W., "What Constitutes Effective Deterrence?" *Journal of Conflict Resolution*, Vol. 3, No. 2, June 1959, pp. 138–145.

Miller, John, "Interview: Osama Bin Laden," *ABC News*, transcript, May 1998. As of August 10, 2007:
http://www.pbs.org/wgbh/pages/frontline/shows/binladen/who/interview.html

Miller, Steven E., Sean M. Lynn-Jones, and Stephen Van Evera, eds., *Military Strategy and the Origins of the First World War*, rev. ed., Princeton, N.J.: Princeton University Press, 1991.

Mintz, John, "U.S. Charges 2 as Bin Laden Aides," *Washington Post*, February 25, 2004, p. A1.

MIPT Terrorism Knowledge Base, referenced data current through July 18, 2005:
http://www.tkb.org/AboutTKB.jsp

Morgan, Forrest E., *Compellence and the Strategic Culture of Imperial Japan: Implications for Coercive Diplomacy in the Twenty-First Century*, Westport, Conn.: Praeger, 2003.

Mueller, John, *Retreat from Doomsday: The Obsolescence of Major War*, New York: Basic Books, 1989.

Mueller, John, and Karl P. Mueller "The Methodology of Mass Destruction: Assessing Threats in the New World Order," *Journal of Strategic Studies*, Vol. 23, No. 1, March 2000, pp. 163–187.

Mueller, Karl P., "Strategic Airpower and Nuclear Strategy: New Theory for a Not-Quite-So-New Apocalypse," in Phillip S. Meilinger, ed., *The Paths of Heaven: The Evolution of Airpower Theory*, Maxwell AFB, Ala.: Air University Press, 1997, pp. 279–320. As of August 10, 2007:
http://aupress.maxwell.af.mil/catalog/books/Meilinger_B29.htm

———, "Totem and Taboo: Depolarizing the Space Weaponization Debate," *Astropolitics*, Vol. 1, No. 1, Spring 2003, pp. 4–28.

Mueller, Karl P., Jasen J. Castillo, Forrest E. Morgan, Negeen Pegahi, and Brian Rosen, *Striking First: Preemptive and Preventive Attack in U.S. National Security Policy*, Santa Monica, Calif.: RAND Corporation, MG-403-AF, 2006. As of August 10, 2007:
http://www.rand.org/pubs/monographs/MG403/

Mulvenon, James, and David Finkelstein, eds., *China's Revolution in Doctrinal Affairs: Emerging Trends in the Operational Art of the Chinese People's Liberation Army*, Alexandria, Va.: CNA Corporation, 2005. As of August 10, 2007:
http://www.cna.org/documents/doctrinebook.pdf

Mulvenon, James C., and Andrew N. D. Yang, eds., *A Poverty of Riches: New Challenges and Opportunities in PLA Research*, Santa Monica, Calif.: RAND Corporation, CF-189-NSRD, 2003. As of August 10, 2007:
http://www.rand.org/pubs/conf_proceedings/CF189/

"Musharraf Warns India of Storm," *Herald Sun* (Melbourne, Australia), May 31, 2002, p. 31.

National Intelligence Council, *Iran: Nuclear Intentions and Capabilities, National Intelligence Estimate*, Washington, D.C.: Office of the Director of National Intelligence, November 2007. As of December 29, 2007:
http://www.dni.gov/press_releases/20071203_release.pdf

National Military Philosophy and Social Science Planning Office, ed., *Ershiyi Shiji Chu Junshi Xue Xueke Jianshe yu Chuangxin* [*Development and Innovation of Military Science in the 21st Century*], Beijing: Junshi Kexue Chubanshe, 2004.

Nelson, Richard W., "Multinational Peacekeeping in the Middle East and the United Nations Model," in Anthony McDermott and Kjell Skjelsbaek, eds., *The Multinational Force in Beirut, 1982–1984*, Miami, Fla.: Florida International University Press, 1991, pp. 3–36.

Office of the Secretary of Defense, *The Military Power of the People's Republic of China*, annual report to Congress, 2005. As of August 10, 2007:
http://www.defenselink.mil/news/Jul2005/d20050719china.pdf

———, *The Military Power of the People's Republic of China*, 2004. As of August 10, 2007:
http://www.defenselink.mil/pubs/d20040528PRC.pdf

Olson, Kyle B., "Aum Shinrikyo: Once and Future Threat?" *Emerging Infectious Diseases*, Vol. 5, No. 4, July–August 1999, pp. 513–516. As of August 10, 2007:
http://www.cdc.gov/ncidod/EID/vol5no4/olson.htm

"The Palestine Resistance and Jordan," *Journal of Palestine Studies*, Vol. 1, No. 1, Autumn 1971, pp. 162–170.

Pan Xiangting and Sun Zhanping, eds., *Gao Jishu Tiaojian Xia Meijun Junbu Zhanzheng* [*The U.S. Military in Local Wars Under High-Tech Conditions*], Beijing: Liberation Army Press, 1994.

Pape, Robert A., *Bombing to Win: Air Power and Coercion in War*, Ithaca, N.Y.: Cornell University Press, 1996.

———, *Dying to Win: The Strategic Logic of Suicide Terrorism*, New York: Random House, 2005.

"Parris Chang Says the US, Japan Will Defend Taiwan," Central News Agency, August 14, 2005.

Peng Guangqian and Yao Youzhi, eds., *Zhanluexue* [*The Science of Military Strategy*], Beijing: Junshi Kexue Chubanshe, 2001.

Peters, John E., James Dickens, Derek Eaton, C. Christine Fair, Nina Hachigian, Theodore Karasik, Rollie Lal, Rachel M. Swanger, Gregory F. Treverton, and Charles Wolf, Jr., *War and Escalation in South Asia*, Santa Monica, Calif.: RAND Corporation, MG-367-1-AF, 2006. As of August 10, 2007:
http://www.rand.org/pubs/monographs/MG367-1/

Pirnie, Bruce R., Alan J. Vick, Adam Grissom, Karl P. Mueller, and David T. Orletsky, *Beyond Close Air Support: Forging a New Air-Ground Partnership*, Santa Monica, Calif.: RAND Corporation, MG-301-AF, 2005. As of August 10, 2007:
http://www.rand.org/pubs/monographs/MG301/

Pollack, Jonathan D., and Chung Min Lee, *Preparing for Korean Unification: Scenarios and Implications*, Santa Monica, Calif.: RAND Corporation, MR-1040-A, 1999. As of August 10, 2007:
http://www.rand.org/pubs/monograph_reports/MR1040/

Posen, Barry R., "Inadvertent Nuclear War? Escalation and NATO's Northern Flank," *International Security*, Vol. 7, No. 2, Autumn 1982, pp. 28–54.

———, *Inadvertent Escalation: Conventional War and Nuclear Risks*, Ithaca, N.Y.: Cornell University Press, 1991.

Press, Daryl G., *Calculating Credibility: How Leaders Assess Military Threats*, Ithaca, N.Y.: Cornell University Press, 2005.

Preston, Bob, Dana J. Johnson, Sean J. A. Edwards, Michael Miller, and Calvin Shipbaugh, *Space Weapons, Earth Wars*, Santa Monica, Calif.: RAND Corporation, MR-1209-AF, 2002. As of August 10, 2007:
http://www.rand.org/pubs/monograph_reports/MR1209/

Pyes, Craig, Judith Miller, and Stephen Engleberg, "One Man and a Global Web of Violence," *New York Times*, January 14, 2001, p. 1.

Ragavan, V. R., "Limited War and Nuclear Escalation in South Asia," *Nonproliferation Review*, Vol. 8, No. 3, Fall–Winter 2001. As of August 10, 2007:
http://cns.miis.edu/pubs/npr/vol08/83/83ragh.pdf

Rapoport, David C., "The Fourth Wave: September 11 and the History of Terrorism," *Current History*, Vol. 100, No. 650, December 2001, pp. 419–424.

Rashid, Ahmed, and Toby Helm, "India Accused of Tyranny, 'War Hysteria': Pakistan's President Draws Ire with Talk of Hindu Terrorists," *National Post* (Canada), May 24, 2002, p. A8.

Report of the DoD Commission on Beirut International Airport Terrorist Act, October 23, 1983, December 20, 1983.

Richburg, Keith B., "Battle Killed 12 Americans, Wounded 78," *Washington Post*, October 5, 1993, p. A1.

Risen, James, "U.S. Pursued Secret Efforts to Catch or Kill Bin Laden," *New York Times*, September 30, 2001, p. A1.

Robinson, Thomas, "The Sino-Soviet Border Conflicts of 1969: New Evidence Three Decades Later," in Mark A. Ryan, David M. Finkelstein, and Michael A. McDevitt, eds., *Chinese Warfighting: The PLA Experience Since 1949*, New York: M. E. Sharpe, 2003, pp. 198–214.

Rosenberg, David Alan, "American Atomic Strategy and the Hydrogen Bomb Decision," *Journal of American History*, Vol. 66, No. 1, June 1979, pp. 62–84.

———, "The Origins of Overkill: Nuclear Weapons and American Strategy, 1945–1960," *International Security*, Vol. 7, No. 4, Spring 1983, pp. 3–71.

Ross, Michael, and Art Pine, "Angry Lawmakers Threaten to Push for Somalia Pullout," *Los Angeles Times*, October 6, 1993, p. A1.

Ryan, Mark A., David M. Finkelstein, and Michael A. McDevitt, eds., *Chinese Warfighting: The PLA Experience Since 1949*, New York: M. E. Sharpe, 2003.

S. R. "Palestinian Report," Middle East Report, No. 4, Middle East Research and Information Project, November 1971, pp. 2, 13–14.

Sagan, Scott D., *The Limits of Safety: Organizations, Accidents, and Nuclear Weapons*, Princeton, N.J.: Princeton University Press, 1993.

Sageman, Marc, *Understanding Terror Networks*, Philadelphia, Pa.: University of Pennsylvania Press, 2004.

Schanzer, Jonathan, *Al-Qaeda's Armies: Middle East Affiliate Groups and the Next Generation of Terror*, New York: Specialist Press International, 2005.

Schelling, Thomas C., *The Strategy of Conflict*, Cambridge, Mass.: Harvard University Press, 1960.

———, *Arms and Influence*, New Haven, Conn.: Yale University Press, 1966.

Schwartz, Lowell, RAND Corporation, interviews with Forrest E. Morgan, Pittsburgh, Pa., March 2006a.

———, "Comments on Jed Peters Draft," email to Forrest E. Morgan, March 16, 2006b.

Schweid, Barry, "State Department Issues New Worldwide Warning," Associated Press, December 21, 1999.

Scobell, Andrew, *China's Use of Military Force: Beyond the Great Wall and the Long March*, New York: Cambridge University Press, 2003.

Seabury, Paul, ed., *Balance of Power*, San Francisco, Calif.: Chandler, 1965.

Shlapak, David A., David T. Orletsky, and Barry Wilson, *Dire Strait? Military Aspects of the China-Taiwan Confrontation and Options for U.S. Policy*, Santa Monica, Calif.: RAND Corporation, MR-1217-SRF, 2000. As of August 10, 2007:
http://www.rand.org/pubs/monograph_reports/MR1217/

Shang Yi, "Zhu Chenghu: Foreign News Agency 'Cites Out of Context,'" *Ta Kung Pao* (Hong Kong), Foreign Broadcast Information Service, trans., July 15, 2005.

"Six Convicted for Role in Assassination Attempt," *Prince George Citizen* (British Columbia), October 5, 2005, p. 14.

Smith, R. Jeffrey, "U.S. Probes Blasts' Possible Mideast Ties; Alleged Terrorists Investigated in Albania," *Washington Post*, August 12, 1998, p. A19.

Smoke, Richard, *War: Controlling Escalation*, Cambridge, Mass.: Harvard University Press, 1977.

Snyder, Glenn, *Deterrence and Defense*, Princeton, N.J.: Princeton University Press, 1961.

———, "The Balance of Power and the Balance of Terror," in Paul Seabury, ed., *Balance of Power*, San Francisco, Calif.: Chandler, 1965, pp. 198–199.

Sokolski, Henry, and Patrick Clawson, eds., *Getting Ready for a Nuclear-Ready Iran*, Carlisle, Pa.: Strategic Studies Institute, 2005. As of August 10, 2007: http://www.strategicstudiesinstitute.army.mil/pdffiles/pub629.pdf

Spacy, William L. II, "Assessing the Military Utility of Space-Based Weapons," *Astropolitics*, Vol. 1, No. 3, Winter 2003, pp. 1–43.

Stallworthy, Lucy, "Analysis: Targeted Killings Often Work," United Press International, February 10, 2006.

Stewart, Richard W., *The United States Army in Somalia, 1992–1994*, Washington, D.C.: Center for Military History, U.S. Department of the Army, CMH Pub 70-81-1, 2002.

Sullivan, Kevin, "Key Defector Warns Again of North Korean War Plans," *Washington Post*, July 10, 1997, p. A23.

Susman, Tina, "Bin Laden's Plush Life in Sudan," *Newsday*, August 26, 1998, p. A3.

Susman, Tina, and Knut Royce, "Bin Laden Link: El Shifa Factory Chief Lives in House He Used to Occupy," *Newsday*, August 27, 1998, p. A3.

Swaine, Michael D., and Ashley J. Tellis, *Interpreting China's Grand Strategy: Past, Present, and Future*, Santa Monica, Calif.: RAND Corporation, MR-1121-AF, 2000. As of August 10, 2007: http://www.rand.org/pubs/monograph_reports/MR1121/

Tellis, Ashley J., *Stability in South Asia*, Santa Monica, Calif.: RAND Corporation, DB-185-A, 1997. As of August 10, 2007: http://www.rand.org/pubs/documented_briefings/DB185/

Tellis, Ashley J., C. Christine Fair, and Jamison Jo Medby, *Limited Conflicts Under the Nuclear Umbrella: Indian and Pakistani Lessons from the Kargil Crisis*, Santa Monica, Calif.: RAND Corporation, MR-1450-USCA, 2002. As of August 10, 2007: http://www.rand.org/pubs/monograph_reports/MR1450/

Teng Jianqun, "Thoughts Arising from the U.S. Military's Space War Exercise," *Liberation Army Daily*, February 7, 2001, in Foreign Broadcast Information Service as "*Jiefangjun Bao* Views U.S. Preparations for Space Warfare," February 7, 2001.

Terraine, John, *The U-Boat Wars, 1916–1945*, New York: Putnam, 1989.

Thies, Wallace J., *When Governments Collide: Coercion and Diplomacy in the Vietnam Conflict, 1964–1968*, Berkeley, Calif.: University of California Press, 1980.

Timmerman, Kenneth R., "The Day After Iran Gets the Bomb," in Henry Sokolski and Patrick Clawson, eds., *Getting Ready for a Nuclear-Ready Iran*, Carlisle, Pa.: Strategic Studies Institute, 2005, pp. 121–125. As of August 10, 2007:
http://www.strategicstudiesinstitute.army.mil/pdffiles/pub629.pdf

Trachtenberg, Marc, "The Meaning of Mobilization in 1914," in Steven E. Miller, Sean M. Lynn-Jones, and Stephen Van Evera, eds., *Military Strategy and the Origins of the First World War*, rev. ed., Princeton: Princeton University Press, 1991, pp. 195–226.

Tuchman, Barbara W., *The Guns of August*, New York: Dell, 1962.

Turner, L. C. F., *Origins of the First World War*, New York: W. W. Norton, 1970.

United Nations Department of Public Information, "Somalia—UNOSOM I: Mission Backgrounder," March 21, 1997a. As of November 1, 2005:
http://www.un.org/Depts/DPKO/Missions/unosomi.htm

———, "Somalia—UNOSOM II: Mission Backgrounder," March 21, 1997b. As of November 6, 2005:
http://www.un.org/Depts/DPKO/Missions/unosom2b.htm

United Nations Security Council, Resolution 751 (Somalia), April 24, 1992. As of April 10, 2007:
http://daccessdds.un.org/doc/RESOLUTION/GEN/NR0/011/10/IMG/NR001110.pdf?OpenElement

———, Resolution 794 (Somalia), December 3, 1992. As of August 10, 2007:
http://daccessdds.un.org/doc/UNDOC/GEN/N92/772/11/PDF/N9277211.pdf?OpenElement

———, Resolution 814 (Somalia), March 26, 1993. As of August 10, 2007:
http://daccessdds.un.org/doc/UNDOC/GEN/N93/226/18/IMG/N9322618.pdf?OpenElement

———, Resolution 837 (Somalia), June 6, 1993. As of August 10, 2007:
http://daccessdds.un.org/doc/UNDOC/GEN/N93/332/32/IMG/N9333232.pdf?OpenElement

"Urgent—US Confirms Arrests in Jordan Related to Potential US Attacks," Agence France Presse, December 15, 1999.

U.S. Department of State, *Patterns of Global Terrorism 2004*, Washington, D.C.: U.S. Government Printing Office, April 2005.

———, Bureau of Near Eastern Affairs, "Background Note: Lebanon," February 2007. As of August 10, 2007: http://www.state.gov/r/pa/ei/bgn/35833.htm

"U.S. Envoy Back for Talks," *St. John's Telegram* (Newfoundland), August 24, 2002, p. A16.

"U.S. Investigations Link Osama Bin Laden to Suspected Algerian Terrorists," Agence France Presse, January 27, 2000.

U.S. Joint Chiefs of Staff, *Joint Doctrine for Space Operations*, Joint Publication 3-14, August 9, 2002. As of August 10, 2007: http://www.dtic.mil/doctrine/jel/new_pubs/jp3_14.pdf

———, *DoD Dictionary of Military and Associated Terms*, Joint Publication 1-02, April 12, 2001, as amended through June 13, 2007. As of August 10, 2007: http://www.dtic.mil/doctrine/jel/new_pubs/jp1_02.pdf

U.S. Policy Planning Staff, "The Problems to Review and Define United States Policy Toward China," memorandum, PPS 39, September 7, 1948, in *Foreign Relations of the United States, 1948*, Vol. VIII: *The Far East: China*, Washington, D.C.: U.S. Government Printing Office, 1973, pp. 146–155.

Van Evera, Stephen, "The Cult of the Offensive and the Origins of the First World War," in Steven E. Miller, Sean M. Lynn-Jones, and Stephen Van Evera, eds., *Military Strategy and the Origins of the First World War*, revised ed., Princeton, N.J.: Princeton University Press, 1991, pp. 59–109.

———, *Causes of War: Power and the Roots of Conflict*, Ithaca, N.Y.: Cornell University Press, 1999.

Waltz, Kenneth N., *Man, the State, and War: A Theoretical Analysis*, New York: Columbia University Press, 1959.

Wang Houqing and Zhang Xingye, eds., *Zhanyixue [The Science of Military Campaigns]*, Beijing: National Defense University Press, 2000a.

———, eds., *Zhanyixue [The Science of Military Campaigns]*, Beijing: Guofang Daxue, May 2000b.

Wang Wenrong, ed., *Zhanluexue [The Science of Military Strategy]*, Beijing: Guofang Daxue Chubanshe, 1999.

Washington, Versalle F., "Setting the Stage," in Robert F. Baumann and Lawrence A. Yates with Versalle F. Washington, eds., *"My Clan Against the World": US and Coalition Forces in Somalia, 1992–1994*, Ft. Leavenworth, Kan.: Combat Studies Institute Press, 2004, pp. 9–22. As of August 30, 2007: http://handle.dtic.mil/100.2/ADA465677

Watts, Barry D., *The Military Use of Space: A Diagnostic Assessment*, Washington, D.C.: Center for Strategic and Budgetary Assessments, 2001.

Weiner, Tim, "U.S. Fury on 2 Continents: The Protagonist; Man with Mission Takes On the U.S. at Far-Flung Sites," *New York Times*, August 20, 1998, p. A1.

White House, "Three Years of Progress in the War on Terror," fact sheet, September 11, 2004. As of August 10, 2007:
http://www.whitehouse.gov/news/releases/2004/09/print/20040911.html

Whiting, Allen S., *The Chinese Calculus of Deterrence*, Ann Arbor, Mich.: University of Michigan Press, 1975.

———, "China's Use of Force, 1950–96, and Taiwan," *International Security*, Vol. 26, No. 2, Fall 2001, pp. 103–131.

Wortzel, Larry M., "Concentrating Forces and Audacious Action: PLA Lessons from the Sino-Indian War," in Laurie Burkitt, Andrew Scobell, and Larry M. Wortzel, eds., *The Lessons of History: The Chinese People's Liberation Army at 75*, Carlisle, Pa.: Strategic Studies Institute, 2003, pp. 327–352.

Xiao Tianliang, *Zhanzheng Kongzhi Wenti Yanjiu* [*Research on War Control*], Beijing: Guofang Daxue Chubanshe, 2002.

Xie Yonggao, Qin Zizeng, and Huang Haibing, "Junshi Hangtian Jishu de Huigu Zhanwang" ["Looking at the Past and Future of Military Space Technology"], *Zhongguo Hangtian* [*China Aerospace*], No. 6, 2002.

Xu Wei and Chang Xianqi, "Shilun Kongjian Weishe" ["A Tentative Discussion of Space Deterrence"], *Zhuangbei Zhihui Jishu Xueyan Xuebao* [*Journal of the Academy of Equipment Command and Technology*], February 2002, pp. 10–13.

Xue Xinglin, ed., *Zhanyi Lilun Xuexi Zhinan* [*Campaign Theory Study Guide*], Beijing: Guofang Daxue Chubanshe, 2001.

Yaphe, Judith S., and Charles D. Lutes, *Reassessing the Implications of a Nuclear-Armed Iran*, McNair Paper No. 69, Washington, D.C.: Institute for National Strategic Studies, 2005. As of August 10, 2007:
http://www.ndu.edu/inss/mcnair/mcnair69/McNairPDF.pdf

Yates, Lawrence A., "Buildup and Withdrawal, October 1993–March 1994," in Robert F. Baumann and Lawrence A. Yates with Versalle F. Washington, *"My Clan Against the World": US and Coalition Forces in Somalia, 1992–1994*, Ft. Leavenworth, Kan.: Combat Studies Institute Press, 2004, pp. 165–200. As of August 30, 2007:
http://handle.dtic.mil/100.2/ADA465677

———, "Operation Restore Hope Phases I and II, December 1992," in Robert F. Baumann and Lawrence A. Yates with Versalle F. Washington, *"My Clan Against the World": US and Coalition Forces in Somalia, 1992–1994*, Ft. Leavenworth, Kan.: Combat Studies Institute Press, 2004, pp. 23–60. As of August 30, 2007:
http://handle.dtic.mil/100.2/ADA465677

Zhang Ming and Li Suoku, "Kongjian Xinxi Zuozhan yu Guojui Kongjian Fa" ["Space Information Operations and International Space Law"], *Zhuangbei Zhihui Jishu Xueyan Xuebao* [*Journal of the Academy of Equipment Command and Technology*], April 2003, p. 35.

Zhang, Shu Guang, *Deterrence and Strategic Culture: Chinese-American Confrontations, 1949–1958*, Ithaca, N.Y.: Cornell University Press, 1992.

Zhang, Xiaoming, "Air Combat for the People's Republic: The People's Liberation Army Air Force in Action, 1949–1969," in Mark A. Ryan, David M. Finkelstein, and Michael A. McDevitt, eds., *Chinese Warfighting: The PLA Experience Since 1949*, New York: M. E. Sharpe, 2003.

Zhanyixue Yanjiu [*Campaign Studies Research*], Beijing: Guofang Daxue Chubanshe, 1997.

Zimmerman, John C., "Sayyid Qutb's Influence on the 11 September Attacks," *Terrorism and Political Violence*, Vol. 16, No. 2, Summer 2004, pp. 222–252.